Max Beerbohm

Max Beerbohm

A Kind of a Life

N. John Hall

Yale University Press
New Haven and London

For information about this and other Yale University Press publications, please contact:
U.S. Office: sales.press@yale.edu   www.yale.edu/yup
Europe Office: sales@yaleup.co.uk   www.yaleup.co.uk

Set in Adobe Garamond by Fakenham Photosetting
Printed in Great Britain by St Edmundsbury Press

Library of Congress Cataloging-in-Publication Data

Hall, N. John.
   Max Beerbohm: a kind of a life/N. John Hall.
      p. cm.
Includes bibliographical references and index.
   ISBN 0–300–09705–0 (alk. paper)
1.   Beerbohm, Max, Sir, 1872–1956.   2.   Authors, English—20th
century—Biography.   3.   Cartoonists—Great Britain—Biography.   4.
Dandies—Great Britain—Biography.   I. Title.
   PR6003.E4 Z69 2002
   824'.912—dc21   2002007034

A catalogue record for this book is available from the British Library.

10 9 8 7 6 5 4 3 2 1

For J. N.

CONTENTS

Plates

A Little Book

Max Beerbohm was an intensely private person. When a friend, Bohun Lynch, threatened to write a book about him in 1922, Max pleaded with Lynch that he keep the book little and that he avoid his person and concentrate on his writings and caricatures. Moreover, as Max's "gifts are small," Lynch is to *underrate* him as writer and caricaturist so that those who do not like his work will not be incensed, and those who do like it might rally round him. Accordingly, I shall keep this book relatively short, and I shall not attempt to ferret out the inner man. The "inner man of Max Beerbohm" sounds oxymoronic. He was very self-aware, but he was not given to introspection or soul-searching. If he did look deeply into himself – and I don't believe he did so very often – he did not tell us about it. Instead, he points us towards his art, his writings and caricatures, all of it highly personal, unmistakably his own. For "Max" – as he is always called – peers out at us from everything he wrote or drew. Virginia Woolf said, "What Mr Beerbohm gave was, of course, himself. . . . He was affected by private joys and sorrows, and had no gospel to preach, and no learning to impart. He was himself, simply and directly, and himself he has remained. . . . He has brought personality into literature, not unconsciously and impurely, but so consciously and purely that we do not know whether there is any relation between Max the essayist and Mr Beerbohm the man. We only know that the spirit of personality permeates every word that he writes. The triumph is the triumph of style." Style is the man, right? But how elusive this man, and, all the more, the so-called inner man. The glittering surface of his work reflects about as much as we shall know of its author. He didn't keep a diary (except for a few desultory notes in Italy, chiefly about the weather, walks into town, and an electric stove); he wrote letters that were for the most part personally unrevealing; he would have nothing to do with modern psychology or self-analysis. His private life remains what he would have wanted it to remain: a puzzle.

I have no difficulty adhering to Max's premise that his gifts were small. He was essayist, critic, parodist, fiction writer, and caricaturist. The essay is considered a "small" form *vis-à-vis* the novel, or even history; criticism is smaller yet. Parody is also a lesser, a "subsidiary art" (Max's term), and to be ranked tops in this genre is a limited, almost suspect, accomplishment. To have written one novel and a handful of short stories, no matter how exceptional, is a smallish accomplishment in fiction (we all know that Dickens would not be Dickens if he had written only *Pickwick* and the Christmas Stories). And caricature is not oil painting; it is not work on the grand scale. So, Max does certain small things extraordinarily well, or, in the case of fiction, he makes but a "small" contribution.

But Max Beerbohm does present a special problem for the prospective biographer: he had the most amusing mind of his generation, and how is one to keep his biography amusing? I shall adopt the obvious and safest strategy, that of quoting him whenever possible, either in small bits or fairly large chunks. For a writer's own words form the prime matter of his or her biography. As Anthony Trollope once wrote, the man of letters is, in truth, ever writing his own biography. And thus, what should emerge here is a biography, not quite "Max Beerbohm by Max Beerbohm," but close to it. Nonetheless, no matter how much I use Max's own words, the choice of quotations will be mine, and, unavoidably, the book will be my version of Max. Every biography is a performance shared by its subject and the biographer. And although I shall let Max perform as much as possible, I shall be in evidence as putting on the show. In this regard, I don't suppose it will hurt to say of myself that for thirty years I have worked on and written about two writers, Trollope and Beerbohm. In 1991 the Trollope involvement resulted in a biography, a long, inclusive, and, as far as I could make it so, impersonal book. It was not of course an "objective" biography – there is no such thing – but I tried to stay very much in the background and would no sooner have thought of using the personal pronoun *I* in the course of it than of including a picture of myself among the book's plates. Reviewers called the writing "modest" and "self-effacing." This biography of Max will be quite different – short, selective, and personal. Some will say quirky.

A caveat, if you will, about reading Max or looking at his caricatures: you and I must try not to be lulled into acceptance of the received idea that because a thing is amusing, or light, or comic, it is not serious or important. The prejudice against comedy goes far in explaining, for example, why the novel-reading world does not – though Max did – rank *Vanity Fair* the greatest novel in English, in effect, the English *War and Peace*. If you are unhappy about pairing these two novels, you are an example of just what I am complaining about. You will probably concede that great comedy is more rare than great tragedy, but the next step, the belief that great comedy is equal to great tragedy, will never be popular. Nonetheless, it is a view held by a few highly respected authorities. Plato has Socrates argue that "the genius of comedy was the same with that of tragedy." Aristotle, for all we know, may have come down on the side of comedy, though unfortunately the text has been lost. (Recall how in Umberto Eco's *The Name of the Rose* the serious of this world are willing to poison their fellows rather than have them get hold of Aristotle's text on comedy.) James Joyce ranked comedy higher. He insisted that comedy "makes for joy, while tragedy makes for sorrow; the sense of possession of joy in the one being superior to the sense of deprivation in the other." Bertolt Brecht, we are told, maintained that "tragedy deals with the sufferings of mankind in a less serious way than comedy," a pronouncement that elicited from one critic the supporting comment that "the comic vision does not give to suffering and to evil a dangerous romantic grandeur or an inevitable dominance." But the preference for comedy is probably temperamental, and not to be taught by argument.

In reading Max we might also take a cue from Harold Bloom on reading, even while we acknowledge that Bloom holds no special brief for comedy, is himself not a Maximilian, and has become something of a crank. Yet his aesthetically driven words on reading seem pertinent: he appropriates Dr Johnson's maxim, *Clear your mind of cant*, i.e. of sectarian thinking; and he urges, *Do not attempt to improve your neighbor or your neighborhood* by your reading. Bloom's additional hope for the recovery of irony would also be germane to reading Max, although, as Bloom with characteristic pessimism rightly observes, "You can no more teach someone to be ironic than you can instruct them to become solitary." There are people – those that can't be left alone in a room with an irony – who simply cannot read Max Beerbohm.

Bohun Lynch's book did not amount to much and was, as Max desired, negligible for biographical purposes. S. N. Behrman and David Cecil, unequivocal biographers, are my predecessors. They were aesthetic appreciators who had in common an unashamed love for Max's work. Both were lucky enough to have known Max. Behrman, a long-time admirer, visited Max five times during the early 1950s, and the two became close friends. Behrman elicited

many reminiscences which he set down in the Memoir of his visits, first published serially in the *New Yorker* and in book form in 1960 as *Portrait of Max*.
It's a delightful work. I should like to have met Behrman – he died in 1972
– who by all accounts was also a delightful person.

David Cecil records how in 1956, some few months after Max's death,
Elisabeth Jungmann, Max's widow, told him that Max had wished him to
write his biography. The result, in 1964, was *Max: A Biography*, a very thorough and loving book. Some critics thought it too long. I for one am grateful for its exhaustive detail, though I do wish Cecil had supplied his sources.
David Cecil I did meet. In 1979 I called on the longtime Oxford professor at
his home in Dorset where he was living in retirement. He told me that in his
opinion the two most underrated of the great English writers were Beerbohm
and Trollope. There you are. I of course concurred, and suggested that the
neglect was of different kinds: Beerbohm by general readers, Trollope by critics, an obvious remark, perhaps. In any case, this book is indebted to Cecil
and to Behrman. But times change, and this biography will be unlike either
of theirs.

My subtitle, *A Kind of a Life*, draws on the passage in *Zuleika Dobson* where
Clio, the Muse of History, lets fall her opinion on Gibbon's *Decline and Fall*:
ὅστις τοῖα ἔχει ἐν ἡδονῇ ἔχει ἐν ἡδονῇ τοῖα (For people who like that kind
of thing, that is the kind of thing they like). It is wonderfully incontrovertible, and I'd like to suggest that it is more than an example of Maximilian wit.
Rather, the words are part of Max's small and comic contribution to the
ongoing debate about beauty. What makes a work of art good or beautiful?
Max's aphorism seems to endorse an unqualified subjectivism, or, worse still,
to be merely a clever enunciation of the infamous "I don't know anything
about art, but I know what I like." On the other hand, if the words are ironic,
and Max is ever ironic, they do not mean that at all. As he said in another
context, One never knows where one is with these ironists.

CHAPTER ONE

A Small Brother

Here's Max Beerbohm on his parents and family: "I adored my father and mother and I adored my brothers and sisters. What kind of complex would they find me the victim of? . . . They were a tense and peculiar family, the Oedipuses, weren't they?" The Beerbohm family were an odd and peculiarly talented family. The father, Julius Ewald Edward Beerbohm, a native of Memel, Lithuania, on the Baltic Sea, came from a merchant family of German, Dutch, and Slavonic origins. Born in 1810, the youngest of eleven children, he was educated at Thuringia, trained in business at Paris, and in 1830 migrated to London where he set up as a City corn merchant. In 1849 he married an Englishwoman, Constantia Draper, the daughter of John Draper, a Lloyd's of London clerk, described by Max as "a deeply religious man, and an ardent bibliophile with no worldly ambitions of any kind; a very lovable character."

Julius and Constantia Beerbohm had four children, Ernest, born 1850; Herbert, born 1852; Julius, born 1854; and Constance, born 1856. Mrs Constantia Beerbohm died in 1858 at the age of thirty-two, whereupon the widower Beerbohm married her sister Eliza (in Switzerland, as marriage to a deceased wife's sister was unlawful in England). She in turn had five children, three of whom survived: Agnes, born 1865; Dora, born 1868; and, on 24 August 1872, Henry Maximilian Beerbohm, the cadet of the family, born when his father was sixty-two. ("Henry" was baptized two months later in All Saints Church, Kensington.) The Beerbohms were living at the time at 57 Palace Gardens Terrace, Kensington, though they would soon move to Clanricarde Gardens, in nearby Bayswater.

Max's father was a charming man, and according to Herbert's biographer, also shrewd, courteous, cultured, dignified, humorous, tolerant, and, business matters excepted, absent-minded. It is known also that Beerbohm *père* was a dandy – nicknamed "Monsieur Su-Perbe-Homme" during his youthful days in Paris. He prospered as a City merchant, published two trade papers, spoke seven languages, and lived until 1892, at which date he was eighty-two and his youngest son twenty. Max's mother was considered even more charming than her husband and was known especially for her hospitality and keen sense of humour. She doted on her youngest child, always, long after he had grown into manhood. He lived in her house until, aged thirty-seven, he married and moved to Italy in 1910. In 1956 Max told Elisabeth Jungmann, "My sister Constance, who slept in my mother's room, always told me that when I was out, my mother didn't sleep until I had come home; I then usually went in to kiss her good night & a moment later she was sound asleep." The bedroom shared by stepmother and daughter would have been in the Upper Berkeley Street house where the Beerbohms lived after 1897. Mrs Beerbohm must have become accustomed to the late hours, for during these years Max, by his own account, dined out, went to dinner parties, or the theatre, just about every night. In these latter years a friend described her as "small and keen-eyed, in her lace cap and black silk dress, looking very dignified but with the wit and humour of a gamin [street arab]." She was always a great favourite with Max's friends.

Constance, the eldest sister, was thought rather "plain" and is described by one friend as "vague and dreamy and imaginative," with literary ambitions. When she grew up she briefly left her stepmother's house, but soon returned to help manage the household and stayed the rest of her life. Agnes, the elder of Max's full sisters, was considered the beauty of the family and is described as "gay and amusing and high-spirited"; she married a Mr Neville, who took her to India; the marriage failed, and she too returned home. Dora, the sister nearest Max in age, some five years older than he, was reportedly the "gayest" of all the family, something of a tomboy, and in her mother's view "the cleverest of all my clever children." She became an Anglican nun, a Sister of Charity at St Saviour's Priory in the East End of London. When she entered the convent in 1893, Max was temporarily dismayed: "My sister is quite young," he wrote to a friend, "and is determined to cut herself off from life. Strange, isn't it?" As it turned out, Dora remained cheerful and funny; she spent annual holidays with her family and later with Max and his wife. Max, writing her obituary in 1940, had long since come to understand the altruistic motives in this favourite sister, who had been "a far more spirited child than I, brighter and more adventurous." In addition to charitable work among the poor, Dora edited and wrote her Order's quarterly journal. She had wide tastes in literature: she idolized Dante, and she read *War and Peace* many times in a French translation, something her younger brother would never have dreamed of doing.

Max grew up in a very female household. By the time he was four, the time to which his memory could later reach back, his brothers were out of the house, his father busily working in the City, and he was home with his doting mother and sisters. He was, by all accounts, a pleasant, happy, well-mannered, and well-behaved child. He returned his mother's and sisters' affection and would remain close to them all his life. W. H. Auden attributes much of Max's adult character to his having grown up in a feminine world, adoring and being adored by his mother and sisters: "One can very well understand why he was pampered," Auden writes, "for few people can have been by nature so adapted to a life of cozy domesticity." How one comes to be by nature so adaptive Auden cannot of course explain, but he is right to assert that when Max came to maturity he was a "charming, affectionate, intensely loyal, good-tempered" man, and, after his marriage, intensely domestic. We hardly need Auden's supporting pronouncement that this domesticity prevailed in him because none of the common threats to a happy home life, like "promiscuity, the bottle, or the race track, seem ever to have tempted him."

Of Max's boyhood, we know little. We get a glimpse from a 1936 BBC broadcast:

> In my earlier years, soldiers had monopolized the romantic side of me. Although, like all my coevals, I wore a sailor suit, my heart was with the land forces; insomuch that I insisted on wearing also, out of doors, a belt with a sword attached to it, and on my breast a medal which, though it had merely the Crystal Palace embossed on it, I associated with the march to Kandahar. I used to watch with emotion the sentries changing guard outside Kensington Palace; and it was my purpose to be one of them hereafter. Meanwhile I made many feeble little drawings of them, which I coloured strongly. But somehow, mysteriously, when I was eight years old or so, the soldiery was eclipsed for me by the constabulary. Somehow the scarlet and the bearskins began to thrill me less than the austere costume and calling of the Metropolitan Police. Once in every two hours a policeman came, on his beat, past the house of my parents. At the window of the dining room I would await his coming, punctually behold him with profound interest, and watch him out of sight. ... [I] looked forward impatiently to being a member of the Force. But the young are faithless. By the time I was eleven years old I despised the Force. I was interested only in politicians – in Statesmen, as they were called at that time.

Max tells how he got his first mental pictures of the politicians of his day from the weekly pages of *Punch*; and how he spent many hours imitating and colouring drawings from that magazine; and how *Punch*, being firmly Liberal and Gladstonian, portrayed Prime Minister Gladstone as "always more muscular than any of his enemies, redoubtable though they too were; and the attitudes he struck were more striking than theirs." This seemed unfair to the Conservatives, and to Max himself: "For my father was a Conservative, and so, accordingly, was I." He claimed to have derived more than a familiarity with the features of politicians from this magazine: "It is from the bound volumes of *Punch* that small boys derive their knowledge of life. That, I suppose, is why small boys are always so old-fashioned in their ideas. ... Even in later years, when they have detected how wide and fluid a thing life is, they do yet conceive many real things through the false conventions of John Tenniel, George du Maurier, Charles Keene, and the rest." In due course, passing people through his own caricatural convention would become the foremost delight of his life.

Max saw his grown brothers regularly, except for the eldest, Ernest, who had emigrated and become a sheep farmer in the Cape Colony, where he is said to have married a "coloured lady." Max never knew him. But his other two brothers little Max idolized. And, by the way, though we call them half-brothers, they were genetically more than this, in that their mothers were sisters. One eighth closer than conventional half-brothers? Herbert, the second eldest son, became one of London's foremost actor-managers. Like Max he had a keen sense of humour and a boyish charm. Otherwise, Herbert was very much Max's opposite: Herbert was not only much older – almost twenty years – he was much bigger; he had carrot-coloured hair; he was flamboyant, vital, untidy, restless, histrionic, extroverted; he was a great host (Max was a great guest); he was a man of huge energies and ambitions, constantly in motion, never still for a moment, reading his letters and scripts as he walked or was driven between home and theatre. He was married, with a wife and three children, but had many love affairs, even a "second family" with five illegitimate children (movie director Carol Reed was his son, actor Oliver Reed a grandson); and yet another son, by an actress, was born to him in 1917, the year of his death at the age of sixty-four. (One could argue that Max had no children because his brother produced more than his share.) Herbert was witty and unpredictable in speech, given to talking in outlandish paradoxes and dazzling *non sequiturs*. He was a natural gambler, an eccentric, a "character," a man of "sanguine radiance." Max told of seeing a guest off in front of his mother's house, in 1908, when a taxi stopped at the kerb: "My brother Herbert stepped out of it in the dreamy yet ample and energetic way that he had of stepping out of taxis. 'Oh, how are you, Mr Tree?' my friend greeted him. 'I?' said Herbert ... 'I? Oh, I'm radiant!' " Coming from anyone else, the epithet would have been absurd, Max and his friend agreed, but Herbert's use of it was "perfectly right and proper."

Herbert's life was the theatre. He took early to the amateur stage, where in 1876 he adopted the name Tree. He wanted, Max explained, "a shoutable monosyllable" for purposes of applause (he was also merely translating the second part of "Beerbohm"). After he made his professional London début in 1878, his reputation rose steadily, enhanced by his versatility as an actor; and in 1887 he became manager of the Haymarket Theatre. In 1897 he moved into his own large, lavish theatre, Her Majesty's – "quite the handsomest playhouse in London." Max told the story that this theatre had had a narrow escape "from never existing at all": while in America with Herbert in 1895, Max, sent by his brother to evaluate a stage version of du Maurier's *Trilby*, reported back that the play was "absolute nonsense" and would be a dismal failure in London. Herbert put the matter out of his mind; but having the final night of their stay in New York free, he decided to see the play. After two acts he went backstage and bought it on the spot, and from the proceeds of the spectacular success of his London production of *Trilby*, starring Dorothea Baird and himself, he built Her Majesty's Theatre. Fifty years later, Max told a friend, "I was right about *Trilby*."

Herbert, in his "incessant zeal" and "large, wholesome appetite for life and art" (Max's words), produced and took the leading roles in an impressive range of plays, from Shakespeare and Ibsen to popular figures like Stephen Phillips and Henry Arthur Jones. He was the leading Shakespearian actor-producer of his era, and the founder of successful annual Shakespeare festivals at the renamed His Majesty's Theatre. Herbert's taste was for lavish productions, huge casts, realistic period costumes, striking sound effects and music, and elaborate staging (his banqueting and forum scenes became legendary); he delighted to have live animals on stage, everything from rabbits and doves to horses and oxen. Tree was the original producer of and star in Wilde's *A Woman of No Importance* and Shaw's *Pygmalion* (the latter a great success, except, in Shaw's view, for "the raving absurdity of Tree's acting. ... He was like nothing human, and wallowed ecstatically in his own impossibility, convinced that he was having the success of his life"). But enough of

Herbert's career. Max himself says that hearing about deceased old actors
(this was before film) was about as charming as hearing about other people's
stuffed birds. Our interest in Herbert revolves around his interaction with
Max.

He recalled Herbert's providing one of the most memorable days of his
childhood, some time in March 1882, when Max was nine:

> I wanted to grow up quickly and belong ... to the great world in which
> Herbert was moving. ... Herbert nobly invited me to spend a Saturday
> morning with him. He had rooms in Maddox Street, sharing them with
> his friend A. K. Moore ... who smoked that pipe and stared at me and
> laughed again and again at the notion that Herbert had so small a brother.
> Herbert went on writing at a table by the window; but this pre-occupation
> I excused, for he told me he was writing something for – *Punch*! And he
> told me that in a few minutes he was going to take his manuscript – and
> me! – round to Bouverie Street and show us both to [the editor] Mr
> Burnand. ... [Mr Burnand] seemed to me the more greatly a prince of
> men because he was not smoking, and because he sat in a chair that swung
> round towards us in a most fascinating manner, and because he did not
> laugh at me. I liked also Mrs Bernard Beere, the famous actress, to whom,
> after another drive in a hansom, I was presented as she lay, in the middle
> of a large room somewhere, on a sofa of crimson velvet, with a great deal
> of lace around her head, and an enormous bunch of hothouse grapes on a
> small table beside her, and a company of important-looking men standing
> and sitting around her. I liked her for giving me so many of her grapes;
> but my enjoyment of these was somewhat marred by the more-than-A.-
> K.-Moorish mirth of one gentleman at the smallness of "Beerbohm Tree's
> brother." This gentleman was of immense height and girth; and I was just
> old enough to think of saying, and just too well-brought-up to say, that *I*
> might as well laugh at the bigness of "Beerbohm Tree's friend." I did but
> look fixedly at the striped shirt collar that he wore; and later, when in
> another hansom, Herbert told me that the gentleman was Mr Edmund
> Yates [writer and youthful friend of Dickens, the cause of his falling-out
> with Thackeray], I merely said that I did not like his striped collar.

The greatest event of that great day was yet to come: we were to lunch
at Herbert's club. Was it the "Arundel," perhaps? The "Savage"? I know
not. I cared not. It was Herbert's club, and I lunched in it, and was

presented to the great Mr Godwin* in it. At first I thought he must be a "conspirator," for he wore a large black cloak and a large soft black hat. But he had the most charming manners, and treated me as an equal, and I quite agreed with the opinion, so often expressed by Herbert in those days, that Godwin was a Master. I left the club in company with these two, and Herbert, after hailing a hansom for me and paying the driver, gave me a ten-shilling piece. The gold seemed to me at that time hardly less wonderful than it would seem in this age of paper. That gold piece soon became some mere silver; that silver, vanishing copper; but the memory of those hours with Herbert was a treasure to be jealously hoarded.

Max gradually learned to appreciate Herbert's eminence. Having so famous a brother was a matter of "awe" to his schoolfellows, and, when in 1887 Herbert became manager of the Haymarket Theatre, that awe increased dizzyingly. Max went to Herbert's opening there:

Ripened judgment has not inclined me to think *The Red Lamp* the greatest play ever written. But I thought it so on its first night – the first night of Herbert's management. And I saw it seventeen times, without changing my opinion. Herbert always let me sit in his dressing-room during the entr'actes, and there I met many of the most interesting men of the period – none of whom interested me so much as Herbert. . . . and it seems to me, as I look back, that even during term-time, when my body was at Charterhouse, my soul was in the Haymarket Theatre.

As Max grew older, he was frequently invited to Herbert's famous suppers where he met not only theatre people but notable painters, politicians, writers, and patrons of the arts. Still, and a little surprisingly, Max records how, with the years, as "the gap between our ages was . . . contracted, each of us found himself . . . more shy in the presence of the other. . . . An old friend of Herbert's once said to him and me, in the course of a dinner in the 'Dome' of His Majesty's: 'You two, when you're together, always seem to be in an attitude of armed neutrality.' I suggested to Herbert that 'terrified love' would be a truer description."

---

* E. W. Godwin, architect and stage designer, was the father of two "love children" with Ellen Terry, one of whom, Gordon Craig, born the same year as Max, was destined to become one of his closest friends.

Julius, Max's other half-brother, was known chiefly as an imperturbable dandy. This formed, from earliest days, a bond with Max, who would himself be a lifelong, one could say fanatic, dandy. And although Max as a child and young boy worshipped both his brothers, for a time he considered Julius more a "god," precisely "because he was so cool and calm and elegant." Max compared the two:

> Herbert seemed always to be in a hurry, Julius never. Herbert would over-pay and dismiss his hansom whenever he came to see us, and at his departure would whistle frantically and piercingly for another. Julius always kept *his* hansom waiting, hour after hour. . . . Herbert talked excitedly, and used to pass his hands through his hair, and leave it all standing up on end. Julius never raised his deep voice, and never put any expression into it, and his straw-coloured hair lay around his head as smoothly as satin. Herbert's necktie was often on one side, and his top hat always lustreless, and he never had a flower in his buttonhole. Julius had always a gardenia or Parma violets, and his hat was dazzling, and his linen was washed in Paris. Also, he had a moustache. Not to have that when one was grown up seemed to me to argue a deficiency in sense of fitness. I knew that Herbert, being an actor, had to be clean-shaven. But I felt that I myself, if hereafter I had to choose between being an actor and having a moustache, should not hesitate.

Had his linen washed in Paris! Less spectacularly, Julius wrote a successful book about his youthful travels in Patagonia. Nicknamed "Poet," he produced Swinburnian (daring, sometimes shocking) verse, seldom bothering to write it down. A compulsive gambler, he engaged in financial speculation, usually with disastrous results. It was said that his only successful venture was to marry a rich young woman – whose fortune he squandered. One of his schemes was to dredge the Nile in search of the Pharaohs' lost jewels. Another was to operate a luxury hotel in Marienbad, and, having left a deposit for the hotel, he subsequently forgot about the entire transaction until his creditors reminded him of it. He played the gaming tables at places like Dieppe, where he sometimes won but usually lost down to his last louis. A friend told of finding brokers seizing Julius's household goods on the ground floor of his London flat while Julius himself was upstairs lying in bed translating a lyric of Heine's into English. Whatever his financial or personal disasters, Julius kept his dandy's priorities till the end. Herbert, wearing a red-brown suit, visited him on his deathbed. "Ginger!" Julius cried in disgust and turned his face to the wall. He died in April 1906, aged fifty-two. Max wrote to an old friend, "Poor Julius! I shall miss him very much, and so will many people. He was such an odd, distinguished creature."

Max in his childhood and youth saw less of Julius than of Herbert. But Julius, aside from serving as a stunning exemplar of dandyism, performed one other very special service for his little brother: he took Max to his first London music hall. It happened after dinner at the Café Royal, and the theatre was the Pavilion, where Max saw not only the newcomer Albert Chevalier, but that classic old stager of the music hall, the Great MacDermott, of whom Max had often heard in his childhood: "And here he was, in the flesh, in the grease-paint, surviving and thriving, to my delight; a huge old burly fellow, with a yellow wig and a vast expanse of crumpled shirt-front that had in the middle of it a very large, not *very* real diamond stud," roaring out "We Don't Want to Fight, But By Jingo! If We *Do*." Enthralled, Max would thereafter regularly attend London music halls. More than half a century after Julius escorted him to his first music hall in December 1890, Max told a BBC radio audience:

> Perhaps you will blame me for having spent so much of my time in Music Halls, so frivolously, when I should have been sticking to my books, burning the midnight oil and compassing the larger latitude. But I am impenitent. I am inclined to think, indeed I have always thought, that a young man who desires to know all that in all ages and in all lands has been thought by the best minds, and wishes to make a synthesis of all those thoughts for the future benefit of mankind, is laying up for himself a very miserable old age.

But we are still in Max's childhood, a happy and much extended childhood. The first extension would be his day school.

CHAPTER TWO

Schoolboy

From 1881 to 1885, Max, *aetat* nine to thirteen, attended Orme Square School, a small, pleasant establishment of some twenty pupils, run by a Mr Wilkinson. Blond, mustachioed Mr Wilkinson delighted Max. Wilkinson cared only for the classics and for cricket. Sports never interested Max, but under Wilkinson he came to love the classics: Wilkinson "was by far the best teacher I ever had; wonderfully interesting and 'enthusing.' He did ... so sympathise with the mind of a small boy.... He gave me a love of Latin and thereby enabled me to write English *well.*" We don't have examples of Max's early written English. Orme Square was a day school, so there were no letters home. But anyone fortunate enough to have been taught Latin at a young age knows that that is when one learns English grammar. And it wasn't just Latin and the classics that made Orme Square pleasant. Mrs Wilkinson taught the boys drawing: "Hers were the only lessons I ever had," Max wrote, "the free hand system: ... And what a trial I must have been to Mrs Wilkinson!" Presumably he improved upon his early *Punch* imitations. Forty years later Max was happy to hear that his great friends the Rothensteins were sending their son Billy to Orme Square School, to follow, as he put it to the boy's mother, "in those old obliterated footsteps of mine." He reported to her that Wilkinson – with whom he occasionally had lunch at the Savile Club – "remains as boyish as ever, making me feel always like a nonagenarian."

Max was lucky all his life, and Orme Square School formed an early chapter in his run of good fortune. But his next five years, 1885 to 1890, at Charterhouse, were not to his liking. They could have been far worse: he could have been sent, as had his three elder brothers, to his father's old school at Schnepfeuthal, Germany, a place the boys found cruel and detestable. But for Max his Charterhouse years were the least happy of his life. Actually, they were really not terrible, they just did not live up to the earlier or later years. For one thing, he was away from home and the cosy little school housed in the side-by-side residences of Mr Wilkinson. Orme Square was just five minutes' walk along the Bayswater Road from Clanricarde Gardens. Charterhouse, a big and famous old school, with some 400 boys, was located in rural Surrey in the village of Godalming (having moved from London in 1872), some forty miles south-west of London. Here he lived briefly at Robinites, and afterwards at Girdlestoneites or "Duckites," so called because the House Master was thought to walk like a duck. The strong emphasis on athletics at his new school ran entirely contrary to Max's tastes and abilities. On the other hand, Charterhouse, like all public schools of the time, still put stress on the classics, and here Max, with his penchant for Latin, felt secure. But no close friendships came his way. He was an odd boy, something of a loner, although not exactly unsocial. School records show him a member of the Library and the *Greyfriar* committees and, in his last year, the Debating Society. He was undoubtedly "different," but the other boys, *mirabile dictu,* seem to have accepted this. Nor did it hurt him, as we have seen, that his brother was a well-known man of the London theatre.

Max was a steady if unspectacular student, who restricted his attention to the subjects he enjoyed and in which he was accomplished. He had a gift for languages ancient and modern, though he preferred the ancient. His best effort came in his third year, 1888, when he won the classics prize in the Remove, the top form in the lower school. In this same term he did poorly in mathematics and natural science. In his last year he ranked 8th overall in classics, 12th in French, 104th (just about the bottom) in maths, and managed to avoid science altogether. Latin aside, what he liked was not directly helpful in schoolwork: he liked comic verse and comic prose. (Ralph Vaughan Williams, who entered Charterhouse the same year as Max did, recalls him reciting from memory the *Nonsense* verse of Edward Lear.) He liked to read, and he pored over Thackeray, his great favourite. Thackeray had also been a Carthusian. Moreover, Thackeray could draw! Here was a model. At Charterhouse, Max thought he would like to become a writer.

During his last year at school, at the urging of one of his masters, Major Alexander Hay Tod, he had printed at Godalming a "classic fragment" in Latin elegiacs called "Carmen Becceriense." The 14-line poem, bulked out to four printed pages by critical notes and scholarly apparatus (in the style of a Latin scholar and Charterhouse master, T. E. Page), is attributed to Lucretius by the editor, "H. M. B." The poem is a spoof on a piano recital by Beccerius, who is Music Master A. G. Becker, an eccentric of volatile temper (reported

to have walked out of a concert after hearing one chord by – the story varies
– either Pachmann or Paderewski, saying he "knew the man was a charla-
tan"). Beccerius/Becker plays the piano with such fervour, such "heavy
blows," that the boys hold their ears; but, because another music master,
G. H. Robinson, laughs, Harmony rushes out of the Hall and Charterhouse
is deprived of Concord. As comic satire of classical verse and scholarship
"Carmen Becceriense" is remarkably mature – a work of which, according to
Auden, any adult humorist could be proud. The notes combine learning and
silliness – e.g. the line *Mixtaque cum mixtis sunt nota mixta notis* is glossed:
"*Nota* from nōtum = a note. Look this word out in your Latin-English.
Conington elegantly: – 'And mixéd notes with mixed notes are mixéd.'" The
poem is tough going for today's reader (the Latin, I am told, is excellently
classical), but as this is Max's first publication, it deserves notice. The impulse
towards satire and parody had begun.

Charterhouse also nurtured Max in his lifelong passion for the right
clothes. School provided him with an opportunity to be extra careful, perfect
in his schoolboy way, in his dress. This obsessive concern with clothes must
have gone back further still. We know that his father was a superb dresser and
his older brother Julius a complete dandy (not Herbert, who was always a
careless, hurried, flurried dresser). But Charterhouse seems to have spurred
Max on. Photographs of him at this time are arresting (see plate 2): every item
of dress from collar and tie to jacket and trousers seems meticulously dapper;
the hair is scrupulously parted towards or in the middle; the pose is formal.
It was too early for any philosophical (much less French) considerations of
the underpinnings of dandyism; but it was not too early for a certain coolness, a certain detachment. This had already set in, and can be seen in the old
group portraits in the Charterhouse archives, showing him baby-faced and
younger-looking than many of his contemporaries but decidedly, almost
alarmingly, self-assured and self-possessed.

As for his attitude of mind during his Charterhouse years, we have his own
words, though only as set down in later times. The earlier the comments, the
more negative they were. Scarcely two years out of Charterhouse, he writes to
an Oxford friend in September 1892:

> I went down to Charterhouse the other day, putting up at an inn in the
> town. After a solitary dinner I walked up the hill and peered through the
> windows of my house where boys were sitting at "preparation" with rough

hair on long forms giggling covertly – just as when I was among them. I suppose if I went there twenty years hence I should see the same thing. Isn't school an awful place?

One wonders why he revisited the scene. Five years later, in the essay "Going back to School," his tone is more light-hearted, but he is still revelling in the fact that he is no longer at school. He explains how a few nights previously, in a hansom cab outside Victoria Station, he noticed another cab laden with "a small hat-box, a newish trunk and a corded play-box," and, inside the cab, he glimpsed "a very small pale boy in a billicock-hat. He was looking at me through the side-window. If Envy was ever inscribed on any face, it was inscribed on the face of that very small, pale boy. 'There,' I murmured, 'but for the grace of God, goes Max Beerbohm!' ":

> It was always the most bitter thing, in my own drive to the station, to see other people, quite happy, as it seemed, with no upheaval of their lives; people in cabs, who were going out to dinner and would sleep in London; grown-up people! The impotent despair of these drives – I had exactly fifteen of them – I hope that I shall never experience a more awful emotion. Those drives have something, surely, akin to drowning. In their course the whole of a boy's home-life passes before his eyes, every phase of it standing out against the black curtain of the future. ... Well do I remember how, on the last day of the holidays, I used to always rise early, and think I had got twelve more whole hours of happiness, and how those hours used to pass me with mercifully slow feet. ... Three more hours! ... Sixty more minutes! ... Five! ... I used to draw upon my tips for a first-class ticket that I might not be plunged suddenly among my companions, with their hectic and hollow mirth, their dreary disinterment of last term's jokes. I used to revel in the thought that there were many stations before G——. ... The dreary walk, with my small bag, up the hill. I was not one of those who made a rush for the few cabs.

As he now sees it, his character at school had "remained in a state of undevelopment":

> As I hovered, in grey knickerbockers, on a cold and muddy field, round the outskirts of a crowd that was tearing itself limb from limb for the sake of a leathern bladder, I would often wish for a nice, warm room and a good game of hunt-the-slipper. And, when we sallied forth, after dark, in the

frost, to the swimming-bath, my heart would steal back to the fireside and
Writing School and the plot of Miss Braddon's latest novel.

He was, he shrewdly concludes, simultaneously too young and too old for his
years. The essay continues to contrast his present happy state with the sad
plight of the schoolboy: he himself has no lines of Xenophon to construe, no
ode of Horace to memorize by tomorrow, no need to master "the intricate
absurdities" in the second book of Euclid; instead he writes at a comfortable
table by a warm fire, and in the evening will go to the theatre to be followed
by supper and wine – "In a word I enjoy myself immensely." Come to think
of it, having suffered himself all the miseries of school, he need not lavish pity
on the present schoolboy: "I am at a happier point in Nature's cycle, that is all."
    Years later, in 1920, at Rapallo in Italy, he would again write of his school
years, this time at the invitation of the school paper. This essay cuts two ways.
He tells how immediately after Charterhouse, he looked back from Oxford at
the school he had just left: "I thought Charterhouse a very fine school, really.
I was very glad of having been there. But ... my delight at having been at
Charterhouse was far greater than had been my delight in being there." And
whereas he was very well content while at Oxford, as he is very well content
at present in Rapallo, he had never been content at Charterhouse. He had
always longed to get school over with. Nor has he any feeling of fraternity
with what he calls the "straitest sect" of former students, those who simply
can't bear the thought of having left Charterhouse, for whom everything
thereafter is "one long anticlimax," those old boys who can't forget so-and-
so's kicking that decisive goal, or the old jokes about the French master, or
the black eye that Simpson gave Thompson. It's all right, Max supposes, for
a boy to have regarded Charterhouse as a home, but he should not be home-
sick for it ever after. Still, he is quite willing, thirty years after the fact, to see
that his years at Charterhouse were good for him. If he hadn't gone there, if
he had had a private tutor, might he not have become "a prig and an egoist"?

> "But," say my young readers, "isn't that just what you *have* become?" To
> a certain extent, yes, perhaps. But I should be much worse if I hadn't been
> at Charterhouse. ... And I am not really priggish when I haven't a pen in
> my hand, believe me. The very fact that I foresaw your distaste for what I
> have written shows that I have a power of getting outside myself. That is a
> very useful power. And it is a power which a shy and sensitive little boy
> learns better at a public school than he could anywhere else. A private tutor

might have made me proficient in French, in Algebra, even in Science. Of these subjects (partly, but only partly, because I had no natural bent for them) I knew next to nothing when I left Charterhouse. The main thing that I had learnt there, and have not yet forgotten, was a knack of understanding my fellow creatures, of living in amity with them and not being rubbed the wrong way by their faults, and not rubbing them the wrong way with mine. I live in Italy nowadays, because I like the sun very much. But whenever I go to England my friends are really pleased to see me. I have not lost that good-humoured give-and-take spirit which only the communal life of a public school could have given me.

This is pretty self-revelatory, if he means it, and I believe he does. (My thesis, throughout, is not that Max was not self-aware – quite the contrary; it is rather that he did not need to search inside himself much, did not agonize about his soul; he knew who he was, what he could do, and was modestly pleased with himself.)

Max denies that school repressed his individuality: "I was a queer child. I didn't care a brass farthing for games. What I liked was Latin prose, Latin verse, and drawing caricatures. Nobody bothered me to play games. Boys and Masters alike (Mr Tod always especially) encouraged me to draw as many and as impudent caricatures as possible. I ought to have been very happy. But – oh, how I always longed to be grown up!" In 1955, some sixty-five years after leaving Charterhouse, he wrote to the son of one of his contemporaries there: "I liked all the Masters with whom I came in contact. They were a very amiable array of men, with an innate gift for teaching . . . and never a one of them showed any resentment of the liberties that my prentice pen took with their personal appearance."

The thing, then, which most helped him get on with other boys – and with masters – was his talent for caricature. The archives of Charterhouse contain scores of drawings, some dashed off on lined exercise-book paper, chiefly of the masters, but also of public figures, politicians like Lord Rosebery and Randolph Churchill, theatre people like playwright A. W. Pinero and actors George Grossmith and John Toole, and also, not surprisingly, the Prince of Wales, and Oscar Wilde. A handful of his drawings got into *Greyfriar*, an impressive and glossy school publication; these included caricatures of new boys, of the boys on "Exeat" (holiday), and of Charterhouse "Types" – the photographer, the debater, the vocalist – and a group of "Boulevard Types," all of which presage "Club Types," his first truly public publications a few years later. The striking thing about these Charterhouse pen and ink productions is their maturity; they are astonishingly like his later work (minus the colour and the decorative backgrounds). Max himself, who had such a sure knowledge of his gifts, thought the Charterhouse drawings pretty good. Writing in 1908 to his favourite among the masters, the same Alexander Hay Tod, he said:

> You were one of my first patrons and collectors; so perhaps, if you happen to be in London next Wednesday, or any day within the three weeks or so, you might like to inspect my "later manner" in caricature [at the Carfax Gallery]. Essentially, I think, this manner is the same as that which I had at Charterhouse; I mayn't have improved it very much but I don't think there's any sad falling off. Anyhow, doing caricatures is still the delight that it was to me in the days when you so self-sacrificingly and colleague-sacrificingly egged me on to further outrages.

When Max left Charterhouse, the Headmaster wrote to Max's mother saying he disliked the prospect of parting with Max, that his moving on would be a loss to the school: "His artistic power will be much missed by many whose portraits he has often drawn and among these I may reckon Yours most faithfully, W. Haig Brown."

To Oxford Max went, in the autumn of 1890.

CHAPTER THREE

Oxford Character

"I was a modest good-humoured boy. It was Oxford that made me insuffer-able." Thus Max in 1897. After Charterhouse, Oxford was heaven. The public school system, he wrote, "makes Oxford and Cambridge doubly delec-table":

> Undergraduates owe their happiness chiefly to the consciousness that they are no longer at school. The nonsense which was knocked out of them at school is all pushed gently back at Oxford or Cambridge. ... Even now much of my own complacency comes of having left school.

Well, yes; but Oxford in its own right, aside from its contrast to Charterhouse, perfectly suited his growing tastes. It was Oxford during the heyday of Oscar Wilde's aestheticism and the Whistlerian ideal of art for its own sake. Walter Pater still held forth at Brasenose College. Max found Oxford the perfect place for the development of his dandyism, his aestheti-cism, and his distinctive spectator persona. He arrived at Merton College to study classics in the autumn of 1890. His rooms were in Mob Quad ("the oldest quadrangle in Oxford"), on the ground floor under the Library; he was pleased to learn, from his scout, that these rooms had been occupied in the late 1860s by his boyhood hero, Lord Randolph Churchill, whose name was carved large on the side table. After a year Max lived out of college in a tiny house "scarcely bigger than a Punch and Judy show" at the far end of Merton Street. His room, as was always to be the case henceforward, was papered in blue and was hung with Pellegrini prints from *Vanity Fair*.

In an essay begun at college and finished in 1895, Max gave a peculiar account of his mental bearings during his university years:

> In the year of grace 1890, in the beautiful autumn of that year, I was a freshman at Oxford. I remember how my tutor asked me what lectures I wished to attend, and how he laughed when I said I wished to attend the lectures of Mr Walter Pater. Also, I remember how, one morning soon

after, I went into Ryman's to order some foolish engraving for my room, and there saw, peering into a portfolio, a small, thick, rock-faced man whose top-hat and gloves of *bright* dog-skin struck one of the many discords in that little city of learning or laughter. The serried bristles of his moustachio made for him a false-military air. I think I nearly went down when they told me that this was Walter Pater. Not that even, in those more decadent days of my childhood, did I admire that man as a stylist. Even then I was angry that he should treat English as a dead language, bored by that sedulous ritual wherewith he laid out every sentence as in a shroud – hanging, like a widower, long over its marmoreal beauty, or ever he could lay it at length in his book, its sepulchre.

The rest of the piece is not easily interpreted. It tells of Max's disillusionment not only with Pater (this was probably true) but with Oxford itself, "a bit of Manchester through which Apollo had once passed," its charm and traditions all lost. What might he do?

To unswitch myself from my surroundings, to guard my soul from contact with the unlovely things that compassed it about, therein lay my hope. I must approach the Benign Mother with great caution. And so, while most of the freshmen were doing her honour with wine and song and wreaths of smoke, I stood aside, pondered. In such seclusion I passed my first term – ah, how often did I wonder whether I was not wasting my days, and, wondering, abandon my meditations upon the right ordering of the future!

With the end of the first term he returns to London: "Around me seethed swirls, eddies, torrents, violent cross-currents of human activity. What uproar! Surely I could have no part in modern life. Yet, yet for a while it was fascinating to watch the ways of its children." This life – best embodied in the Prince of Wales – seemed "to have no time for thought, the highest energy of man. Now, it was to thought that *my* life should be dedicated." He would seek only the pleasures of the intellect, which, for him, meant the pleasures of the imagination:

It is only (this is a platitude) the things one has not done, the faces or places one has not seen, or seen but darkly, that have charm. It is only mystery – such mystery as besets the eyes of children – that makes things superb. ... It was, for me, merely a problem how I could best avoid "sensations," "pulsations," and "exquisite moments" that were not purely intellectual. I would not attempt to combine both kinds, as Pater seemed to fancy a man might. I would make myself master of some small area of physical life, a life of quiet, monotonous simplicity, exempt from all outer disturbance. I would shield my body from the world that my mind might range over it, not hurt nor fettered.

This is strange stuff. The truth is he was not at all disillusioned; he delighted in Oxford, the city and its university. Whenever he mentions Oxford in his later writings, private or public, the special enchantment the place engendered is immediately apparent. His one novel, *Zuleika Dobson*, has Oxford as its subject. Its famous set piece, where Max, the historian of Zuleika's visit, pauses half-way through his story to meditate on the place, builds towards the exclamation: "... that mysterious, inenubilable spirit, spirit of Oxford. Oxford! The very sight of the word printed, or sound of it spoken, is fraught for me with most actual magic." In a word, he loved the place.

Still, in some sense, his talk about detaching himself was true enough. Although the gloomy solitariness hinted at in the essay was altogether fanciful, and although he was popular with a small set of friends (he belonged to the Merton College Myrmidon Club and actually spoke once or twice at the Essay Society), he did "unswitch" himself from much of his surroundings. He rarely went to lectures; he boasted that he never wore the cap and gown; he did not work at his studies (he managed only a Third in Honour Moderations in 1892 and would eventually leave Oxford without a degree in 1894); he seldom ventured into any circle beyond his Merton associates; he remained altogether removed from athletics or physical exertion of any sort. Aloofness was of course part of dandyism, and dandyism was something he did, in his way, work at. And while Max was always a pleasant person, during these college years he was probably not the delightful person he would become. I don't think many found him "insufferable" as he himself entertainingly claimed, but during his Oxford years he did cultivate some fashionable Wildean affectations, the taste for the precious, the paradoxical, the flippant, and these were not to everyone's taste. I myself find it hard to be impressed by such recorded exchanges as his reply – "What river?" – when he was asked during Eights' Week if he were going down to the river. And there is the anonymous testimony of an elderly cleric, Max's contemporary at Merton: "We thought the fellow put on too much side." Detachment came at the cost of being misunderstood by people who did not know him well.

On the other hand, after his Oxford years he would become, in spite of his cool, detached character, enormously popular in London society. The truly radical "unswitching" in his life would come only in 1910 when he married and retired to Italy.*

The great good that Oxford did for Max was to let him be himself, to let him grow into himself. Oxford meant freedom; it meant being grown up. It meant being leisurely, doing what he wanted, making a few special friends, cultivating his gifts for conversation and wit, developing his writing and drawing skills, indulging his obsession for dandified dressing. It has been argued, chiefly by David Cecil, that Max, as we know him, was a persona, a "mask," a personality that he created. Cecil believes that Max "instinctively desired to dramatize himself"; that he enjoyed "cutting a figure" and was a disciple of the aestheticism of his day which said that a man's dress and manners should be cultivated "in accordance with his ideal of the delightful and the beautiful." All this tended to make Max "artificial." He chose and assumed "a mask that represent[ed] his personal ideal, his conception of what, taking account of his capacities and limitations, he should aspire to be." An exponent of this doctrine of the mask (Yeats was another) will thereby "endue his life with beauty and meaning: if he retains the mask and consistently acts in character with it, he may even ultimately assimilate his nature to it, become substantially the personality he presents to the outer world." If Cecil is right, Max quite literally "made" himself. He did not simply grow up to be what he was automatically, the way most of us do, quite passively, the result of the nature/nurture mix that comes our way. Rather, Max early on knew what he wanted to be and created himself in that image; over the course of time (much like his own fairy-tale character, Lord George Hell) he grew to become his mask. It's an inviting reading of the facts. Another great admirer and student of Max, W. H. Auden, thinks it is nonsense: he confesses himself "astonished" that both of Max's biographers, S. N. Behrman as well as Cecil, talk of Max "as a man who deliberately adopted and cultivated a mask." Auden elaborates, "To say that a man wears a mask is to say that the person as he appears to be to others, perhaps even to himself, differs from the person he really is." This, Auden goes on, was simply not the case:

---

* A friend, noting Max's name among those who attended Herbert Beerbohm Tree's funeral in 1917, said quite unfairly that "Max . . . is too detached to know that Herbert is dead."

Max Beerbohm ... at an astonishingly early age ... knew exactly the sort of person he was, and he never showed the slightest desire to be anyone else. Lucky enough to be equally gifted in two artistic media, and without any ambition to transcend his limitations, he made his caricatures and his writings between them say everything that was in him to say. The behaviour and conversation of most people vary a little in according to the company they happen to be in, but Max's were the same wherever he was. Indeed, if there does seem something not quite human about him, something elfish, it is because, as an adult, he retained the transparency of a child. Intentionally or unintentionally, Oscar Wilde's wisecrack about him is acute: "Tell me, when you are alone with Max, does he take off his face and reveal his mask?"

So, was Max merely being himself, or did he prepare a face to meet the faces that he met? Did he, while at Oxford – or earlier – say to himself, "I shall be not so much a participant but rather a detached, playful observer of human life"? Did he in this manner "create" himself, beginning with admiration, *a distans*, for Oscar Wilde? Disinclined as I am to fence sitting, I yet confess to seeing something in both views. Pushed to choose, I lean towards Auden. But notice that Cecil's position almost merges into agreement with Auden in Cecil's words about the mask-wearer ultimately assimilating his nature to the mask, becoming the personality he has created. The reconciling view might be that Max saw what he wanted to be and went after it, only to find that he had been that person all the time.

Did Max himself ever comment directly – at the time – on this issue? He came close, just once. Writing to a friend, he reports urgings (probably imaginary) of conscience arising from his partly feigned obsession with a fifteen-year-old female music-hall singer:

> She has shewn me what a small distorted career mine has been. After all what have I done since I came to Oxford with power to make myself? What have my pleasures been? To dress carefully, to lie in a canoe in the summer and read minor verse by the fire in winter, to talk of Oscar, to sit down to dinner looking forward to rising from it drunk, to draw more or less amusing caricatures – a few friends, a few theatres and music-halls and cigarettes a day – and there you have my life. Accompanied by a sense of humour, and utter absence of the moral sense and an easy temper, it has been fairly happy I suppose.

In any case, at Oxford Max quickly grew into what he either made of himself or was, at least *in potentia*, all along. Moreover, he became confirmed in his intention to become a writer and a caricaturist. He toyed – no more than that, certainly – with the thought of going into law. It was something to say when asked what he might do with his life. But the truth was, he didn't want to go to work, he wanted to go on drawing and writing. In some ways he wanted to be in a position analogous to that of certain college professors who are honest enough to say, every once in a while, "Thank God I don't have a real job."

At Oxford Max formed the two deepest and most consequential friendships of his life, with Reginald Turner and William Rothenstein.

"Reggie" Turner, two years Max's senior at Merton, came of uncertain parentage. Although commonly believed to be the illegitimate son of Edward Lawson (once Levy), later Lord Burnham, Turner was much more probably, as Hart-Davis convincingly argues, the son of Burnham's uncle, Lionel Lawson, wealthy part-owner of the *Daily Telegraph* and owner of the Gaiety Theatre. His mother may have been a French actress, Miss L. Henrie, who acted in the Gaiety. Turner left Oxford with his degree in 1892, and was later called to the Bar, but never practised. His real talent lay in journalism, which he produced abundantly for the *Telegraph*. His ambition was to be a novelist, but although he sometimes produced a novel a year, his books were never successful. Max seemed to be the only one who thought Turner's novels any good. Turner liked to say that while for most authors first editions were rare, in his case second editions were.

As Merton undergraduates Max and Reggie quickly became close friends, and Max would all his life consider Reggie the "dearest of all my friends." Turner introduced Max to the lure of the continent, and together they visited Rouen, Paris, and Dieppe (the place that became Max's August holiday town). Max judged Turner to be the wittiest, most amusing man he ever met, a talker who could break into "ludicrously adequate blank-verse" or even rhyme, as the subject demanded. He was an "incomparable" mimic, and his performances left his hearers debilitated with laughter. Others – Osbert Sitwell, Somerset Maugham, Harold Acton – corroborate this verdict. Turner's stories and witticisms are lost in the retelling, and I shall hazard only one example: amid a crowd of passengers reboarding a train, Reggie on spotting his compartment stopped abruptly and caused a collision with an

American tourist who angrily exclaimed "Jesus Christ!" "Shh!" came Reggie's reply, "I'm traveling incognito." But Reggie was more than just a funny man. Practically everyone who knew Turner, including Oscar Wilde, thought of him as a faithful and extremely generous friend (he was forever sending people presents).

Max's affection for Turner is attested to in their lifelong correspondence, plentiful because Turner lived mostly abroad. Max's *Letters to Reggie Turner* (1964) form a closely printed 300-page book. We don't have quite everything: Max had gone through the letters (recovered from Reggie's estate in 1946 by Selwyn and Tania Jepson) and given his approval for their publication after his death provided they were purged of passages he marked as possibly offending or causing pain or evincing "certain youthful extravagances." Editor Hart-Davis scrupulously followed Max's wishes and destroyed the excised material. It's tantalizing but useless to speculate on what has been obliterated from the record. Turner as correspondent inspired trust, and Max's letters to him, whatever their irony and playfulness, are (along with those of Max to his wife) the frankest and most self-revealing of his writings.

The other great friendship formed at Oxford was with Will Rothenstein. Born (like Max) in 1872, Rothenstein was the son of a Jewish cloth merchant from Bradford in Yorkshire. At seventeen he went to study art at the Académie Julian in Paris, where he was befriended and encouraged by Whistler, Conder, Degas, Lautrec, Forain, and Fantin-Latour. He returned to England in 1893 to undertake a commission from publisher John Lane to make portraits in lithograph of eminent Oxford characters. Max describes Rothenstein's "apparition":

In the Summer Term of '93 a bolt from the blue flashed down on Oxford. It drove deep, it hurtlingly embedded itself in the soil. Dons and undergraduates stood around, rather pale, discussing nothing but it. Whence came it, this meteorite? From Paris. Its name? Will Rothenstein. Its aim? To do a series of twenty-four portraits in lithograph for the Bodley Head, London. The matter was urgent. Already the Warden of A, and the Master of B, and the Regius Professor of C, had meekly "sat." Dignified and doddering old men, who had never consented to sit to any one, could not withstand this dynamic little stranger. He did not sue: he invited; he did not invite: he commanded. He was twenty-one years old. He wore spectacles that flashed more than any other pair ever seen. He was a wit. He was brimful of ideas. He knew Whistler. He knew Edmond de Goncourt. He knew everyone in Paris. He knew them all by heart. He was Paris in Oxford. It was whispered that, so soon as he had polished off his selections of dons, he was going to include a few undergraduates. It was a proud day for me when I – I – was included. I liked Rothenstein not less than I feared him; and there arose between us a friendship that has grown ever warmer.

Rothenstein, in his memoirs, described Max at Oxford:

A baby face, with heavily lidded, very light grey eyes shaded by remarkably thin and long lashes, a broad forehead, and sleek black hair parted in the middle and coming to a queer curling point at the neck; a quiet and finished manner; rather tall,* carefully dressed; slender fingered, with an assurance and experience unusual in one of his years.

Rothenstein observed that though "I had more experience of life than he, his seemed to have crystallized into a more finished form than my own. So had his manners, which were perfect. ... Outside Merton only few undergraduates knew him. ... His caricatures were sometimes seen in Shrimpton's window in the Broad; and in time, through these, he acquired some reputation outside his own small circle; for he was fastidious in the choice of friends. My Balliol friends scoffed when I spoke of him as the most brilliant man in Oxford." From Rothenstein we learn that it is not quite true that Max took no exercise: "He shared a canoe with a Merton friend, L. M. Messell, and did sometimes strike the water of the Cher with his paddle. Perhaps it was merely a gesture; at least it was made in the Cher. Further afield I never knew him to go." Rothenstein's other comments fit nicely with what we know from other sources: "He kept himself aloof; going nowhere he seemed to know about everyone. ... He always declared he had read nothing – only [Thackeray's] *The Four Georges*, and Lear's *Book of Nonsense* – and later, Oscar Wilde's *Intentions*, which he thought beautifully written."

Max, who always caricatured his friends, frequently drew Turner and Rothenstein. Both were good subjects in that they were considered stun-

---

* A relative judgement: Rothenstein was a short man. Max, though often thought of as small, and he himself encouraged people to so regard him, was in fact 5 feet 8½ inches tall.

ningly ugly. When Max was asked what Turner thought about the huge nose he gave him, he replied – unconvincingly – that "when you exaggerate as much as that, there can be no offense in it." (See plate 14.) Rothenstein is often shown as a Lilliputian among the Gullivers. (See plate 23.) In old age Max admitted, "My caricatures of him were very cruel, I am afraid. He knew they were, and yet he took it manfully. . . . One day Sickert said to me, 'Your caricatures of dear Will and of Oscar Wilde were so deadly. I know how Oscar feels about them – he can't bear them – but doesn't Will resent them? Isn't he angry?' 'More frightened,' I said . . . 'than angry.'"

It's time for Oscar Wilde.

CHAPTER FOUR

The Divinity

All writers begin by imitating other writers. Max began his public writing career borrowing from and adapting the prose manner of Oscar Wilde. Thackeray's influence, though earlier and in the long run deeper, was less prominent in the 1890s. Moreover, Wilde influenced not only Max's prose, but (if you are on Cecil's side in the argument about the mask) also his pose, his persona. I am not saying the influence was altogether good, just that it was paramount. From Max's last years at Charterhouse and well into his college years at Merton, he engaged in what he called a "long period of distant adoration and reverence" for Oscar Wilde. In 1888 he had actually met the great man at a dinner given by Herbert, but this was as Herbert Tree's little schoolboy brother. Closer acquaintance was five years off. Moreover, in the late 1880s Wilde was not yet the great, and of course nothing of the tragic figure he would become. He was a poet of slight standing, the author of some engaging fairy tales and a few essays; chiefly he was a personality, an outspoken advocate of aestheticism. Also a striker of poses, he was regarded in some quarters as little more than a buffoon. Then, just before Max went up to Oxford in the autumn of 1890, *The Picture of Dorian Gray* made its magazine appearance, and Wilde was suddenly much better known and much more notorious. Better known because the novel was so much talked about; notorious because of its constant hinting at unspeakable "unnatural" sins. Until his disgrace and downfall five years later, Wilde would rise higher and higher: *Dorian Gray* would make its book appearance in 1891; in the same year *Intentions*, a collection of four earlier essays, would establish him as a serious critic, heir to Pater's mantle; next there would follow a series of plays: *Salomé*, written in French and denied the English stage for its "perversity," would bring only notoriety; but four society dramas were to put him at the top of London's literary establishment: *Lady Windermere's Fan*, *A Woman of No Importance*, *An Ideal Husband*, and *The Importance of Being Earnest*. On the night of his arrest, two of his plays were being performed in the West End. To his followers, especially to young men followers, he was very special indeed. André Gide, who was about Max's age, met this "prodigious being" in 1891: "His gesture, his look triumphed. His success was so certain that it seemed that it preceded Wilde and that all he needed to do was go forward to meet it. His books astonished, charmed."

Which of Wilde's writings astonished and charmed young Max? *The Picture of Dorian Gray* and certainly its preface, with Wilde's version of art for art's sake:

> They are the elect to whom beautiful things mean only Beauty. . . .
> All art is at once surface and symbol. . . .
> All art is quite useless.

The emphasis on beauty and on the uselessness of art had enormous appeal to Max, especially as it capped the English aesthetic tradition of Rossetti, Swinburne, and Pater. Max did have his reservations about *Dorian Gray* itself; but he was not, like the early critics, worried about secret sins. His complaint was about the book's contradictory and (as Wilde put it) "terrible" moral: that excess destroys. "Let us be happy without being good" is among the lines Max inscribed in a copy of the novel.

Max's primary allegiance was to Wilde's *Intentions*, which he treasured always, long after he had outgrown *Dorian Gray*. Reggie Turner gave Max for his twenty-first birthday a copy specially bound in vellum: "How very nice of you to think of my birthday," Max wrote back, "how very clever to think of the one thing of all others I should love." And of the four essays that comprise *Intentions*, "The Decay of Lying" made the most lasting impression on Max. A dialogue, with Vivian as Wilde's spokesman, it argues for Art over Nature or Life: "Art takes Life as part of her rough material, recreates it, and refashions it in fresh forms, is absolutely indifferent to fact, invents, imagines, dreams, and keeps between herself and reality the impenetrable barrier of beautiful style, of decorative and ideal treatment." The modern emphasis on Facts is all wrong, especially as they "are usurping the domain of Fancy, and have invaded the Kingdom of romance." The essay is largely an attack on realism, and Max, himself a fantasist, warmed to Wilde's argument:

> Art never expresses anything but itself.
> All bad art comes from returning to Life and Nature, and elevating them into Ideals. Life and Nature may sometimes be used as part of Art's rough material.
> Life imitates Art far more than Art imitates Life.

What Wilde was doing for British aestheticism, which by this time was somewhat old news, was adding a comic element. He does so in the outlandishness of his extremes and the marvellous and continual flow of sometimes absurd paradoxes. Max would take up this formula of aestheticism and comedy and put the emphasis on the comic. It is comedy that saves him from being ridiculous (as Oscar sometimes was). For Max, Wilde would be the jumping off point, the inspiration. "Great writers," David Lodge observes, "do not copy other writers; they borrow and transform the tricks they admire."

In early 1893, at rehearsals for *A Woman of No Importance*, which Herbert was producing, Max came to know Wilde himself and soon moved into Wilde's inner circle. As it happened, Max already knew two key members of the group, Reggie Turner and Robert Ross; and he may have met Lord Alfred Douglas. All three were important to Wilde's story, itself so important to Max's story.

Lord Alfred "Bosie" Douglas went up to Magdalen College, Oxford, in autumn 1890, the same year Max went up to Merton. When the book edition of *Dorian Gray* was published the following April, Douglas read it nine times, and in June he went to Tite Street and met Wilde. Bosie soon became the consuming passion of Wilde's life. A moody, headstrong, self-centred young man, he had undeniable charm, and, with his pale complexion and blond hair, was considered beautiful. Max reported to Reggie his impressions of Bosie: unstable, but charming, clever, and nice. A year later Max pronounced him "very charming, always beautiful and seldom sober." Max was seeing chiefly the good side of Bosie. He had a ferocious temper that could be loosed on the slightest provocation; he was, in Richard Ellmann's words, "totally spoiled, reckless, insolent, and, when thwarted, fiercely vindictive." In the opinion of almost everyone, Douglas was the real villain in Wilde's life.

Robert Ross, Canadian by birth but brought up in England, met Wilde in 1886 at Oxford while being tutored for university. Fifteen years younger than Wilde, Ross probably introduced him to homosexual practices. In 1888 Ross went up to King's College, Cambridge. There he was considered effeminate, the prototype of the new "Long haired Kingsman" – in spite of his having rowed for the college boat. A group of "hearties," athletic types, dunked him in the college fountain; he suffered a breakdown in his health, explained by

Oscar Browning as "a violent brain attack, the result of the outrage preying on his mind. . . . They were afraid he would kill himself." Ross left Cambridge and turned to journalism and art criticism. Dubbed the "faithful disciple," Ross was with Wilde when he was arrested, met him on the shores of France on his release from prison, and was with him when he died in Paris in 1900. He was also Wilde's literary executor. It was he who brought out *De Profundis* in 1905. And it was Ross who in 1901 at the Carfax Gallery in Ryder Street would give Max his first one-man exhibition of caricatures.

Of Turner, we need here add only that he too qualified as a faithful disciple of Oscar Wilde; like Ross, Turner was with Wilde when he was arrested, met him on release from prison, and attended him on his deathbed.

At about the time that Max and Wilde became friends, Wilde's latest creation, the original French edition of *Salomé*, was published in purple wrappers. A one-act play, it was forbidden stage production by the Lord Chamberlain, on the ostensible grounds that it depicted biblical personages, but in reality because of what critics saw as its decadence and indecency. Reggie gave a copy of the book to Max, who replied,

> The book they have bound in parma violets and across whose page is the silver voice of the Master made visible – how could it not be lovely? I am enamoured of it. It has charmed my eyes from their sockets and through the voids has sent incense to my brain: my tongue is loosed in its praise. Have you read it? In construction it is very like a Greek play, I think: yet in conception so modern that its publication in any century would seem premature. It is a marvellous play. If Oscar would re-write *all* the Bible, there would be no sceptics.

And then Oscar himself offered Max the more valuable gift of encouragement. It came, fittingly enough, in connection with an article Max wrote about Wilde. Anonymous and misleadingly entitled "Oscar Wilde by an American," it appeared in the *Anglo-American Times* of 25 March 1893. Juvenilia aside, it was Max's first publication. He wrote to Turner, "My article . . . consists of fulsome praise of the Master and filthy abuse of his disciples. . . . Behold, high and sheer into the air rise the walls of the Temple of Fame: against them is a ladder placed and on the first rung of it rests my foot." He soon had good warrant for this claim: two weeks later, Max reports

to Reggie, "Oscar thinks my article (which he has read in proof . . .) 'incomparably brilliant,' though he was rather hurt by my reference to *Dorian Gray*."
(Max had said, "We have heard the grumble that the idea of an inanimate complicated by an animate personality developed in the story of *Dorian Gray* had been done before. . . . All this is likely to be true, but I cannot see that it matters. So long as a writer has assimilated all his material in a right way and presents it to us attractively, we have no cause to complain.") Within a few days, Max is again writing, "Oscar himself (of whom I have seen a good deal this vac) liked [the article] very much and said he thought it 'incomparably clever.'" And a week later, describing a meal with Oscar, Bosie, and Herbert, Max tells Reggie, "Oscar talked a great deal about my article – said that he knew no other undergraduate who could have written it, that I had a marvellous intuition and sense of the phrase, that I must take to literature alone, and that my style was like a silver dagger. I am becoming vainer than ever."
Here's a sample of this début piece:

Mr Wilde is indolent and so his writings are few; he has a most fastidious literary taste and so he has produced nothing which is not in its way perfect. Yet what a born writer he is! He is so versatile that he has hardly ever attempted two things of a like kind. He is a writer of poetry, and he is a writer of plays; a critic of books, and of paintings, a philosopher, an essayist and a teller of fairy tales; two or three of the few well-written short stories in this language are by him; he has introduced a new form of novel, has lectured upon art and touched politics with a light hand. . . . the love of beauty for its own sake, which has absorbed his whole system and inspired everything he has written, is a very rare thing indeed. . . . No writer has pleaded with greater zeal and consistency for the preference of Aesthetics to Ethics, or preached more fervidly that the road to Happiness lies behind the broad gates of Beauty.

Style like a silver dagger? foreshadowings at best?
Max's second article and the first under his own name, "The Incomparable Beauty of Modern Dress" (later expanded as "Dandies and Dandies"), was a more Wildean performance still. It appeared in June 1893 in the *Spirit Lamp*, an undergraduate Oxford publication, edited by Bosie Douglas. Here's a passage, on Beau Brummell:

We are struck by the utter simplicity of his attire. The "countless rings" affected by D'Orsay, the many little golden chains, "every one of them slighter than a cobweb," that Disraeli loved to insinuate from one pocket to another of his vest, would have seemed vulgar to Mr Brummell. For is it not to his fine scorn of accessories that we may trace that first aim of modern dandyism, the production of the supreme effect through means the least extravagant? In certain congruities of dark cloth, in the rigid perfection of his linen, in the symmetry of his glove with his hand, lay the secret of Mr Brummell's miracles. He was ever most economical, most scrupulous of means. . . . Mr Brummell was, indeed, in the utmost sense of the word, an artist. No poet, nor cook nor sculptor ever bore that title more worthily than he. . . . And really, outside his art, Mr Brummell had a personality of almost Balzacian insignificance. There have been dandies, like D'Orsay, who were nearly painters; painters, like Mr Whistler, who wished to be dandies; dandies, like Disraeli, who afterwards followed a less arduous calling.

In early 1894 Max wrote another piece on Wilde, "A Peep into the Past," this one wholly satirical. Max, twenty-one, relates in reporter-like style a visit to "Mr Wilde, the old gentleman," a "relic of the Victorian age," who, his star having set, has long outlived his reputation. Wilde was thirty-nine and at the height of his fame. The article shows him still struggling on, an early riser, an old writer most regular in his habits. But there are hints of a dangerous kind: his place on Tite Street shows "womanly care and taste" and "the constant succession of page-boys, which so startles the neighbourhood"; and when Max is ushered into Wilde's little study, "I fancied that I heard the quickly receding *frou-frou* of tweed trousers, but my host I found reclining, hale and hearty, though a little dishevelled, upon the sofa." The piece had been destined for the first number of the *Yellow Book*, but was supplanted by the far more lively – and more Wildean – "A Defence of Cosmetics." Later, after the scandal, "A Peep into the Past" became virtually unpublishable. (A pirated edition of 300 copies appeared in New York in 1923.)

Wilde made good subject matter, but he was more important as literary model. It's hard to imagine what Max's early essays would have been like had it not been for Wilde's influence. Sometimes the Wildean flavour is very direct:

From "1880": "To give an accurate and exhaustive account of that period would need a far less brilliant pen than mine."

From "King George the Fourth": "We are born into a poor, weak age. We are not strong enough to be wicked, and the Nonconformist Conscience makes cowards of us all."

From "A Defence of Cosmetics": " 'After all,' as a pretty girl once said to me, 'Women are a sex by themselves, so to speak.' "

But more often you will find in these essays the Wildean tone muted; it is marshalled, tamed, made more delicate, more subtle, the humour less broad. Still, Wilde's influence is unmistakable, and the prose of these early essays is quite different from that of the later essays; it is also, in my judgement, less likely to hold up. It was a stage Max had to go through; he had to write "A Defence of Cosmetics" and "Dandies and Dandies" before he could write "Quia Imperfectum" and "A Clergyman." The early Max is sometimes, for my taste, a tad too flippant, too paradoxical, too clever. But he had needed a model, and he could have done worse than Wilde, surely.

I must pursue the Wilde involvement further because it is crucial. Max continued to get more from Wilde's books than from the man. His friendship with Wilde, whom he had earlier referred to as "the Master" and "the Divinity," is more difficult to assess than his indebtedness to him as a writer. The most striking aspect of their friendship was the disciple's failure to subscribe to the Oscar myth (or whatever we may choose to call it). He did regard knowing Wilde as a privilege, but not a great privilege. Max held back. He tells Reggie, "I am sorry to say that Oscar drinks far more than he ought: indeed the first time I saw him ... he was in a hopeless state of intoxication. He has deteriorated very much in appearance: his cheeks being quite a dark purple and fat to a fault." (See plate 4.) He later reports what he calls Oscar's "fatuous" carrying-ons in the theatre, wearing vine leaves in his hair and loudly proclaiming the actress "Juno-like" and the actor "Olympian quite," while waving a cigarette around his head. Some indication of Max's disenchantment comes across when he tells Reggie how surprised he is to learn that Oscar so disapproved of Max's caricatures of him: "How I wish he had written to me on the subject and how I could have crushed him. Don't you think it fearful cheek on my part? So long as the man's head interests me, I shall continue to draw it. He is simply an unpaid model of mine and as such he should behave. ... Are all Irishmen sensitive, I wonder?" This was in October 1893. A few days later Max writes to Ross: "Poor Oscar! I saw him the other

day, from a cab, walking with Bosie and some other member of the Extreme
Left. He looked like one whose soul had swooned in sin and revived vulgar.
How fearful it is for a poet to go to bed and find himself infamous." In his
very old age, more than half a century after Wilde's death, Max would tell
Samuel Behrman, "As Oscar became more and more successful, he became
... arrogant. He felt himself omnipotent, and he became gross not in body
only – he did become that – but in his relations with people. He brushed
people aside; he felt he was beyond the ordinary human courtesies."

Wilde's *A Woman of No Importance* was first produced by Beerbohm Tree at
the Haymarket Theatre in April 1893. Max reported to Reggie Turner: "The
first night was very brilliant in its audience. . . . Balfour and Chamberlain and
all the politicians were there. When little Oscar came on to make his bow
there was a slight mingling of hoots and hisses, though he looked very sweet
in a new white waistcoat and a large bunch of little lilies in his coat." Max
observed, in Wildean fashion, "The piece is sure of a long, of a very long run,
despite all that the critics may say in its favour." Attending again on the
second night, Max saw, in the Royal Box, the Prince of Wales (later King
Edward VII). The Prince went backstage and told Wilde, "Do not alter a
single line," leading him to rhapsodize, "What a splendid country where
princes understand poets."

The splendid country did not understand homosexuality, and two years
later Wilde was undone. But for a good many years prior to his fall, Oscar
Wilde represented what a later age would call "closeted" or, in Wilde's case
semi-closeted, homosexuality. The word "homosexuality" was not in use; the
terms were "inversion" and "perversion." Homosexual behaviour was labelled
effeminate or unnatural or sodomitical; the popular slang term was buggery;
its devotees called it Uranian, or Greek love, or, in the phrase that Wilde was
to make famous, the love that dare not speak its name. Just what was Max's
relationship to homosexuality? Clearly he was drawn to the homosexual
milieu. However, he seems immediately to have understood that his role
would not be that of participant, but that of the cool onlooker. Max's stance
towards the Uranian world is complicated and enigmatic; and the evidence is
not plentiful. It is useful to recall that almost all homosexuals were closeted
in those years. (One story said that on the night of Oscar's arrest 600 prominent gentlemen crossed the Channel to France.) Note also that everyone who
has thought about it or written about it says that Max, if he was homosexual,

was a celibate homosexual. I don't know where they get their conviction, but I think they are right. Others argue that he was a "normal" though low-keyed heterosexual; others that he was a celibate heterosexual; and still others contend that he was asexual, in which latter two cases he was a "posing heterosexual." I don't like all of this speculation, but it has to be engaged. The case for Max as a (celibate) homosexual comprises a number of verifiably accurate but ambiguous facts. See what you make of them.

All his life Max was close to homosexual men, and in his youth he moved easily in a circle that was about as openly homosexual as you could find: Turner, Ross, Douglas, and Wilde. He attended the Wilde trials and was sympathetic to Wilde always. He seems to have fitted in perfectly with the kind of world often associated with homosexuality; he had the requisite devotion to art, to beautiful things, to cleverness, word play, humour, irony, preciosity, a sense of pose. He was utterly aloof from athletics or strenuous activity of any kind; he affected a kind of languid indifference towards the "outside" world of politics or business. He was a rigorous dandy – fault-finders would say a fop. The writers of his time that he most admired were Wilde, Henry James, and Lytton Strachey. (This last is supposed to be an argument for homosexuality?) His early letters to Reggie Turner can be read as tinged with homosexual overtones: Max talks a great deal about Oscar Wilde, Ross, and Douglas; he recounts, for example, how he had made a lengthy visit to Ross and had "a long comfortable chat about 'certain forms of crime' [sodomy] and John Gray [partly the original for Dorian Gray]"; he misses Turner sorely, "Oxford simply yawns for you and I want you to see a beautiful new lampshade which I have acquired. It is of green silk made out of the green cloth of the roulette-table." Yet again, "Write and tell me a great deal about yourself; you so seldom write to me now, and I am rather hurt." Also, "I have had a rather gay term but my gaiety has been all enjoyed in the company of out-college men – especially that of Dennis Brown and Bosey Douglas. The latter is charming – a very pretty reflection of Oscar – and we get on together very nicely. ... Oscar came to see me the other day with Douglas (at whose house he is staying) ... he behaved quite quietly and gentlemanly and the visit was quite a success." A follow-up letter says, "You need not, by the way, be jealous of Alfred Douglas as he does not peculiarly fascinate me: he is for one thing obviously mad (like all his family I believe) and though he is pretty and clever and nice I never judge my friends from an Aesthetic, an Intellectual or an Ethical standpoint: I simply like them or dislike: that is all." To his other great friend, Will Rothenstein, Max writes of dining with Bosie, "Aren't you, dear straightlaced timid wonderful Will, very shocked?"

On the other hand, Max in many letters seems to be encouraging Reggie Turner towards a possible latent heterosexuality; he tries to nurture Reggie in a make-believe love affair with a fictitious Miss Cumberledge; and he tells him at all too great length of his own romantic infatuation with the young music-hall mimic, Cissie Loftus. He undertook to mitigate Ross's influence on Turner. From New York in 1895 Max writes to Ross only half jokingly imploring him "not to look after Reggie Turner while I am away. He is very weak and you, if I remember rightly, are very wicked. ... Also keep Bosie away from him (give my love to Bosie). Bosie is more fatal to Reg than you – if anything. All this is quite serious. I really think Reg is at rather a crucial point of his career – and should hate to see him fall an entire victim to the love that dares not tell its name." The letter is balanced, non-judgmental, playful, yet self-distancing. (And, we should add, altogether ineffective. Wilde would christen Turner "the boy-snatcher of Clement's Inn.") In 1898, writing to Reggie, Max asks after Bobbie Ross, "Please give him some mulierastic [i.e. heterosexual] equivalent for my love." Twenty-five years later Max was still keeping his distance from homosexuality, refusing to review Frank Harris's biography of Wilde: "All that raking-up of the old Sodomitic cesspool [especially the involvement of "renters," male prostitutes] – the cesspool that was opened in 1895, and re-opened in recent years by various lawsuits – seemed to me a disservice (howsoever well-intended) to poor old O.W.'s memory."

Make up your own mind. I am withholding my own views on Max's sexuality until we consider his three engagements and marriage.

Although the sad story of 1895 has been told many times, a précis of the Wilde trials here will help, Wilde being so material to Max's development. The best place to follow Wilde at this time or any other time of his life is in Richard Ellmann's magisterial biography (we never say "definitive" nowadays). In a small section called with bald irony "Kind Friends," Ellmann says, "Beerbohm's life often converged with Wilde's at this time [1894]." Ellmann recounts how Max "rejoiced in *Dorian Gray* as a mock-sacred book, to be set for examinations." So far, so good. But then, Ellmann goes on, "Another of his procedures was less innocent." Ah ha – what's this? "[Max] became friendly with Robert Hichens, and early in the summer of 1894

Hichens showed him the manuscript of *The Green Carnation*. Neither he nor Hichens understood how dangerous the book would be for Wilde, but Beerbohm could not have been totally unaware of the risks." Notice how Beerbohm seems more guilty than Hichens. *The Green Carnation* did Wilde no actual harm. It was not cited in the Wilde trials, and Ellmann in his exhaustive study does not mention it again. Hichens, homosexual himself, had written a moderately smart parody of Wilde and Douglas. Wilde was at first amused by the book, telling Ada Leverson, "Hichens I did not think capable of anything so clever." The only real problem Wilde had with *The Green Carnation* was that some people thought he had written it. Ellmann sees the Hichens novel as a "small but noticeable contribution" to the growing disfavour Wilde was encountering. But Max? What was his "less innocent procedure" here? Getting to know Hichens? Having seen the work in manuscript? Ellmann says that Wilde "perhaps" suspected Max of having helped write the book. The suspicion is Ellmann's, not Wilde's. Ellmann, in mid-paragraph, goes on to quote a passage from a letter Max wrote to Reggie on 12 August 1894 where Max, also in mid-paragraph, without any transition from a running account of his own activities, offers this bit of news: "Oscar has at length been arrested for certain kinds of crime. He was taken in the Café Royal (lower room). Bosie escaped, being an excellent runner, but Oscar was less nimble." Rupert Hart-Davis in a helpful footnote tells us this "all-too-prophetic joke almost certainly refers to the police raid on a club at 46 Fitzroy Street, London, on this very day, when eighteen men were arrested, including two in female dress." But Ellmann leaps to this conclusion: "Beerbohm may have awaited with unconscious excitement the removal of the master from the London scene, leaving the field open to the disciple." How can one argue down anything prefaced by the word *unconscious*? It all depends on who is telling whose story, doesn't it?

But forward to the trial. Lord Alfred Douglas was the third son of John Sholto Douglas, Eighth Marquess of Queensberry, a man peculiar, brutal, litigious, and, for what it's worth, militantly atheistic. Son and father were equally key players in the drama. Queensberry, the super-manly originator of the Queensberry rules for boxing, was appalled that his son should be involved with Wilde. He wrote to Alfred, threatening to disown him if this "most loathsome and disgusting relationship" did not cease: "I should be quite justified in shooting [Wilde] at sight. ... Your disgusted so-called father, Queensberry." Alfred, one inch taller than his father, fired back a telegram: "WHAT A FUNNY LITTLE MAN YOU ARE." Queensberry's mood was made even fiercer when, in October 1894, his eldest son and heir, Drumlanrig, committed suicide, apparently for fear of being blackmailed over homosexual relations with Lord Rosebery, then Foreign Secretary under Gladstone. Meanwhile, Wilde and Douglas continued their stormy love affair. When *The Importance of Being Earnest* opened in February 1895, Queensberry planned a demonstration, but the police were alerted, and he was forced to content himself with leaving a bouquet of vegetables at the stage door. He then left a card at the Albemarle Club, "For Oscar Wilde posing Somdomite."* Wilde, foolishly and against the advice of all his friends except the fatal Douglas, who urged him on, sued Queensberry for libel.

When the scandal broke, Max was in America, acting ineffectually as secretary for his brother. To Reggie Max wrote, "Poor, poor Oscar! How very sad it is. And I cannot bear to think of all that must have happened – the whisperings and hastenings hither and thither ... I suppose he was exasperated too much not to take action." Max pleads for a full account, and regrets that Wilde had not got the eminent George Lewis as his counsel. At the trial, with barrister Edward Carson (the man who, years later, almost by himself would "create" Protestant Northern Ireland) acting brilliantly for the defence, the judge and jury ruled for Queensberry. Revelations at the trial led to Wilde's arrest for indecency and sodomy. Max was back in London in time to attend the second trial, where he heard Wilde, now the defendant, cross-examined about the "love that dare not speak its name," words taken from a poem by Douglas. Wilde, dropping his flippancy, said this love consisted in "such great affection of an older for a younger man as there was between David and Jonathan, such as Plato made the very basis of his philosophy, and such as you find in the sonnets of Michelangelo and Shakespeare. It is that deep, spiritual affection that is as pure as it is perfect...." Max reported to Reggie (who like many other homosexuals had fled the country):

> Oscar has been quite superb. His speech about the Love that dares not tell his name was simply wonderful, and carried the whole court right away, quite a tremendous burst of applause. Here was this man, who had been for a month in prison and loaded with insults and crushed and buffeted,

---

* Queensberry's carelessly aristocratic mis-spelling of "Sodomite" has long been noted. Earlier generations (and Wilde himself) probably read the card as "For Oscar Wilde ponce and Somdomite."

perfectly self-possessed, dominating the Old Bailey with his fine presence and musical voice. He has never had so great a triumph.

Max added that he had seen Bosie the night before he fled to France, on the eve of the trial: "He seemed to have lost his nerve."

This trial ended in a hung jury; another trial was scheduled. Between trials Max, hoping for news of Oscar or for "amelioration" of some kind, went to the office of the police inspector who had arrested Oscar: "The walls were covered with a grisly collection of criminal souvenirs – oh, knives and pistols and bludgeons, all the implements of crime – and there among them, as though it were evidence against the inspector's latest malefactor, was one of my own caricatures of Oscar." That drawing, originally published in *Pick-Me-Up* in September 1894, is pretty hideous. "I hadn't realized till that moment," Max confessed, "how wicked it was. I felt as if I had contributed to the dossier against Oscar."

The third trial led to Wilde's conviction and a sentence of two years' imprisonment with hard labour.

While Oscar was in jail, Max published a Wildean fairy tale, *The Happy Hypocrite*, a kind of reversal of *Dorian Gray*. Lord George Hell is an ageing Regency rake, whose face reflects his dissolute life. He is "greedy, destructive, and disobedient"; he stays out too late at Carlton House, eats and drinks too much, is overly fond of fine clothes; he is thirty-five years old "and a great grief to his parents." Falling in love with the innocent, girl-like young woman Jenny Mere, Lord George has himself fitted with a saintly mask, for she had vowed to marry only a man with a saint-like face. Masked, Lord George carries on an idyllic courtship and wins her. They marry and live and love in a cottage. Then a former mistress of Lord George appears. Jealous and wrathful, she pulls off his mask, but his face has become saintly – art, or artifice, has transformed him. The man has become his mask. *The Happy Hypocrite* is hardly Beerbohm at his best; it may be parodying the sentimental, but it comes curiously close to being seduced into what it is parodying.*

---

* *The Happy Hypocrite* has been often reprinted, and frequently dramatized, beginning in December 1900 when Mrs Patrick Campbell put it on at the Royalty Theatre to good notices. Its ten-week run was interrupted for a fortnight following Queen Victoria's death on 22 January 1901: "I shall insist," Max wrote to Reggie, "that when I die *More Leaves from the Highlands* shall be withdrawn from circulation temporarily." In 1936 Vivien Leigh played Jenny Mere in a production at His Majesty's Theatre; and in 1940 Deborah Kerr took that role in a BBC radio adaptation.

In May 1897 Wilde was released from prison. (Max's suggestion for evading reporters, a "decoy-brougham which should be driven out of the prison-yard with blinds drawn down," was not adopted.) At Dieppe Ross and Turner awaited Wilde's arrival, talking, Reggie wrote to Max, "of your *mots* and dilating on your great sanity.... In [Wilde's] room we have put a lot of flowers. All the books we have collected are on the mantelpiece, and your own two works are in the centre to catch his eye." Max had sent Wilde four books including his own *Works* and *The Happy Hypocrite.* Wilde would write to Turner, "I have just read Max's *Happy Hypocrite*, beginning at the end, as one should always do. It is quite wonderful, and to one who was once the author of *Dorian Gray,* full of no vulgar surprises of style or incident." To Max Wilde wrote:

> I cannot tell you what a real pleasure it was to me to find your delightful present waiting for me on my release from prison, and to receive the charming and sweet messages you sent me. ... *The Happy Hypocrite* is a wonderful and beautiful story, though I do not like the cynical directness of the name.... But in years to come, when you are a very young man, you will remember what I have said, and recognise its truth, and in the final edition of your work, leave the title unchanged. ... The implied and accepted recognition of *Dorian Gray* in the story cheers me. I had always been disappointed that my story had suggested no other work of art in others.

In 1898 Wilde sent Max an inscribed copy of *The Ballad of Reading Gaol.*

Early in 1900 the old Marquess of Queensberry died, quarrelling till the end with his sons. On his deathbed he "gathered himself to spit" at Percy, his second-eldest son and heir to the title, who had put up bail money for Wilde. Queensberry left Douglas a large inheritance, which the young lord spent lavishly. He did nothing for Wilde at the time, and had done nothing for him after his release from prison beyond living with him for a short disastrous time during the autumn of 1897.

Oscar Wilde died in Paris on 30 November 1900, attended by Turner and Ross. Turner wrote immediately to Max, who replied by return of post:

> I am, as you may imagine, very sorry indeed; and am thinking very much about Oscar, who was such an influence and an interest in my life. Will you please lay out a little money for me in flowers for his grave? I will repay

you. . . . I hope to be able to write something nice about Oscar in my next article for the *Saturday*. . . . I suppose really it was better that Oscar should die. If he had lived to be an old man he would have become unhappy. Those whom the gods, etc. And the gods *did* love Oscar, with all his faults. Please give my sympathy to Bobbie, and tell him how much less happily Oscar might have died.

Max's *Saturday* piece was nothing special. Coming as it did as part of his weekly theatre review, it concerned itself with Wilde's dramaturgy: his death extinguished the hope that we would have more Wildean plays. Max's best tribute to Wilde would come in an article for *Vanity Fair* in March 1905, occasioned by the publication of *De Profundis*. This book, Max insists, shows Wilde still "A Lord of Language":

Fine as are the ideas and emotions in *De Profundis*, it is the actual writing – the mastery of prose – that most delights me. Except Ruskin in his prime, no writer has achieved through prose the limpid and lyrical effects that were achieved by Oscar Wilde. One does not seem to be reading a written thing. The words sing. There is nothing of that formality, that hard and cunning precision, which marks so much of the prose that we admire, and rightly admire. The meaning is artificial, but the expression is always magically natural and beautiful. The simple words seem to grow together like flowers. . . . The prose of *Intentions* and of his plays, and of his fairy-stories, was perfect in its lively and unstudied grace. It is a joy to find in this last prose of his the old power, all unmarred by the physical and mental torments he had suffered.

In 1909 Wilde's remains were removed from Bagneux to Père Lachaise Cemetery, where in 1912 the Jacob Epstein monument was placed. Max thought the sculpture a monstrosity.

CHAPTER FIVE

Aesthete Triumphans

Oscar Wilde has taken us somewhat ahead of the story. We had Max at Oxford, determining upon a career in writing and in caricature. As it turned out, he would never spend so much as an hour doing anything else for a living. His two careers ran in tandem throughout his productive years. This brings us to the nagging question: in which of his arts did he excel? in which did he think himself better? The ease, the pleasure with which he drew may have led him in early years to rank his writing, which was always hard work, as more important. Still, he was not a person to depreciate a thing because it came easily. I believe that early on he quite rightly saw his abilities "with pen and pencil" as equal, different of course, but of about the same calibre, and indeed growing, with the years, more like each other. He would have waved aside as meaningless the question of his being better in one or the other. During his lifetime his sister arts were equally prized by astute people. Later generations continue to be undecided. That bit of posterity which we currently inhabit probably knows him best as a caricaturist because the caricatures are frequently reprinted. If someone writes a biography of, say, Coleridge, there among the plates you will find Max's caricature of Coleridge. Similarly with Wordsworth, Rossetti, Tennyson, Browning, Swinburne, James, Whistler, Shaw, Sargent, Yeats, Wells, Conrad, Kipling; and also with lesser-knowns like Gosse, Chesterton, Belloc, Harris, Moore, Douglas, *et al.* And of course Wilde. On the other hand, there are still men and women, that little band of people with their heads screwed on right, who know and admire the prose along with the caricatures, and who invariably protest that they can't make up their minds. Their ambivalence hasn't helped Max's reputation with the larger public: most people cannot or do not want to believe in Max's kind of twofold eminence. It's too much for them.

But this is not a chapter on Max's later reputation. It's about his initial success. And success came first with the caricatures, and it came with a rush. This was in 1892, when Max was twenty years old. He had shown one of his sisters – most likely Constance – a series of drawings of "Club Types." She showed them to the editor of the *Strand Magazine*, who accepted them for publication. Nothing could have been more fortunate. This inexpensive (6d.) monthly miscellany was hugely successful; its initial issue in January 1891 sold 300,000 copies, a figure that soon rose to a spectacular half a million. The magazine, which specialized in the detective story and featured Arthur Conan Doyle, became a national institution. In printing Max's caricatures the *Strand* ("the Mirror of the Century") offered them the widest possible audience. During September, October, and November 1892 three dozen of his drawings appeared. At the time he knew next to nothing of club types, and he was later amused at having made all the habitués of Whites ageing Regency bucks "remembering Beau Brummell" and having filled the Travellers' Club with "bronzed and bearded men exchanging tales of adventure by flood and field in distant quarters of the globe." Although Max was quite adept at types, they were never his forte; he was a "portrayer of character," as Edmund Wilson would put it; he specialized, as the Rupert Hart-Davis *Catalogue of the Caricatures of Max Beerbohm* so graphically demonstrates, in "actual people," some 800 of them, most of them contemporaries and acquaintances. Nonetheless, it all began with "Club Types." Their publication, Max said, dealt "a great, an almost mortal blow to my modesty."

We have seen how Max's career as a writer got off to an unheralded start in April 1893 with an article on Oscar Wilde published anonymously in the little-read *Anglo-American Times*, followed soon by another article (with his name), on modern dress, in an undergraduate Oxford magazine. The real thing was about to start, and it would do so in the *Yellow Book*. A great deal has been written about this magazine, probably more than it deserves. For the *Yellow Book* has served, quite out of proportion to its actual importance, as the very embodiment of "The 1890s" in literature and art. But the magazine is crucial to the development of Max's writing career. It was the brain child of three people: John Lane, the publisher, whose firm called itself the Bodley Head and featured finely printed books by "advanced" and "aesthetic" authors; an American writer, Henry Harland, who was to be literary editor; and Aubrey Beardsley, who was to be art editor. An illustrated quarterly, with each issue as big as a book and selling for five shillings, it was devoted entirely to literature and art – no news or politics. The originators claimed, a little disingenuously, that they did not intend the magazine to be the organ of Decadence or of any movement; but they admitted to a plan to publish unconventional material, even, as Beardsley said, some that was "a little risqué." To do so and get away with it, the magazine hoped to dilute the unconventional with much that was conventional: the established and respectable Henry James would set off a decadent writer like Arthur Symons; and Frederick Leighton, president of the Royal Academy, would balance, if that were possible, Aubrey Beardsley himself.

Max came to join the *Yellow Book* stable of writers and artists through the efforts of the enthusiastic Will Rothenstein. For Rothenstein, having completed his portraits of Oxford celebrities, settled into London and made it his business to promote his new friend. He escorted Max to meet the more or less anti-establishment artists. "It was to him," Max wrote, "that I owed my first knowledge of that forever enchanting little world-in-itself, Chelsea, and my first acquaintance with Walter Sickert and other august elders who dwelt there." The others included Wilson Steer and Henry Tonks, who, like Sickert, were admirers of French Impressionism. Rothenstein, Max continues, "took me to see, in Cambridge Street, Pimlico, a young man whose drawings were already famous among the few – Aubrey Beardsley, by name." Beardsley was, of all the men Rothenstein introduced him to, the one whose work most appealed to him. Max liked the frail, precocious, modest Beardsley, and the two became close friends. Altogether above prudery, Max admired all phases of Beardsley's very original art, including the controversial works. Beardsley, in turn, encouraged Max to write and draw professionally.

Rothenstein also took Max to the Bodley Head to meet John Lane and various of the publisher's writers. These included, most spectacularly, Wilde, but also Arthur Symons, Richard Le Gallienne, John Davidson, Lionel Johnson, Henry Harland, authors labelled "decadent," especially by those who disapproved of them. (Actually the only decadent whose writing Max truly admired was Wilde; the others were too much like Enoch Soames.) These men gathered at the Crown in Cranborne Street, where, it was said, they rubbed shoulders with "prostitutes and confidence men." An even more favourite meeting place was in Regent Street. Max wrote:

By [Rothenstein] I was inducted into another haunt of intellect and daring, the domino room of the Café Royal. There, on that October evening – there in that exuberant vista of gilding and crimson velvet set amidst all those opposing mirrors and upholding caryatids, with fumes of tobacco ever rising to the painted and pagan ceiling, and with the hum of presumably cynical conversation broken into so sharply now and again by the clatter of dominoes shuffled on marble tables, I drew a deep breath and "This indeed," said I to myself, "is life!"

John Lane was to be Max's first publisher, and Max would be grateful always to his "discoverer." Privately, Max and Rothenstein spoke slightingly of Lane, Max labelling him "Art's middleman" and "that poor fly in the amber of modernity." Rothenstein, for his part, reported that in Paris Lane "mistook St Sulpice for Notre Dame and fell asleep over some music of Brahms" and at the Louvre made comments that provoked the irascible Rothenstein into telling him "never to mention Art again." In August 1893 Max told Rothenstein that Lane had written to him saying, "How lucky I am to have got hold of this young Beardsley: look at the technique of his drawings! What workmanship! *He never goes over the edges!*" But whatever his limitations, Lane, together with Beardsley, proposed that Max contribute to the *Yellow Book*, and to its very first issue. Editor Harland had his doubts. Max was still an undergraduate. Should he be there alongside Henry James and Edmund Gosse? Beardsley and Lane prevailed, and, as it turned out, Max would play a key role in the magazine's début.

The effort to suggest balance didn't work. It seldom does. A little sensationalism will outweigh much that is unsensational. The first issue of the *Yellow Book* offered contributions from Henry James (whose story had pride of place), and other "establishment" figures including George Saintsbury, Edmund Gosse, Arthur Waugh, and William Watson. There was art work by Leighton, Sickert, Laurence Housman, Will Rothenstein, and Whistler's disciple, Joseph Pennell. But there was sensation enough, and the *Yellow Book* was branded as decadent and indecent. Three culprits caused most of the furore: Beardsley, Symons, and Max. Beardsley's cover depicted a leering woman, masked and adorned with the prostitute's beauty mark; this was followed inside by another drawing, "L'Education sentimentale," which Max described for Reggie: "Aubrey has done a *marvellous* picture for the Yellow B. . . . A fat elderly whore in a dressing-gown and huge hat of many feathers is reading from a book to the sweetest imaginable little young girl, who looks before her, with hands clasped behind her back, roguishly winking." Symons provided "Stella Maris," a poem not about the Virgin Mary but about a "Juliet of the night" and her "chance romances of the street" – including an explicit memory of love-making. And Max contributed an essay called "A Defence of Cosmetics" that sparked, strangely, as much antagonism as Beardsley or Symons.

If the projectors really thought they would simply annoy the establishment and not provoke it to serious anger, they were wrong. *The Times* thundered that the *Yellow Book*, this "organ of the New Literature and Art," was "a combination of English rowdiness with French lubricity" – though, oddly, it praised "Stella Maris." The *Westminster Gazette* called for "an act of Parliament to make this kind of thing illegal." *Punch* rose up in verse and singled out Max as the "popinjay," "the little busy bore" who attempted to improve on Nature. The *World* attacked "a Mr Beerbohm" whose defence of cosmetics, with its humorous phrases such as "the respunite sex" and "the veriest sillypop," amounted to "pure nonsense." Max, doubtless with Harland's concurrence, answered in a long letter to the magazine's editor, deploring the fact that what in the entire volume raised "the most ungovernable fury" was his essay: one reviewer dropped "the usual prefix of 'Mr' as though I were a well-known criminal and referred to me as 'Beerbohm,'" while another called his essay "the rankest and most nauseous thing in all literature."

Let's have a look at this "bomb thrown by a cowardly decadent." Here are some lines, including the very first, from the essay that made the name Max Beerbohm known as a writer. "A Defence of Cosmetics" begins:

> Nay, but it is useless to protest. Artifice must queen it once more in the town, and so, if there be any whose hearts chafe at her return, let them not say, "We have come into evil times," and be all for resistance, reformation, or angry cavilling. For did the king's sceptre send the sea retrograde, or the wand of the sorcerer avail to turn the sun from its old course? And what man or what number of men ever stayed that inexorable process by which cities of this world grow, are very strong, fail, and grow again? Indeed, indeed, there is charm in every period, and only fools and flutterpates do not seek reverently for what is charming in their own day. ... It is the times that can perfect us, not we the times, and so let all of us wisely acquiesce. ...
>
> For behold! The Victorian era comes to its end and the day of *sancta simplicitas* is quite ended. The old signs are here and portents to warn the seer of life that we are ripe for a new epoch of artifice. Are not men rattling the dice-box and ladies dipping their fingers in the rouge-pot?

Today, the piece continues, there has been in England a wonderful revival of cards and "that other great sign of a more complicated life, the love of cosmetics":

No longer is a lady of fashion blamed if, to escape the outrageous persecution of time, she fly for sanctuary to the toilet-table; and if a damsel, prying in her mirror, be sure that with brush and pigment she can trick herself into more charm, we are not angry. Indeed, why should we ever have been? Surely it is laudable, this wish to make fair the ugly and overtop fairness, and no wonder that within the last five years the trade of the makers of cosmetics has increased immoderately – twenty-fold, so one of these makers has said to me. We need but walk down any modish street and peer into the little broughams that flit past, or (in Thackeray's phrase) under the bonnet of any woman we meet, to see over how wide a kingdom rouge reigns.

Accordingly,

This is a time of jolliness and glad indulgence. For the era of rouge is upon us, and as only in an elaborate era can man, by the tangled accrescency of his own pleasures and emotions, reach that refinement which is his highest excellence, and by making himself, so to say, independent of Nature, come nearest to God, so only in an elaborate era is woman perfect. Artifice is the strength of the world, and in that same mask of paint and powder, shadowed with vermeil tinct and most trimly pencilled, is woman's strength.

The lyric silliness swells:

Was it not at Capua that they had a whole street where nothing was sold but dyes and unguents? We must have such a street, and, to fill our new Seplasia, our Arcade of the Unguents, all herbs and minerals and live creatures shall give of their substance. The white cliffs of Albion shall be ground to powder for Loveliness, and perfumed by the ghost of many a little violet. The fluffy eider-ducks, that are swimming round the pond, shall lose their feathers, that the powder-puff may be moonlike as it passes over Loveliness' lovely face. Even the camels shall become ministers of delight, giving many tufts of their hair to be stained in her splendid colour-box, and across her cheek the swift hare's foot shall fly as of old. The sea shall offer her the phucus, its scarlet weed. We shall spill the blood of mulberries at her bidding. . . .

And the conclusion:

All these things shall come to pass. Times of jolliness and glad indulgence! For Artifice, whom we drove forth, has returned among us, and, though her eyes are red with crying, she is smiling forgiveness. She is kind. Let us dance and be glad, and trip the cockawhoop! Artifice, sweetest exile, is come into her kingdom. Let us dance her a welcome!

Had the critics missed ironies so obvious? Max, in his letter to the editor, claimed it was all a hoax misunderstood by the public. If he had signed the article D. Cadent, or Parrar Docks, or appended a note saying that the manuscript had been picked up not a hundred miles from Tite Street (Wilde's address), the critics would have called it a "very delicate bit of satire." However, the piece is too engaged, I think, to be completely satiric. The prose is too comely, if I may be allowed that word, to be merely a sustained joke. Rouge as a stand-in for Aesthetics? It is worth recalling that, like Wilde, like Whistler, Max was all for artifice, for art as an improvement on nature.

Whatever the cosmetics article "meant," it succeeded. It was a large part of the notoriety, the *succès de scandale* provoked by the *Yellow Book*. The first volume sold well for so expensive a periodical. Max next contributed an article on George IV. Then, in January 1895, he was interviewed at home by the fashionable magazine, *The Sketch*. The article began:

> Mr Max Beerbohm left Oxford only last term to plunge into the delights of literature in London. In that short space of time, by his curious contributions to the *Yellow Book*, he has gained a more than merely esoteric fame. Indeed, he may be said to occupy in literature somewhat the same position as does Mr Aubrey Beardsley in art. The success has been a success of astonishment.

Max goes over the now old business of how the critics missed the joke of the "Cosmetics" piece; he talks of his George IV article as having been "more nearly understood"; it treated history "as a means of showing one's own cleverness [as] . . . has been done by the best historians from Herodotus to Froude and myself." And no, he is not going to abandon his "queer" words – like "oscillant" as in "Style should be oscillant"; no, they are not an affectation, and yes he does occasionally invent words, like "pop-limbo" and "bauble-tit," sometimes "merely because the cadence of a sentence demands it." He insists that his caricatures are not really cruel: "The caricaturist simply passes his subject through a certain grotesque convention. . . . I never pretend that my caricatures are meant for portraits." This *Sketch* interview appeared with a silly photograph of himself in a sailor suit, aged about eight. It was a clever, in some ways Wildean piece, with an anonymous interviewer who was altogether sympathetic. No surprise this, for the interviewer was his friend Ada Leverson, a witty, clever, unconventional woman, hostess and friend to many writers, most notably Oscar Wilde, who gave her the nickname "Sphinx." (She and her husband sheltered Wilde between trials, helped him financially, and met him on the morning of his release from prison, this meeting prompting Wilde's now famous quip, "Sphinx, how marvellous of you to know exactly the right hat to wear at seven o'clock in the morning to meet a friend who has been away!") More on Ada Leverson later, when we look at Max's involvements with women.

It was an exciting time for Max, who would go from strength to strength. In all he contributed four essays and one longish fairy tale to the *Yellow Book*. When the time came in 1896 for his first book, four of the seven essays reprinted there were from this source, and all were in his *Yellow Book* manner. This book, published by John Lane, was a thin, small, almost square affair in deep red covers, its pages having more than ample margins. It was called *The Works of Max Beerbohm*.*

From the *Yellow Book* were reprinted the Cosmetics article, renamed "The Pervasion of Rouge," along with "King George the Fourth," "1880," and "Poor Romeo!" Of the other pieces, "A Good Prince" had first appeared in *Savoy*, "Diminuendo" in *Pageant*, and the lead essay, "Dandies and Dandies," was compounded from articles in the *Spirit Lamp*, *Vanity*, *Unicorn*, and *Chap-book*. A bibliography appended to the volume, ostensibly by John Lane, has more than sixty entries, chiefly of caricatures, the "life-work," the Preface says, of "Mr Beerbohm . . . [whose] advancing years, powerless to rob him of one shade of his wonderful urbanity, had nevertheless imprinted evidence of their flight in the pathetic stoop, and the low melancholy voice of one who, though resigned, yet yearns for the happier past." The book, including the odd title and the bibliography, amused the people who liked that sort of thing. Meanwhile, as Max's own fortunes rose, the *Yellow Book* foundered. When the magazine was scarcely a year old, the Wilde trials hit, and its

---

* In the days before computers, the old Catalog of the New York Public Library, with its millions of 3 × 5 cards, had inscribed in pencil atop the printed card for this book, in a librarian's legible hand, "*Not* Collected Works!"

position was seriously endangered, though Wilde had never been a contributor. In Vigo Street a mob stoned the bay windows of the Bodley Head,
incensed by an erroneous headline: "Arrest of Oscar Wilde. *Yellow Book*
under his arm" (it was in fact a paper-bound French novel). Beardsley was
fired and his drawings – even though they did not go over the edges – were
expunged from the volume then in press. The *Yellow Book* "turned grey
overnight" and would fold in 1897, after thirteen "volumes."

In the mean time, Max was publishing many caricatures. Drawing came
effortlessly. In addition to the handful of caricatures he drew for the *Yellow
Book*, *Savoy* (a kind of rival to the former), and *The Sketch*, he provided eight
caricatures for the *Pall Mall Budget*, and thirty for *Pick-Me-Up*. His first
public showing was at the Fine Art Society's exhibition in 1896, "A Century
and a Half of English Humorous Art, from Hogarth to the Present Day," to
which he contributed six caricatures. Then, at the close of 1896, Leonard
Smithers, the man who was to take John Lane's place as nineties publisher of
daring material (he would publish Wilde after Lane dropped him; Smithers
also dealt in pornography), brought out Max's first book of drawings. Called
Caricatures of Twenty-Five Gentlemen, with an appreciative introduction by
Punch cartoonist L. Raven-Hill, it was dedicated "To the Shade of Carlo
Pellegrini," the *Vanity Fair* artist whose early work had inspired Max. The
caricatures, all but two drawn specifically for inclusion in the book, are black-
and-white line drawings intended for reproduction by wood engraving.
Among his twenty-five subjects were politicians Chamberlain, Rosebery,
Harcourt; writers, theatre people, and artists George Moore, Arthur Wing
Pinero, George Alexander, Herbert Beerbohm Tree, Aubrey Beardsley,
Paderewski, and George Brodrick (the Warden of Merton); also the man
whom he would attack always, Kipling; and his two very favourite targets,
Shaw and, in a class by himself, the Prince of Wales. Oscar Wilde, alas, could
not be represented. That would have been impossible and also in bad taste.
You do not hit a man (even jokingly), much less a friend, when he is down.
I do find the inclusion of Lord Queensberry surprising. People liked the
book.

Thus 1896 saw Max with two books published, one in each of his sister arts,
and famous at twenty-four; it was his *annus mirabilis*. Max had more than
one foot on the ladder of fame by this time; he was about half-way up. Later
he wrote that he had had "a pleasant little success of esteem. I was a – slight

but definite – 'personality.'" This "personality" existed not only as "Max" artist/writer but literally as a person, as someone of note in Edwardian London. He had been forever meeting people at Beerbohm Tree's lavish supper parties in the Dome of Her Majesty's Theatre, but now his own circle of friends was growing apace. He had been a member of Wilde's intimate clique, and of the *Yellow Book* group, when, of a sudden, he was invited to one of the Sunday parties at Edmund Gosse's house. It was tantamount to a ticket "to the inner temple of letters." As Max explained it, "My *Works* had just been published; and to Gosse, whom I had met often enough, I sent a copy. He was not quick to patronize young men who had done nothing, nor those who had done nothing good. . . . I remember when I received my summons to Delamere Terrace I felt that my little book really had not fallen flat. The drawing-room was very full when, carefully dressed for the part of brilliant young dandy, and very calm, and very shy, I made my entry." Gosse took immediately to Max and for a time fancied himself a kind of adviser to the young man, something that was altogether beyond his reach. (This may explain why Max's caricatures of Gosse always turn him into a hard-to-please schoolteacher.) But the two became fast friends, and Max was frequently a guest from this time on. At Gosse's he met everybody: Henry James, John Singer Sargent, George Moore, Thomas Hardy, Fred Benson, Austin Dobson, A. E. Housman, W. B. Yeats, Stephen Phillips, Rider Haggard, Maurice Hewlett, Arthur Waugh, J. M. Barrie, J. A. M. Whistler, Joseph Pennell, and countless others. The very first party Max attended had sixty guests. Nearly everybody seemed to like him. He was in demand as a guest.

More importantly, Max found himself in demand as a writer: "Frank Harris . . . engaged me to kick up my heels in the *Saturday Review*, Alfred Harmsworth was letting me do likewise in the *Daily Mail*." Harmsworth (later Lord Northcliffe) had started the *Daily Mail* in 1894 as a compact halfpenny morning newspaper and had made it a tremendous hit. He would later (1908) take over *The Times* and emerge as easily the most influential newspaper proprietor in the land – the "Czar of the Northcliffe Press." Shortly after Max's success with his *Works*, Harmsworth put at his disposal a column in the *Daily Mail*. Max came on board in December 1896 and had *carte blanche* to write about anything he wished – fire brigades, sign-boards, knighthoods. The pieces all had the kind of smart-alecky hook that

Harmsworth liked. "What I want every morning in the paper," Harmsworth said, "is something new and strange." Max's article on the Oxford/ Cambridge boat race says, "Rivers have their uses. They are serviceable for purposes of commerce, scenery, suicide, and the like, but it is a shame that they should ever pass near a great University." He also used his column to descant on books and art. He prefaced a slating of Hall Caine's *The Christian* by protesting that Caine's preliminary puffings of his novel were not, as some had alleged, a disgrace to literature: "One should be grateful to any man who makes himself ridiculous." In August 1897 Max's connection with Harmsworth brought him an invitation to the publisher's country house in Kent. To Reggie Max reported,

> Harmsworth is wholly delightful. ... Mrs Harmsworth also very nice. They have a charming house, and many, many servants. ... My toilets knocked 'em all silly. On Sunday, flannel coat, white waistcoat, purple tie with turquoise pin, duck trousers and straw hat. ... Altogether a pleasant visit, and I got away without tipping more than one person. I hope to see much of the Harmsworths – cigarettes and a telephone by one's bedside, and an enormous peach with one's morning-tea, and a glass of sherry-and-bitters on one's dressing-table at nightfall, and bound volumes of *Vanity Fair* in the library, and two small alligators in one of the innumerable hot-houses, and generally all the things which are indispensable to a scholar and a gentleman.

In 1906 Harmsworth would send Max to Italy to write a series of travel articles for the *Daily Mail.* The time in Italy roused Max to determine to live there, something he did four years later. That move would radically change his life.

Frank Harris was a prominent member of the Wilde set (though a decidedly heterosexual one), faithful and helpful to the last. Irish-born, he had arrived in London via the US and Europe in 1882, and had become editor of the *Evening News*, the *Fortnightly Review*, and, eventually, the *Saturday Review*. Everyone agrees that he was a superb editor although many found his personal flaws disconcerting. Bernard Shaw, who wrote for the *Saturday* under Harris, called him a buccaneer and a ruffian but forgave him because he "had the supreme virtue of knowing good literary work from bad and preferring the good." Max also prized Harris as an editor and as a talker; he liked Harris personally, though he was under no illusions about Harris's character.

Harris was an inveterate philanderer: "Women like men to be confident," Max said, "and Frank did not lack confidence." Max also considered him an egomaniac: "When you believe yourself omnipotent, it is hard ... to reconcile yourself to mere potency. Like all deeply arrogant men, Harris possessed little or no sense of reality." An inveterate liar, Harris told the truth, Max said, only "when his invention flagged." Still, Max remained fond of Harris. Aesthetics over ethics. (He drew Harris many times. One caricature from this early period connects Harris with Shakespeare, on whom he wrote and lectured widely – one of his lectures was called "Shakespeare, Shaw, and Frank Harris." During a crowded luncheon in 1896 Max heard Harris's voice booming above the din, "like the organ of Westminster Abbey, with infallible footwork." Harris was exclaiming: "Unnatural vice! I know nothing of the joys of unnatural vice. You must ask my friend Oscar Wilde about them. But, had Shakespeare asked me, I should have had to submit!" Whereupon Max drew a caricature titled "Had Shakespeare asked me ..." showing, from behind, a naked muscular Frank Harris, thinking over a proposition from a spindly-legged, sheepish-looking Shakespeare.)

At any rate, rambunctious Frank Harris in 1896 hired Max to write, now and then, on anything he pleased, for the *Saturday Review*. This was a considerable privilege. The *Saturday* was important – some would say self-important – sophisticated, authoritative, and attention-getting. The drama critic was George Bernard Shaw. Max contributed essays on subjects as various as Madame Tussaud's, Prangley Valley, and Jerome K. Jerome.

Max was also writing for other publications, most notably a London magazine called *To-Morrow*. In 1899 he brought out a second collection of essays, cautiously selecting less than half of his recently published pieces. He called the book *More*. Again published by John Lane, it reprinted twenty essays, as compared to seven in *The Works*, but as the newer ones were much shorter, the second book was only slightly longer than the first. The mood, the style, is much the same, a youthful smartness predominating. *More* is dedicated to Ouida, the prolific Victorian novelist (Marie Louise de la Ramée), and Max's essay on her is representative of the book. Because so much of his writing career would be as critic, the essay "Ouida" is of special interest as an early exercise in and discussion of criticism:

> The good critic, with a fastidiousness which is perhaps a fault, often neglects
> those who can look after themselves; the very fact of popularity ... often

repels him; he prefers to champion the deserving weak. And so, for many years, the critics, unreproved, were ridiculing [Ouida] a writer who had many qualities obvious to ridicule, many gifts that lifted her beyond their reach.

But Max, his friend George Street, and Stephen Crane, "three intelligent persons," had defended Ouida and then, belatedly, many critics praised a late novel of hers. Max claims that Ouida is a writer of intense vitality – like Meredith and Swinburne; she cannot stop to express herself artfully; she "is not, and never was, an artist. ... The artist presents his ideas in the finest, strictest form, paring, whittling, polishing." But Art in a writer is not everything – can even imply a certain limitation. Many consciously artistic writers lack force of intellect or of emotion; and "reticence, economy, selection, and all the artistic means may be carried too far. Too much art is, of course, as great an obstacle as too little art." Case in point, Walter Pater, who "in his excessive care for words is as obscure to most people as are Carlyle and Browning, in their carelessness." Then, coming back upon himself, Max says

> Well! For my own part, I am a dilettante, a *petit maître*. I love best in literature delicate and elaborate ingenuities of form and style. But my preference does not keep me from paying due homage to Titanic force, and delighting, now and again, in its manifestations. I wonder at Ouida's novels, and I wonder still more at Ouida. I am staggered when I think of that lurid sequence of books and short stories and essays which she has poured forth so swiftly, with such irresistible *élan*.

The little book snappily titled *More* appealed, even more than *The Works* had done three years earlier, to a small but enthusiastic readership. The *Critic* said Max treated his varying subjects "cleverly, seriously sometimes, with cheerful impertinence; but always with an artistic touch." The *Dial* claimed, a bit tortuously, that Max had made criticism of *More* impossible because the critic of such a book would have to assume Max's point of view to do so, and the result would be "imitative and therefore silly in anyone except the gifted author." The *Academy*, while complaining of the unevenness of the essays, shrewdly observed that Max "is often very Thackerayan," a compliment that delighted him.

He continued to turn out caricatures regularly. These changed and developed in two ways, both suggested by the ever-helpful Rothenstein in the mid-1890s: the use of colour and the addition of "decoration" or background. Thereafter most of Max's drawings incorporated full or partial colour wash. And many of them, perhaps a third, had settings, backgrounds, story-lines – decoration. It would be almost ten years before a second collection of caricatures was published, but he drew hundreds of caricatures for about two dozen newspapers and magazines. In 1901 he had his first one-man exhibition, at the Carfax Gallery in Ryder Street, through the good offices of his old friend Robbie Ross. "You are indeed a delightful dealer to deal with," he wrote to Ross. There were 110 caricatures in all (those that sold went for an average of five guineas each), politicians, artists, writers, aristocrats, actors: everyone, or so it seemed – Salisbury, Balfour, Chamberlain, Campbell-Bannerman, Hichens, Leno, Yeats, Harmsworth, Moore, Irving, Gilbert, Kipling, Beerbohm Tree, Sickert, Nicholson, Shaw, Max himself. He was acclaimed England's foremost caricaturist. Three years later another Carfax exhibition, which featured, among others, the twenty caricatures published simultaneously (and in colour) as *The Poets' Corner*, prompted the *Athenaeum* to call Max "our only caricaturist": Max's drawing of Omar Khayyám, the reviewer assserts, is "as idyllic and charming as it is funny, the Wordsworth is tenderly sympathetic, and the Dante has an almost Giottoesque dignity"; Yeats introducing George Moore to the Queen of the Fairies is "exquisite in its observation"; the Verlaine is "sublime"; and Max's presentation of Rossetti drawing in his back garden is the masterpiece of the collection, "an important historical document for which future historians of the Pre-Raphaelites will be grateful." Amen.

For Max, the 1890s were special years indeed. When he looked back at them he could hardly believe his run of good luck. And he always connected these years with Will Rothenstein. When Max was seventy and living in wartime England, he wrote a letter to Rothenstein in which, after reflecting on legendary figures of the nineteenth century, he says, "Oh, give me legends, fairly recent legends, all the time! Thank Heaven, we ourselves have a legendary touch about us! We are ex-Arcadians, greatly envied by the young." Their Arcadia had been the London of the 'nineties.

CHAPTER SIX

A Better Model

Two chapters back I said that Oscar Wilde was the strongest artistic influence on Max's early writing. This just might be, not exactly wrong, but misleading. Influence is an uncertain business. We must go back beyond Wilde and pick up on the earlier influence of Thackeray. We have seen how at Charterhouse Max devoured Thackeray and that he regarded *Vanity Fair* as the greatest of all English novels. The Thackerayan influence on his writing, it is true, was eclipsed by that of Wilde for much of the 1890s, but Thackeray was on (and in) his mind.

Like Wilde, Thackeray provided, in one essay at least, a subject as well as a stylistic model: "King George the Fourth," written for the *Yellow Book* in 1894, argues ironically against Thackeray's portrayal of that Prince:

> All that most of us know of George is from Thackeray's brilliant denunci-
> ation. Now, I yield to few in my admiration of Thackeray's powers. He
> had a charming style. We never find him searching for the *mot juste* as for
> a needle in the bottle of hay. Could he have looked through a certain
> window [Flaubert's] by the river at Croisset or in [Pater's] quadrangle at
> Brasenose, how he would have laughed! He blew on his pipe, and words
> came tripping round him, like children, like pretty little children who are
> perfectly drilled to the dance, or came, did he will it, treading in their
> precedence, like kings, gloomily. And I think it is to the credit of the read-
> ing mob that, by reason of his beautiful style, all that he said was taken for
> the truth, without questioning. But truth is after all eternal, and style tran-
> sient, and now that Thackeray's style is becoming, if I may say so, a trifle
> 1860, it may be not amiss that we should inquire whether his estimate of
> George is in substance and fact worth anything at all.

Even at this early stage Max has a Thackerayan tone. Easy, natural, unpretentious, graceful, light, witty. But how does one demonstrate these qualities?
Writers on style always cheat. They do not, as they often profess, take a
random paragraph and say only So-and-So could have written that: instead

they take Dickens at his most typical or most memorable, the opening paragraphs of *Dombey* or *Bleak House*, the dialogue of Mrs Gamp or Mr
Micawber; they choose Wilde at his cleverest and most paradoxical and epi-
grammatic from *Intentions* or *The Importance of Being Earnest*. They choose
Thackeray inveighing against snobbism and hypocrisy, immersing us all,
himself included, in Vanity Fair, as in this passage about Becky Sharp and her
husband living on nothing a year:

> If every person is to be banished from society who runs into debt and
> cannot pay – if we are to be peering into everybody's private life, specu-
> lating on their income, and cutting them if we don't approve of their
> expenditure – why, what a howling wilderness and intolerable dwelling
> Vanity Fair would be! Every man's hand would be against his neighbour
> in this case, my dear sir, and the benefits of civilization would be done
> away with. We should be quarrelling, abusing, avoiding one another.
> Our houses would become caverns; and we should go in rags because we
> cared for nobody. Rents would go down. Parties wouldn't be given any
> more. All the tradesmen of the town would be bankrupt. Wine, wax-
> lights, comestibles, rouge, crinoline petticoats, diamonds, wigs, Louis
> Quatorze gimcracks, and old china, park hacks and splendid high-
> stepping horses – all the delights of life, I say – would go to the deuce,
> if people did but act upon their silly principles, and avoid those whom
> they dislike and abuse. Whereas, by a little charity and mutual forbear-
> ance, things are made to go on pleasantly enough: we may abuse a man
> as much as we like, and call him the greatest rascal unhung – but do we
> wish to hang him therefore? No. We shake hands when we meet. If his
> cook be good we forgive him, and go and dine with him; and we expect
> he will do the same by us. Thus trade flourishes – civilization advances:
> peace is kept; new dresses are wanted for new assemblies every week; and
> the last year's vintage of Lafite will remunerate the honest proprietor who
> reared it.

This is unmistakable Thackeray. And, to me, it is the kind of writing that
echoes through all of Max. I'm not just making this up. Max himself, in old
age, when asked who had influenced his writing, said unhesitatingly, Wilde
and Thackeray. Reading Thackeray at Charterhouse, Max said, "had given
[me] all unconsciously a feeling for how English could be written." And
again, "Thackeray gave me an ideal of well-bred writing."

Today we are pretty sure that we can spot the Wildean influence. We are not sure that we can recognize the Thackerayan. But it was not always so. For roughly a hundred years after the appearance of *Vanity Fair* (say, until 1950) people knew Thackeray almost as well as they knew Dickens; and I suppose it must be admitted that Thackeray's admirers always considered their author, like themselves, more sophisticated, more educated in taste. However that may be, and sadly, Thackeray's appeal has dropped off in latter days, and he is not the great name he once was. He is too allusive, too subtly ironic. Moreover, he is an author great because of a single wonderful novel, rather than because of a whole series of novels – as with Dickens, Trollope, or Hardy. But for those with a Thackerayan sensibility there is no one quite like him, and *Vanity Fair* remains one of those few books that genuinely reward constant rereading. It is said that certain people – some dentists, for example – give their lives a steadying perspective by an annual reading of *Don Quixote*. The same holds for a yearly reading of *Vanity Fair*. It offers a salutary corrective; it makes one smile at one's own foibles and pretensions: what Thackeray would lump together as our humbug and flunkeyism. But unless you have been reading Thackeray, what good does it do to say that he was the most important and abiding influence on Max? It may help to remind today's readers of some of the things that wise people a generation or two back were saying of Thackeray, because their assertions seem so nicely to apply to Max: V. S. Pritchett, for instance, declares that "the pleasure of Thackeray is the sense of Style, the intimacy of an educated mind." Gordon Ray, Thackeray's biographer, affirms the ironic wit, the "sustained verbal brilliance" and "unpretentious ease" of the writing. As for substance, again according to Ray, Thackeray saw human beings as inherently flawed, with wickedness and folly often prevailing; success is "so largely dependent on luck, so little on moral worth, that it is the emptiest of accolades." What to do? mitigate one's discontent, Thackeray implies, by pursuing the satisfactions of private life: "the cultivation of family affections, the contemplation of beauty, the enjoyment of such good things of the earth as food and wine." In Max's case add the enjoyment of the Italian sunshine and the sensuous pleasure of applying colour wash to caricatures. Max was affected, Virginia Woolf says, by private joys and sorrows only.

In 1940 Max wrote to R. C. Trevelyan that he thought of establishing at Charterhouse a prize for the best essay that would (a) write the death of Dickens's Little Nell as Thackeray would have written it and (b) write the death of Thackeray's saintly old Colonel Newcome as Dickens would have written it. (Colonel Newcome, like his creator, and like Max, had been to Charterhouse School.) Max boasts to Trevelyan that he would have done Thackeray's Dickens well enough forty years ago and even now he could do a Dickensian version of Thackeray. And he writes the latter out for Trevelyan. I give first the original Thackeray:

> At the usual evening hour the chapel bell began to toll, and Thomas Newcome's hands outside the bed feebly beat time. And just as the last bell struck, a peculiar sweet smile shone over his face, and he lifted up his head a little, and quickly said "Adsum!" [I am here] and fell back. It was the word we used at school, when names were called; and lo, he, whose heart was as that of a little child, had answered to his name, and stood in the presence of The Master.

Here is Max's Dickens:

> And now, of a sudden, lo, the westering sun shone through the dormer window of the room, in crimson splendour. Simultaneously, there came the tolling of the Chapel's bell, the ancient curfew of the Pension House, that place which was for young and old alike, and where as boy the aged warrior himself had dwelt as he was dwelling now. It was the signal for the muster-roll. The Colonel heard it, and the sound found him responsive to the call of it. He sat erect and in a strong full tone uttered the old-time answer, "'Ere I am," and he whose heart was pure as driven snow stood at the golden judgment bar of Heaven, and was enrolled among the host angelic, where no tears are.

This burlesque of Dickens, with its over-writing, clichés, wordiness, cock-neyism, and overheated sentimentality is, like all parodies, cruel. Max's oft-repeated claim that in his parodies and his caricatures he mocked what he loved is sometimes disingenuous. This informal parody, thrown off in a letter, reveals not so much Dickens as the kind of writing Max did not care for, the kind of thing he had always avoided. In the great rivalry that Victorians, Edwardians, and even early moderns saw between Dickens and Thackeray, Max was (like his other most-admired Victorian novelist, Trollope) an unreformed Thackerayan.

We can continue to hold that Oscar Wilde was the dominant artistic force in Max's early writings, but we must see Wilde's influence as a kind of heavy overlay upon the earlier and as yet underdeveloped influence of Thackeray. When Max came entirely into his own – I will not offend by saying when he came to his senses – when his prose settled into the "classic Max" style, by the time he was twenty-six or twenty-seven, when the Wildean impulse had largely burned itself out, or rather, when the highly Wildean characteristics of his early work were supplanted by simplicity and clarity, here the Thackerayan model reasserted itself, and did so till the end.

CHAPTER SEVEN

Butterfly

One more early hero and influence, J. A. M. Whistler. Max thought Whistler a great, independent-minded, devoted artist; he also admired him as art critic, aesthete, dandy, satirist and wit, altogether a fascinating and amusing person, even in his looks (see plate 12). During the 1890s no visual artist loomed larger in Max's imagination. Max was of the view – one not shared by many – that Whistler was also a superb writer. In 1904 Max published an essay on Whistler's *The Gentle Art of Making Enemies* (1890), a book he had treasured and reread many times. This essay, "Whistler's Writing," is instructive as an example of Max's extravagant praise of what he liked.

That no one had done justice to Whistler's prose is not, Max insists, surprising. To begin with, many people think *The Gentle Art* unworthy of the great man and wish it could be "blotted out of existence." Those who hold this view, Max avers, probably love and understand painting, but do not understand or love writing. People who contend or hope that beneath Whistler's prickly surface was to be found "the quintessence of the Sermon of the Mount"* are deluding themselves:

> So far as he possessed the Christian virtues, his faith was in himself, his hope was for the immortality of his own works, and his charity was for the defects in those works.... He was inordinately vain and cantankerous. Enemies, as he had wittily implied, were a necessity to his nature; and he seems to have valued friendship (a thing never really valuable, in itself, to a really vain man) as just the needful foundation for future enmity. Quarrelling and picking quarrels, he went his way through life blithely. Most of these quarrels were quite trivial and tedious. In the ordinary way,

---

* The closest Max himself came to sounding (very quietly) like the Sermon on the Mount was at a party given by the novelist G. B. Stern in 1931. She and he had disagreed about the character of a mutual acquaintance, and she, on saying goodbye to Max, apologized for her spirited defence of the man. Max told her, "No, if two people can't agree about a third person whom they both know, the one who likes him is right, always."

they would have been forgotten long ago, as the trivial and tedious details in the lives of other great men are forgotten. But Whistler was great not merely in painting, not merely as a wit and dandy in social life. He had, also, an extraordinary talent for writing. He was a born writer. He wrote, in his way, perfectly; and his way was his own, and the secret of it has died with him. Thus, conducting them through the Post Office, he has conducted his squabbles to immortality.

A small immortality of course, and of consequence only to those "few people interested in the subtler ramifications of English prose as an art form." Not only are most others turned away by the nastiness of Whistler's published writings, they are kept from taking his writing seriously because they can't believe that an artist can excel in two arts: "When a man can express himself through two media, people tend to take him lightly in his use of the medium to which he devotes the lesser time and energy, even though he use that medium not less admirably than the other." They think him an amateur in his secondary art, though, Max argues, "You do not dispose of a man by proving him to be an amateur." (There were people who thought Max a professional writer but amateur caricaturist.) For an amateur writer like Whistler, "His very ignorance and tentativeness may be, must be, a means of especial grace"; Max will concede nothing beyond admitting that "in his writing [Whistler] displays to us his vanity; whilst in his painting we discern only his reverence. In his writing he displays too his harshness – swoops hither and thither, a butterfly equipped with sharp little beak and talons; whereas in his painting we are conscious only of his caressing sense of beauty."

Just what was Whistler's writing like? Why all the fuss over this oddly printed, contentious – some thought half-insane – little book? Unquestionably, both its matter and its manner charmed Max. *The Gentle Art* reprinted, for example, the famous *Ten O'Clock Lecture* (1885), offering Whistler's version of art for art's sake: Art "is selfishly occupied with her own perfection only – having no desire to teach – seeking and finding the beautiful in all conditions and in all times":

No reformers were these great men [Tintoretto, Veronese, Velasquez] – no improvers of others! Their productions alone were their occupation, and, filled with the poetry of their science, they required not to alter their surroundings. ... In all this their world was completely severed from that of their fellow-creatures with whom sentiment is mistaken for poetry; and for whom there is no perfect work that shall not be explained by the benefit it confers upon themselves. Humanity takes the place of Art, and God's creations are excused for their usefulness. Beauty is confounded with virtue, and, before a work of Art, it is asked "What good will it do?" Hence it is that nobility of action, in this life, is hopelessly linked with the merit of the work that portrays it; and thus the people have acquired the habit of looking, as who should say, not *at* a picture, but *through* it, at some human fact, that shall, or shall not, from a social point of view, better their mental and moral state. So we have come to hear of the painting that elevates, and of the duty of the painter – of the picture that is full of thought.

This debunking of the reforming and improving uses of art was all to Max's tastes, as were Whistler's attacks on the notion that Nature pure and simple is the end-all of art.

The occasionally "dignified" side of Whistler's writing also appealed to him – such as the celebrated passage on the evening mist that "clothes the riverside with poetry, as with a veil, and the poor buildings lose themselves in the dim sky, and the tall chimneys become campanili, and the warehouses are palaces in the night, and the whole city hangs in the heavens, and the fairyland is before us." This, Max comments, "is as perfect, in its dim and delicate beauty, as any of his painted 'nocturnes.'" But Max makes no secret of his liking, preferring even, Whistler's hostile, contemptuous style, which, though often in bad taste, was just as perfect in its own murderous way. Whistler's most famous target was John Ruskin, "learned in many matters ... save his subject":

We are told that Mr Ruskin has devoted his long life to art, and as a result – is "Slade Professor" at Oxford. In the same sentence, we have thus his position and its worth. It sufficeth not, Messieurs! a life passed among pictures makes not a painter – else the policeman in the National Gallery might assert himself. As well allege that he who lives in a library must needs die a poet.

Lesser figures, like the art critics for the *Saturday* and the *World*, did not escape; nor did Oscar Wilde, whom Whistler quite justly accused of appropriating his ideas. Wilde replied that Whistler ought to "remain, as I do, incomprehensible. To be great is to be misunderstood." Whistler came back in his best alliterative mode:

What has Oscar in common with Art? except that he dines at our tables and picks from our platters the plums for the pudding he peddles in the provinces. Oscar – the amiable, irresponsible, esurient Oscar – with no more sense of a picture than of the fit of a coat, has the courage of the opinions ... of others!

Wilde retorted,

With our James vulgarity begins at home, and should be allowed to stay there.

To which Whistler replied, famously,

A poor thing, Oscar, but for once, I suppose, your own.

Max's judgement was that after Whistler's attacks, his enemies

never again were quite the same men in the eyes of their fellows. Whistler's insults always stuck – stuck and spread round the insulted, who found themselves at length encased in them, like flies in amber. You may shed a tear over the flies, if you will. For myself, I am content to laud the amber.

Thus Max in 1904. In 1896 he had met Whistler where everybody met everybody: at Edmund Gosse's house. He was delighted to encounter in the flesh this peculiar, combative man of genius. Whistler had also the special fascination of being a survivor from Max's favourite period, that of the Pre-Raphaelites, a period he himself would later capture in (friendly) amber in *Rossetti and His Circle*. And when, in the autumn of that same wonderful year, Max started writing for the *Saturday Review*, he did so *à la* Whistler.

His first target was an elderly, self-important drama critic and part-time poet and playwright named Clement Scott. Max's review, "An Unhappy Poet," leads off with an "exquisite" quatrain from Scott, beginning "Bexhill-on-Sea is the haven for me ...".:

Every great poet [Max writes] has had some one impulse, to which may be traced all that is finest in his work. It is a function of criticism to determine in each case what that impulse was. Some poets are propelled by a love of Liberty or of Truth or of Pleasure, or their native land; others ... by a love of Nature. Wordsworth loved Nature in all her manifestations. ...

Swinburne was the poet of the sea. Mr Clement Scott is the Poet of the Seaside.

Perhaps, Max suggests, Scott's poetic impulse works against him as drama critic and as dramatist:

> Cooped in the gilded confinement of a stage-box, Scott's soul becomes restless and intractable. The glare of the foot lights blinds his clear poetic vision. ... Like Shelley and Tennyson, and how many others! he has assayed to write plays. Like them, he lacks the dramatist's touch. Unable to originate in this line, he has to fall back upon adaptations from the drama of that city which once, in a patriotic spasm, he branded "thoughtless Paris." That he should have dallied with the fair houri, Boulogne-on-Sea, is not to be wondered at. But Paris! "Thoughtless Paris!" An inland-town, too!

Max suggests that Scott leave such things alone, and that the drama world should "raise some great fund which will enable him to flee away, with his broken heart and his split infinitives, to the shores of Bexhill-on-Sea, there to work out his genius."

Whistler himself liked the article, and doubtless also the sequel, reminiscent of his own newspaper squabbles. First, Reggie Turner wrote ironically defending Scott. Then Scott published a long response headed "COME OUT OF YOUR HOLE, RAT!" (in which he appealed to Turner's "defence"). Max replied in a signed letter, "HOLD, FURIOUS SCOT," twitting him for "hinting darkly that there was some one, a desperate relative [Beerbohm Tree] who had urged me on to assail him. But herein, to adopt his own mode of speech, Mr Scott has planted his cloven hoof upon a mare's nest." The whole business has a distinctly Whistlerian ring to it – as do many of Max's subsequent criticisms in the *Saturday Review* and the *Daily Mail.*

In 1897 Max actually took on the Master himself. In a *Saturday* essay, "Papillon Rangé" (Steady Butterfly), he asks why Whistler has edged towards a demand for public acceptance, something he would never have stooped to in the past; he has always had the esteem of his fellow artists and has always "scored" off the critics: "Why should he now accept homage from men who stand in precisely the same relation to art as did they whose disparise he was wont to punish so prettily and swiftly? ... why, you may ask, should he, a great artist, have cared a fig for the mob's ridicule? Why should he not have

been, like his peers, indifferent, aloof, unruffled?" Max's identification with
Whistler and his strategies – perhaps unwitting at this point in his career –
seems apparent:

> When, nowadays, critics prate of [Whistler's] "marvellous knowledge of
> the limitations of his medium," they mean really that marvellous knowl-
> edge of his own limitations, that divine caution, which has ever withheld
> him from (perhaps) higher tasks and has left him content with absolute
> monarchy in his own sphere.

Whistler's riposte in the *Saturday* to "your new gentleman – a simple youth,
of German extraction –" said that he had heard most of this long ago; he was
"vastly intrigued" by a slip in Max's "Limburgher" French (*"Fais l'entrer"* for
"Let him enter") and complained of the unusual word *tewed* ("Yiddish, I
daresay – don't let him translate it").

This was not bad at all. Max replied:

> We will not imitate M. Whistler's manner; the airiness of the youthful irre-
> sponsible beau is antiquated now; the white plume that used to stand out
> so bravely against the dark locks is now almost indistinguishable, the
> boyish impertinences even have lost their charm as do the girlish gigglings
> of a maiden aunt; but "it intrigues us vastly," if we may imitate without
> understanding M. Whistler's English, we are, in other words, curious to
> know why M. Whistler should parry thrusts that do not, he avers, go near
> his skin.

The old warrior in Whistler did not deign to reply; he may have sensed the
great admiration underneath it all – although in the past such a consideration
would not have prevented him from getting in the last word. Max had done
well not to be encased in amber.

CHAPTER EIGHT

Around Theatres

Everyone who knows anything about Max Beerbohm knows that George Bernard Shaw labelled him "the incomparable Max." The occasion, in the spring of 1898, was Shaw's stepping down as drama critic for the *Saturday Review*. He felt he had done it long enough – four years – and, besides, he was now a dramatist rather than a drama critic. The idea that Max take over for Shaw came from the deputy editor, John F. Runciman, who was running the magazine while editor Frank Harris was abroad on holiday. Shaw immediately agreed and wrote to Harris saying that he wished to hand the job over after the present season; he then sent Max a postcard saying that he was leaving and that Max was "the only man to carry on the business." Max wrote back that he was very much pleased with the great compliment, but that Shaw ought to reconsider his retirement: "You may be tired of the job, but 'stale' you certainly are not – you are a weekly marvel of freshness and agility." Moreover, Max feels uncertain about the task:

> My mind is not very fertile, and any success I may have had is due to my own shrewdness in not doing much. ... I might come an early and a nasty cropper off the hebdomadal tightrope. Also, I have no enthusiasm for the theatre – in fact I don't care a damn about the theatre. This would handicap me for decent criticism. Also, I have a big brother at Her Majesty's, and he would be rather compromised by my position, and I by his. Also I am an amiable person, and might be unable to speak ill of any bad actors, except those I have never met. And I have met so many, so many!

But the greatest difficulty would be following "in your large and deep footprints." Nonetheless, as the position is a "dignified" one, and the prospect of regular emolument very nice, he will wait and see whether Shaw remains adamant and Frank Harris agrees.

Shaw then decided upon an immediate changing of the guard. He had developed a foot infection that required surgery. Harris telegraphed Shaw, asking him to stay on through the season, but Shaw fired back a letter to

Runciman, instructing him to tell Harris to stop being a "damned idiot": "I have a big cleft in my instep. .... there is nobody but Max to take up the running ... you can't do better." Shaw wants a smooth succession, "duly boomed as an important event."

Max was not an unknown quantity to Runciman or Shaw or Harris. For the past two years he had been writing, on Harris's invitation, occasional articles in the *Saturday*, "tilting at this or that personage as the fancy seized me." And now, just as Shaw was insisting on Max as his successor, Max in a two-part article was tilting "fervidly" at G.B.S. himself. Shaw, in a throwaway at the end of a letter suggesting Max begin his reign by reviewing a maiden effort at playwrighting by the actor George Bancroft, addressed himself to the first half of Max's criticism:

> I have read your article on my plays with some anxiety for your salvation. You must go on a vestry [become a borough councilman, like himself] at the first opportunity. You have been badly brought up, & can only taste life when it is fried in fine art. Follow my glorious example, & go into the Park every Sunday morning with a kitchen chair & a red flag. That is all your genius needs to sun away the north light of the studio.

Max wrote back that he did not think reviewing the Bancroft play – "a debut within a debut" – a good idea; besides, the second half of his article about Shaw was scheduled for the next *Saturday*. That piece, it turned out, was even more critical of Shaw than the first. Max had found particular fault with *Mrs Warren's Profession*. Some critics there are, he wrote, for whom the mere presence of a serious theme makes for great drama: "Drag in a brothel, and they will never have seen so great a play." But Shaw's play, with a brothel as its very basis, while "well and forcibly written," was not a good play: "No amount of stage-craft, and good dialogue and philosophic grip will enable a man to write a serious play that can be anything but ridiculous, unless the man can also draw human characters." Shaw's "men are all disputative machines, ingeniously constructed, and the women, who, almost without exception, belong to the strange cult of the fountain-pen, are, if anything, rather more self-conscious than the men." As for his informing philosophy, "it rests, like Plato's *Republic*, on a profound ignorance of human nature." Max thinks Shaw should stay with the true bent of his genius, farce. He is a funny Irishman: "He may try, and try again, to be serious, but his nationality will always prevent him from succeeding in the attempt. When he writes seriously, is always Paddy *malgré lui.*"

Shaw doubtless dismissed this criticism as cheerfully as he had the earlier. In the very issue containing Max's harshest words on his plays, Shaw in a farewell article was generously welcoming Max. (Reading the letters and articles, one could be excused for thinking Shaw and Max stage-managed the whole thing; I don't think they did.) Drama criticism, Shaw wrote, had made a slave of him for too long: "The subject is exhausted; and so am I. . . . The younger generation is knocking at the door; and as I open it there steps sprightly in the incomparable Max."

Max (now and for ever dubbed "the Incomparable") stepped in the following week with his first regular column, entitled "Why I Ought Not To Have Become a Dramatic Critic." This article seems less odd, less saucy, when you put it in the context of his replacing a showman like G.B.S. Max begins by "inconsolably" mourning Shaw's departure: "For, with all his faults – grave though they are and not to be counted on the fingers of one hand – he is, I think, by far the most brilliant and remarkable journalist in London." Then too, he, Max, although he has been from his cradle at the fringe of the theatre world (because of his brother), has no great love for the theatre as such. He is completely innocent of any theories on the theatre. He can't comprehend why people insist on regarding a visit to the theatre as a treat and finds inexplicable the phenomenon of men and women queuing at a pit-door: "I confess that I have never regarded any theatre as much more than the conclusion to a dinner or the prelude to a supper." Accordingly, he is appalled at the thought of going to the theatre under the obligation "to keep my attention fixed, never taking my eyes from the stage except to make a note upon my cuff." He won't know how to fill up his column; unlike G.B.S., he will not be able to branch off into discussions of ethical, theological, or political questions: "I have not that well-considered attitude towards life which gave a kind of unity to G.B.S.'s worst inconsistencies about art. In a word, I don't quite know what to do with the torch that G.B.S. has handed to me." Furthermore, "Most of the elder actors have patted me on the head and given me six pence when I was 'only *so* high.' Even if, with an air of incorruptibility, I now return them their sixpences, they will yet expect me to pat *them* on the head in the 'Saturday Review.'"

Especially troubling in this connection is his own particular bent:

I have a satiric temperament: when I am laughing at any one I am generally rather amusing, but when I am praising anyone, I am always deadly
dull. Now, such is the weakness of my character that I cannot say in print
anything against a personal acquaintance. ... Therefore, in criticising an
average production, I shall be obliged to confine myself to slating such
members of the cast as I have never met. If they have acted well, this will
undoubtedly be hard on them. Even if they have not acted well – and I for
one shall not know whether they have or not – their punishment will be
out of all proportion. The only advice I can offer them, meanwhile, is that
they should make haste and meet me.

Altogether, he writes, his position is unfortunate. He consoles himself with
the thought that other callings are more uncomfortable and dispiriting:
"Whenever I feel myself sinking under the stress of my labours, I shall say to
myself, 'I am not a porter on the Underground Railway.'" The irony here
runs almost too close to the surface. He had little trouble criticizing the work
of friends; he decidedly had a knack, as he himself later admitted, for digression, "the easy expedient of gliding from the matter in hand as soon as it
becomes wearisome into the discussion of some more or less irrelevant
subject."

And thus in May 1898 Max embarked on the only regular job he ever held.
He did so with trepidation, telling Will Rothenstein that he was going "on
the streets of journalism ... an intellectual prostitute." He asked to be paid
more than the £6 Shaw had been paid, for "I have less experience of the
theatre and so will find the work more difficult." The *Saturday*, understandably, did not see it this way and paid Max £5 a week. But for Max this was a
lot of money, and he was very glad to get it. It would make him less of a
burden on his mother and sisters. His tastes were relatively modest: dinner
now and then at Solferino's, drinks at the Café Royal, hansom cabs, the
occasional telegram, the upkeep of his dandy's wardrobe. He had not antici-
pated staying long on the job; he feared he might be fired when the *Saturday*
changed hands, as it did six months later. But in fact his tenure lasted until
1910, when he fired himself and went to live in Italy.

As he settled into his work, Max developed, he admitted, a "vivid interest"
in the theatre that surprised even him. He believed that he got better as he
went along, and when he later collected many of his reviews in *Around
Theatres*, he suggested that anyone dipping into the volumes would do well

to begin "about the year 1901." But the weekly writing stint remained a
burden. His valedictory article in 1910 described that burden:

> Writing has always been uphill work to me, mainly because I am cursed
> with an acute literary conscience. To seem to write with ease and delight is
> one of the duties which a writer owes to his readers, to his art. And to con-
> trive that effect involves very great skill and care; it is a matter of technique,
> a matter of construction partly, and partly of choice of words and cadences.
> There may be – I have never met one – writers who enjoy the act of
> writing; but without that technique their enjoyment will not be manifest.
> I may often have failed in my articles here, to disguise labour. But the
> effort to disguise it has always been loyally made. And thus it is that
> Thursday, the day chosen by me (as being the last possible one) for writing
> my article, has for twelve years been regarded by me as the least pleasant
> day of the week. On Wednesday I have had always a certain sense of
> oppression, of misgiving, even of dread. On Friday – the danger past, the
> sun shining, my feet dancing! And yet (such is habit, and so subtle a thing
> the human organism), whenever I have let pass a Thursday I have felt
> uncomfortable, unsatisfied, throughout the day. Even during my annual
> holiday, away from England, when I have kept no count of the days of the
> week, I have always recognized Thursday by the vague feeling of inanition
> in me, of impatience – the sort of feeling a clock may have when it has not
> been wound up. And I am wondering now, as I write, just how I shall feel
> next Thursday, and on the Thursdays to come. ...
>
> Is love of my readers as strong in me as my hatred of Thursdays? It is
> not half so strong.

Ten years later, to an enquiry about doing theatre criticism for "a new and
small, though energetic" American magazine, he answered, "I ceased many
years ago to write dramatic criticism; and by the time I was utterly sick and
tired of the drama, and have remained so ever since." His "terms" for writing
anything remotely connected with the drama would be $5,000 a word.

In 1930, for the American edition of *Around Theatres*, his prefatory note
goes over similar ground:

> ... let me claim for my years of bondage merely this: that without them I
> could not have had the delicious sense of freedom that filled me when they
> were over – that fills me even now whenever I think of them. My interest

in theatres didn't survive my freedom by a single moment. I never go to the theatre of my own accord. But when I am invited to one, or taken to one, I never fail to revel there. Whether the play and the acting be good, or bad I don't care a straw. All that matters is that I shan't have to sit down subsequently and write well-reasoned opinions of the affair. Bliss! Rapture!

Enough of background, complaints, excuses, and the sharpening of writing skills. What did he come up with? How good was the criticism? Fair questions, but one more exculpation, if you will. It draws upon Oscar Wilde's "The Critic as Artist," wherein he asks whose fault it is that the critic has such second-rate materials to deal with: "The poor reviewers are apparently reduced to be the reporters of the police-court of literature, the chroniclers of the doings of the habitual criminals of art." And while it is incontestable that a weekly critic of any art form has always a lot of dross to deal with, the London theatre during the twelve years of Max's servitude was in a particularly bad way. It was the time of ridiculous melodramas, empty farces, weak adaptations from the French. If the test of time means anything (and Max thought it did), playwrights whose work he dutifully reported on week after week in the *Saturday Review* have not scored very high. Name, please, a single play by any of the following: Frederick Fenn, S. M. Fox, Walter Frith, Sydney Grundy, Anthony Hope, G. R. Sims, Sergius Stepniak, A. Bisson, R. C. Carton, Lady Bell, Philip Carr. Yes, occasionally there comes along some relief, in the shape of a Shaw play, or one by J. M. Barrie, and of course revivals – of Ibsen and Shakespeare and some of the classical Greeks; but for the most part it was Cosmo Gordon Lennox, St John Hankin, Charles McEvoy, Felix Salten and their like who occupied Max for twelve years, nearly 500 reviews, enough to fill four fat volumes. How silly the talk of Max as the exquisite trifler who produced so little.

How did he keep it up so long? In an interview granted to a reporter for the *World* in 1900, Max said the trick was to be "unfailingly careful 'to give himself airs,'" to say "relatively little," to avoid the fatal mistake of "underrating himself," and to indulge in as much irrelevant digression as possible (Sardou's *La Sorcière* with Sarah Bernhardt, for example, prompts an essay on old age). Years later, when he was seventy, Max told a correspondent that he had failed to cultivate enough modesty as a reviewer, that he wished too much for his reader to admire him, "And it served me right that, so far as I am aware, he didn't." Max says he was never an enlightened judge of excellence in drama: "I knew what was good, but I was apt to be puzzled as to the constituents of its goodness, and was a foggy eulogist. Badness is easy game, and to badness I always turned with relief. Badness is auspicious to the shower-off. Its only drawback is that it isn't worth writing about."

To take "badness" first: yes, he had, as he never hesitated to confess, a satiric temperament that made it easy for him to be rough on writers and actors whom he found wanting. A prime example was playwright Arthur Wing Pinero, who had risen to the head of his profession in 1893 with *The Second Mrs Tanqueray.* He wrote 54 plays in 55 years, everything from farces and comic operas to serious, Ibsen-inspired dramas. That Pinero was the reigning playwright during Max's days as a young man and as *Saturday* drama critic distressed Max. While admitting Pinero's talent for dramatic construction ("technique"), he complained that when Pinero fell under the spell of Ibsen "and began to take life, and his art, and himself, in laudably grim earnest," he made a big mistake, "For he was not a born thinker: his mental processes were vague." It is one thing for a playwright to present a bore on stage and see how he "devastates" his fellows in the play, but quite another thing to devastate his audience: "I implore [Mr Pinero], once and for all, to clear his mind of the delusion that a dull thing expressed at great length becomes amusing." Pinero's "literary style" also annoyed Max:

In an unlucky moment, years ago, some rash creature hazarded the opinion that Mr Pinero wrote well. ... The consequence is that Mr Pinero, elated, has been going from bad to worse, using longer and longer words and more and more stilted constructions under the impression that he was becoming more and more literary.

Pinero's literary style amounted to nothing but "the lowest and most piteous form of journalese"; he ought to hire someone "to translate his next MS into passable English."

Other playwrights were even easier game than Pinero, who after all had considerable talent. Stephen Phillips, for instance, dreamed of reviving poetic drama. After Beerbohm Tree gave Phillips's *Herod* a sumptuous production in 1900, the public was eager for his *Paolo and Francesca.* When it appeared in 1902, Phillips was "greeted as the successor of Sophocles and Shakespeare." Max thought not: the British public's attitude to poetic drama was "We needs must try to love the highest when we see it [Tennyson]. Nor must we miss any opportunity of seeing it. It is for our good. Duty calls. Let us not hold back. Courage! Forward! On!"

Of course Rudyard Kipling too came in for more than his share of dispraise. For Kipling was in Max's eyes a man of great talent who debased that talent, an "apocalyptic bounder who can do such fine things but mostly prefers to stand (on tip-toe and stridently) for all that is cheap and nasty." Max turned in disgust from "the smell of blood, beer, and 'baccy'" which he found exuding from Kipling's pages; he especially loathed Kipling's "manliness." And so, when a production of Kipling's early novel *The Light that Failed* appeared on the boards in 1903 – Ah, that mine adversary would write a play – Max leapt to the attack. His review hangs on the fact that the novel was adapted for the stage by a woman, Julia Constance Fletcher, writing under the name "George Fleming." Might not "Rudyard Kipling" also be a pseudonym for a woman? In *The Light that Failed*, Max says,

> men are portrayed in an essentially feminine manner, and from an essentially feminine point of view. They are men seen from the outside, or rather, not seen at all, but feverishly imagined. ... "*My* men – *my* men!" cries Dick Heldar when a regiment of soldiers passes his window. He is not their commanding officer. He was at one time a war-correspondent. ... He had always doted on the military. And so has Mr Kipling. To him, as to his hero, they typify, in its brightest colours, the notion of manhood, manliness, man. And by this notion Mr Kipling is permanently and joyously obsessed. That is why I say that his standpoint is feminine.

In novels written by men, Max contends, "virility is taken for granted"; in the novels of (inept) women writers, the male characters are constantly acting in a "manly" fashion, ever in dread of "a sudden soprano note in the bass." "They must, at all costs, be laconic, taciturn, as becomes men. Their language must be strong but sparse. ... In real life, men are not like that. At least, only the effeminate men are like that. The others have no preoccupation with manliness. They don't bother about it." And so Max finds it remarkable that "these heroes, with their self-conscious blurtings of oaths and slang, their cheap cynicism about the female sex, their mutual admiration for one another's display of all those qualities ... were not ... fondly created out of the inner consciousness of a lady-novelist." Miss Fletcher offers "a marvellously close adaptation of the book," capturing, Max says, the "inconfusible" vulgarity that is Kiplingese (though he regrets that she omitted "Dick's immortal description of his inamorata as 'a bilious little thing'").

Kipling was not a playwright, but Max in his drama criticism inserts whenever possible some gratuitous attack on him. We read in an aside, for example, that had Kipling been a Frenchman, he would still be a mere journalist, known only as "a particularly virulent Anti-Semite, Chauvinist, and fulminator against 'perfide Albion.'" Again:

> Signally precocious in artistic execution, [Kipling] has always been signally backward in intellectual development. As a young man he took exactly the same kind of interest in soldiers and sailors and steam-engines as most of us take between the ages of five and ten. Last year [1903] I was amused to find that he had just reached the undergraduate stage: he was trying his hand at literary parodies. ... these parodies, so dull and feeble that no undergraduate editor would have accepted them on their merits, were blazoned forth, day after day, as a special feature of a newspaper that has a huge circulation among quite grown-up persons.

Elsewhere Max finds reason to mention Kipling's "The Absent-Minded Beggar," a "banjo melody" of Tommy Atkins, serving his country in the Boer War, a war Kipling staunchly supported, while Max was appalled by it: "Mr Kipling can receive no greater tribute than that his poem has electrified the land without the help of that other Great man ["the Great MacDermott," a music-hall performer who read poems on stage]. ... However, why should I be sneering at Mr Kipling? Reaction against him and all his works will set in soon enough. He will not be less under-rated than he has been over-rated." Max proudly counted himself as one of that "acute and upright minority" of "haters of Mr Kipling's work." A play by St John Hankin provides occasion for the observation that there are people – Max professes not to be one of them – who think that "two or three years under the refining influences of an university would have done [Kipling] all the good in the world." In 1907 Max devoted a column to Oxford: he was distressed to find that his alma mater had "learnt to play the big drum" and to "advertise herself so heartily" by conferring an honorary doctorate on Kipling: "No doubt it was a very popular move. ... But it is not the business of an university such as Oxford to make popular moves. Mr Kipling's gift has its fit reward, I think, in the applause of a crowd that will soon cease to remember him. ...The idols of the market-place need no wreaths from an university." Why not an honorary

degree for Henry James, "a writer as signally fit for it as Mr Kipling is unfit"? In old age, Max felt almost guilty about his attacks: "Friends of his and
mine kept telling me that he was pained and shocked by what I wrote, but I
couldn't stop. As his publication increased, so did my derogation. He didn't
stop; I *couldn't* stop. I meant to. . . . Why did I go on persecuting him? . . . I
had to do it. He was a great genius who didn't live up to his genius, who misused his genius." Why did Max do it? I'll let those who love to spy out unconscious motives do so on their own.

Max's negative drama criticism is better, or at least certainly more fun,
than the positive. He was a very fussy critic. Not easily pleased, he wanted
"beauty, reality and intelligence" on the stage, and, frequently enough, he
seems not to have found them. His praise of what he thought worthwhile
could be lavish, but his negative criticisms preponderate. Even the classics, so
beautiful to read, were often disappointingly staged. Of Milton's *Samson
Agonistes*, he wrote:

> For good downright boredom, mingled with acute irritation, commend
> me to the evening I spent last Tuesday in the theatre at Burlington House.
> The Milton Tercentenary has produced a fine crop of dullness and silli-
> ness, but nothing quite so silly and dull as this performance of "Samson
> Agonistes."

Of course he did like some things. After only a few weeeks on the job, he
reviewed Edmond Rostand's *Cyrano de Bergerac*. The play was presented at
the Lyceum Theatre, in French, with the famed Coquelin as Cyrano. Paris
had just declared the work a classic, and Max felt inclined to agree:

> Even if I could, I would not whisk from the brow of M. Rostand, the tal-
> ented boy-playwright, the laurels which Paris has so reverently imposed on
> it. For even if "Cyrano" be not a classic, it is at least a wonderfully ingeni-
> ous counterfeit of one, likely to deceive experts far more knowing than I
> am.

Max lauds Rostand as a "gifted, adroit artist, who does with freshness and
great force things that have been done before; and he is, at least, a monstrous
fine fellow." The character of Cyrano will survive "because he is practically a
new type in drama." Beauty loved by grotesque is an old theme, Max said,
but not grotesque as stage-hero. As for Coquelin in the part of Cyrano, "Even
if one does not like the play, it will be something, hereafter, to be able to bore

one's grandchildren by telling them about Coquelin as Cyrano." Max felt
that *Cyrano* could not be adequately presented in English: it was too "charged
with its author's nationality," and "to translate it were a terrible imposition
to set anyone. ... To adapt it were harder than all the seven labours of
Hercules rolled into one." When the play was produced in English, in 1900,
Max was predictably unhappy with it: "Cyrano, in the original version, is the
showiest part of modern times – of all times, maybe. ... The English critic,
not less than the English actor, is dazzled by him. But, though he shut his
eyes, his brain still works, and he knows well that an English version of
Cyrano would be absurd. Cyrano, as a man, belongs to a particular province
of France and none but a Frenchman can really appreciate him."

Max also praised – with reservations – the plays of J. M. Barrie: *Quality
Street* (1901) and especially *The Admirable Crichton* (1902), which he called
"quite the best thing that has happened, in my time, to the British stage."
Peter Pan appealed to the fantasist in Max:

> To remain, like Mr Kipling, a boy, is not at all uncommon. But I know
> not any one who remains, like Mr Barrie, a child. It is this unparalleled
> achievement that informs so much of Mr Barrie's later work, making it
> unique.

Shaw. I am saving Max on Shaw.

Ibsen. Max, like most knowledgeable people, viewed Ibsen as the dominant force in the theatre in the last half of the nineteenth century. And yet –
you knew there would be a qualification – Max always saw Ibsen's great plays
as somehow diminished by the author's personality; he writes, in 1899, that
Georg Brandes's book on Ibsen

> enables us to *see* Ibsen, and seeing him to – alas! no; somehow, not to love
> him. Sorrowfully, we admit that he is not attractive. ... The personality of
> Ibsen has no magic for us. That he was great, we know well. ...[But] one
> finds in him ... that wrong-headedness, that incapacity for seeing life in a
> dispassionate way, which is characteristic of so many great artists. ... Such
> narrowness is not found in the very great artists. Shakespeare and (no! not
> Mr W. B. Yeats) Goethe are the two most obvious examples of men whose
> greatness was so transcendent as to make them dispassionate. They saw
> things, of course, within the limits of their own temperaments, but their
> temperaments were so wide as to let them see all things clearly and, as it

were, in the round. Ibsen cannot see thus, and therefore one cannot reckon him among the very greatest. He is a Titan, not a god. The gods cannot lose their tempers; the Titans cannot keep theirs. Ibsen fails of supreme greatness because he cannot keep his temper.

On Ibsen's death in 1904 Max's obituary article touches on this same note:

> There is something impressive, something magnificent and noble, in the spectacle of his absorption in himself – the impregnability of that rock on which his art was founded. But, as we know, other men, not less great than Ibsen, have managed to be human. ... Innate in us is the desire to love those whom we venerate. To this desire, Ibsen, the very venerable, does not pander.

Maeterlinck. Perhaps surprisingly, Max relished the early and late plays (and other writings) of the Belgian man of letters Maurice Maeterlinck. In 1898 he praised the "marvellous and lovely" *Pelléas and Mélisande* precisely because it "appeals not at all to the reason, only to the sense of beauty and to the sense of mystery." In 1909, in a review of *The Blue Bird*, it is still Maeterlinck's feeling for mystery that draws Max to him, the refusal to provide answers to "things in general":

> For a proper appreciation of Maeterlinck, you must have, besides a sense of beauty, a taste for wisdom. Maeterlinck is not less a sage than a poet. Of all living thinkers whose names are known to me, he has the firmest and widest grasp of truth. He more clearly than any other thinker is conscious of the absurdity of attempting to fashion out of the vast and impenetrable mysteries of life any adequate little explanation – any philosophy. He sees further than any other into the darkness, has a keener insight into his own ignorance, a deeper modesty, a higher wisdom.

Maeterlinck is neither optimist nor meliorist nor pessimist. His early "shudders" overcome, Maeterlinck now, as in this play, takes the world as "a very-well-worth-while place" in spite of everything: "If we are but puppets of destiny, and if destiny is, on the whole, rather unkind, still there seems to be quite enough of joy for us to go on with."

If I had to choose for anthologizing one piece from all Max's vast drama criticism, it would be his memorial tribute to music-hall performer Dan Leno. It is an instance of that rare thing, criticism that can be inspiriting even when the reader knows nothing of who or what is praised. Dan Leno, whose career began at the age of four as the "infant wonder," rose to become London's supreme music-hall singer and dancer; in November 1901 he gave a command performance before King Edward VII and Queen Alexandra, earning himself the designation "the King's Jester." Max, who in many ways preferred the music hall to the theatre, as more honest, less pretentious, nearer to life, was a great admirer of Leno. And so, when Dan Leno died in 1904, aged forty-three, Max needed no prompting. He wrote:

> So little and frail a lantern could not long harbour so big a flame. Dan Leno was more a spirit than a man. It was inevitable that he, cast into a life so urgent as is the life of a music-hall artist, should die untimely. . . . His theme was ever the sordidness of the lower middle class, seen from within. . . . Yet in his hand, how glorious it blazed, illuminating and warming! All that trite and unlovely material, how new and beautiful it became for us through Dan Leno's genius!

The secret of that genius, Max writes, lay partly in the many droll things he said, partly in the way they were uttered, but above all in the delight that came from the man himself:

> The moment Dan Leno skipped onto the stage, we were aware that here was a man utterly unlike any one else we had seen. Despite the rusty top hat and broken umbrella and red nose of tradition, here was a creature apart, radiating an ethereal essence all his own. He compelled us not to take our eyes off him, not to miss a word that he said. Not that we needed any compulsion. Dan Leno's was not one of those personalities which dominate us by awe, subjugating us against our will. He was of that other, finer kind: the lovable kind. He had, in a higher degree than any other actor that I have ever seen, the indefinable quality of being sympathetic. I defy any one not to have loved Dan Leno at first sight. The moment he capered on, with that air of wild determination, squirming in every limb with some deep grievance, that must be outpoured, all hearts were his. That face puckered with cares, whether they were the cares of the small shopkeeper, or of the landlady, or of the lodger; that face so tragic, with all the tragedy that is writ on the face of baby-monkey, yet ever liable to relax its mouth into a sudden wide grin and to screw up its eyes to the vanishing point over some little triumph wrested from Fate, the tyrant; that poor

little battered personage, so "put upon," yet so plucky with his squeaking voice and his sweeping gestures; bent but not broken; faint but pursuing; incarnate of the will to live in a world not at all worth living in – surely all hearts went always out to Dan Leno.

Many people, thinking of Max and the theatre, leap directly to his short memoir, "Savonarola Brown," written seven years after Max had ceased to be a drama critic. For some, this piece is worth more than all the almost 500 drama reviews put together. I myself cannot so easily discount the many good things in the theatre criticism. But "Savonarola Brown" is enticing. Max begins by recounting how at Charterhouse he had briefly known Brown, who suffered greatly from the Christian name Ladbroke, with which his unimaginative parents, who lived at Ladbroke Crescent, W., had saddled him. Some fifteen years later the two men met frequently at the theatre, Max in his capacity of drama critic for the *Saturday*, Brown as a tireless student of the theatre and would-be author of a play about Savonarola (hence the nickname). One night, as Brown and Max walk away from the theatre together, they debate the nature of tragedy. Brown, who has completed four acts of his play, insists that his characters live their own lives; he doesn't know how the play will end. Max argues that Brown ought to follow the laws of tragedy:

"... the catastrophe *must* be led up to, step by step. My dear Brown, the end of the hero *must* be logical and rational."

"I don't see that," he said, as we crossed Piccadilly Circus. "In actual life it isn't so. What is there to prevent a motor-omnibus from knocking me over and killing me at this moment?"

At that moment, by what has always seemed to me the strangest of coincidences, and just the sort of thing that playwrights ought to avoid, a motor-omnibus knocked Brown over and killed him.

Max finds himself named Brown's literary executor and in possession of the unfinished play. He says frankly that he was a trifle disappointed; he wishes Brown had been "more immune from influences." (*Savonarola* is a clumsy pastiche of Shakespeare's Roman plays and of *Hamlet*.) On the other hand, it boasts an impressive Dramatis Personae: Savonarola himself, and Lucrezia Borgia, who has set her cap at the monk – this is the main plot line – but also St Francis of Assisi, Leonardo da Vinci, Lorenzo de Medici,

Cosimo de Medici, Pope Julius II, a court Fool, *et al.* There are poisoned rings, prison scenes, mistaken murders, funeral orations, and telling dialogue:

ST. FRANCIS [TO DANTE]
How fares my little sister Beatrice?
DAN.
She died, alack, last sennight.
ST. FRAN.
                 Did she so?
If the condolences of men avail
Thee aught, take mine.
DAN.*
They are of no avail.

Max once said that in Shaw's plays he most enjoyed the stage directions. Brown's are striking in their own way:

Re-enter Guelfs and Ghibellines fighting. SAV. and LUC. are arrested by Papal officers. Enter MICHAEL ANGELO. ANDREA DEL SARTO appears for a moment in a window. PIPPA passes. Brothers of the Misericordia go by, singing a Requiem for Francesca da Rimini. Enter BOCCACCIO, BENVENUTO CELLINI and many others, making remarks highly characteristic of themselves, but scarcely audible through the terrific thunderstorm which now bursts over Florence and is at its loudest and darkest crisis as the Curtain falls [on Act III].

Comic parodies of Shakespeare's tragedies are not generally successful. *Savonarola: A Tragedy* is about as close as you can come.

---

* While "Savonarola Brown" was going through the press for its book appearance (in *Seven Men*), Max told his publisher, William Heinemann, that "these abbreviations, absurd tho' they are – or rather just *because* they are absurd, ought to be preserved. Banish your fear that I shall address you as 'Hei' or that I shall be offended if you don't call me 'Beer,' and agree with me that these abbreviations are helpful to the general effect of ridiculousness herein aimed at."

CHAPTER NINE

Most Salient Phenomenon

Bernard Shaw, like Oscar Wilde, deserves a separate chapter. And here I shall be straying into territory in Max's life that I promised myself to stay out of, namely the inner man. I shall do so only briefly, clearly flagging the trespass, and offering apologies in advance. Encouragement comes from an odd quarter: Max himself. He saw his feelings about Shaw as terribly ambivalent, and he said so many times. This ambivalence extended to both the man and his works.

Max on Shaw's writings. We have already seen Max, just as he was being put into Shaw's place as drama critic for the *Saturday Review*, expressing his reservations about G.B.S. as playwright: his characters were mere puppets, disputative machines lacking flesh and blood. But when Max came to review regularly for the *Saturday*, in some twenty discussions of Shaw's plays he was much more generous. Still, he could never quite make up his mind. In 1903, reviewing at length the book publication of *Man and Superman*, he compliments and disparages. What Shaw calls a play is not a play at all; if this were a play, it would suffer from "a tyrannous preoccupation" with its message. But *Man and Superman* is really a Dialogue in the manner of Socrates. As such it is " 'as good as a play,' infinitely better, to my peculiar taste, than any play I have ever read or seen enacted," and Shaw ought to stick to dialogues. Shaw sent Max a letter longer than the article, beginning "My dear Max: This won't do ... the spasms of compliment almost draw tears; but the whole thing is wrong." Shaw's argument, and Max's counter-argument in his equally lengthy letter of reply, would need to be re-presented in their entirety to make sense. Even given whole, they are tortuous to follow. It's sufficient to say that Shaw closed by telling Max to stand for a borough council, quit drama criticism, and *draw* for a living. And Max, saying he would cherish Shaw's letter for its "engaging sophistries," closed by saying he would not go in for politics: "Such limitations as I have I must guard jealously."

Max's reviews waver for twelve years. On balance he writes much more in praise than in dispraise. He excoriates West End managers for not producing

Shaw's plays. He attacks Shaw's "exasperating" imitators. Of *John Bull's Other Island* he announces, here is "Mr Shaw at his Best" and shame on critics (like his earlier self) who would cry, "Not a play." To the contrary, Shaw "has an instinct for the theatre, and he can with perfect ease express his idea effectively through the dramatic form." Shaw, a master of dialogue, is additionally a subtle thinker; and he is clear: "We never have to pause to consider what is meant by the last line." Max complains of certain brainless critics who had always opposed Shaw on all points, but who are now – because he is becoming popular – reduced to finding imagined faults such as "brutality" and "blasphemy" in *Major Barbara*. Max goes so far as to retract some of his earlier criticisms, most notably his insistence that plays like *Mrs Warren's Profession* and *The Devil's Disciple* were impossible to stage; he now discovers that "they gained much more than they lost by being seen and not read." Moreover, this "old superstition" had lingered in his brain, and when *Man and Superman* was published, he called it a "Dialogue," quite unfit, even without the Hell Scene, for staging. But on seeing the work produced on stage, he decides that "as a piece of theatrical construction it was perfect." He closes: "There! I have climbed down. Gracefully enough to escape being ridiculous?" And when the Hell Scene itself was finally staged, at the Court Theatre in 1907, Max wrote, with no irony, "We do not deserve Mr Shaw. ... From first to last the high pressure of thought never lacks perfect expression; the close logical sequence of ideas is never obscured, is only illuminated, by the admirable rhetoric and the admirable wit. In point of literary style, this play is very much the best thing that Mr Shaw has done."

Then, in his last year on the job, 1910, provoked by *Misalliance* – admittedly not considered one of Shaw's best plays – Max slips back into his old adversarial stance:

> There never was any reality in Mr Shaw's typical young men and women (I except Anne Whitefield ...) ... these alternately impudent and whining young men, and the invariably priggish and hectoring young women, all of them as destitute of hearts as they are of manners, and all of them endowed with an equal measure of chilly sensuality, evoke in us a rather strong desire to see no more of them. Some comfort we take in our certainty that we shan't, at any rate, run up against them in the actual world.

Even if, Max continues, we allow Shaw his present practice of writing debates instead of plays, this one fails utterly: *Misalliance* "is about anything and everything that has chanced to come into Mr Shaw's head. It never progresses, it doesn't even revolve, it merely sprawls." Max closes by saying that "to condemn a work of Mr Shaw's is for me a new and disagreeable sensation." He reflects, nearly retracts, then decides, "No! I have given very satisfactory reasons why I don't like 'Misalliance.'"

In truth, satisfactory reasons both pro and con seemed to haunt him. When in 1924, a dozen years after retiring from the *Saturday*, Max collected selections of his criticism into *Around Theatres*, he wrote in the preface:

> One thing I never could, from first to last, make up my mind about; and that thing was the most salient phenomenon "around theatres" in my day: "G.B.S." Did I love his genius or hate it? ... I went wavering hither and thither in the strangest fashion, now frankly indignant, now full of enthusiasm, now piling reservation upon reservation, and then again frankly indignant. My vicissitudes in the matter of G.B.S. were lamentable. But they amuse me very much. The satiric temperament again.

The vicissitudes were permanent. When in 1946 a Festschrift was being prepared for Shaw's ninetieth birthday, Max declined to contribute an essay. He wrote to Stephen Winsten, editor of the book, saying he thought it was about time a book should be written to Shaw rather than about him and that he wished he could be among the contributors:

> But I think that no great man at the moment of his reaching the age of ninety should be offered anything but praise. And very fond though I am of G.B.S., and immensely kind though he has always been to me, my admiration for his genius has during fifty years and more been marred for me by dissent from almost any view that he holds on anything ... I remember that ... G.B.S. ... having commented on the adverse criticisms of his old friends ... said, "And Max's blessings are all of them thinly disguised curses." I remember also a published confession of my own that I was always distracted between two emotions about him, (1) a wish that he had never been born, (2) a hope that he would never die. The first of these two wishes I retract. To the second one I warmly adhere. Certainly he will live for ever in the consciousness of future ages. If in one of those ages I happen to be re-incarnate I shall write a reasoned estimate of some aspect of him and of his work. But now I merely send him my love.

Winsten printed the letter in the Festschrift. (Shaw, incidentally, had declined an invitation to a celebration organized in London in 1942 for Max's seventieth birthday: through his secretary he replied, "Mr Bernard Shaw asks me to say that he suffered too much from the celebration of his own seventieth birthday sixteen years ago to make himself a party to a repetition of the same outrage at the expense of an old friend who never harmed him.")

In 1954 Max told his new friend Sam Behrman, "In [Shaw's] plays ... the dialogue is vortical and, I find, fatiguing. It is like being harangued; it is like being a member of one of those crowds he used to exhort on street corners. He used the English language like a truncheon. It is an instrument of attack. ... No light and shade, no poetry. His best work, I think, appears in his books of drama and music criticism and his stage directions."

Max on Shaw the person. Was there a personal animus? They first met, as Max told the story from a distance of sixty years, around 1895:

> I had just come down from Oxford – Shaw made an immense journey by bicycle to see me, because he had heard that I had done some caricatures. He came to be caricatured. I had indeed done some caricatures, I was beginning to achieve a little reputation as a caricaturist, but I hadn't really, at that time, done anything very good, you know. Still, Shaw would rather have had a presentment by anybody, no matter how incompetent, no matter how malicious, than no presentment at all.

An early (but undatable) entry on Shaw in a notebook Max kept reads: "Inhuman – uncomfortable – never playing with dog or child or talking about the weather – or talking on nonsense that wasn't intellectual – or doing nothing." But, whatever Max's reservations, the two men became good, though never intimate, friends. Until Max deserted the capital in 1910, he dined frequently with Shaw and his wife. The letters between Max and G.B.S. are filled with the kind of sprightly banter that only friends can exchange: Shaw sends him a postcard pointing out that he had "that snag tooth nipped off (there was only one, in spite of malicious exaggerations) and replaced by a symmetrical imposture. Your caricatures are now waste paper; and serve you right." When Shaw, having contributed to a book of essays on Max's brother Herbert, offers to return his author's fee, Max writes back: "The money, my dear friend, is yours. ... This notion ... is entirely monstrous – though beautiful, of course. Curb yourself. Or get someone to curb you. Spend a week or two in some nice little private lunatic asylum. Why not come here? My wife and I would watch over you with the greatest care and unfailing presence of mind."

But in corresponding with others about Shaw, Max shows himself of two minds. In 1926 he tells mutual friend Henry Arthur Jones, "I entirely understand your feelings about his vagaries. It is very queer that a man should be so gifted as he is (in his own particular line nobody has been so gifted, I think, since Voltaire) and so liable to make a fool of himself." On the other hand, he reminds Jones, Shaw "is entirely free from any kind of malice." Ten years later he advises Grant Richards not to worry that in a forthcoming book he had given too much room to G.B.S.: "After all, he is the most remarkable of living writers. And the fact that he is neither an artist, in any sense of the word, nor a human being in *very* many senses of the word, doesn't detract from his immense value to the world. And one of his great good points, his genuine kindness and helpfulness, comes out strong in your account of him."

The insistence that Shaw was not an artist went back a long way. Once Max found it confirmed from a surprising quarter. In early 1914 Max met Shaw dining at Philip Sassoon's:

... he seemed [Max tells Reggie Turner] decidedly uncomfortable at being caught by me there. Also, poor man, he got almost nothing to eat. No special dish had been ordered for him. The eye of Mrs Shaw (who was next to me) kept wandering up and down the menu, in fearful anxiety for him. It was only towards the end of dinner that he got a potato and some beans. Of course, meanwhile, I talked a lot to Mrs Shaw about him, as always, and with much affection and admiration, but also, at one point, with considerable frankness. "He is *not*," I said, "an artist." At this her face beamed suddenly more than ever. "Oh," she exclaimed, "how glad I am to hear you say that. That is what *I* always tell him. He is a REFORMER."

Reforming, propagandizing: this was exactly what Max opposed in art. He did not believe utterly in art for art's sake – for that matter neither did Wilde – but he thought the emphasis all wrong in Shaw. As for Mrs Shaw, Max liked her, and she liked him. Her devotion to G.B.S. was unyielding, however; and on one occasion she purchased a caricature Max had recently drawn of her husband (showing that most staunch of teetotallers slightly tipsy), waited until Max was visiting them, and then, in front of his face, tore the drawing in two.

Max recounted to Turner how he had gone to Madame Tussaud's to see G.B.S. in wax:

I thought it might form a good basis for a caricature. Some days later I was lunching at his place, and mentioned the effigy to him; at which he flushed slightly, waved his hands, and said that he had *had* to give Tussaud* a sitting, as "it would have seemed so *snobbish* to refuse"! Considering that it had been the proudest day of his life, I was rather touched by his account of the matter. I am afraid he is afraid of me.

The record does not show that Shaw was afraid of Max. He seems to have regarded him as a talented, friendly phenomenon – and utterly unthreatening. The negative side of Max's criticism of his plays Shaw breezily dismissed. He did tell Max, "William Morris used to say of me that it was a mercy I couldn't draw caricatures. You are the body of his fear." But Shaw seems positively to have enjoyed Max's many caricatures of himself, captions and all. One such accompaniment to a caricature in *Vanity Fair* for 1905 reads, "Magnetic, he has the power to infect almost everyone with the delight he takes in himself."

A couple of years before Max died, Shaw himself having finally died, Samuel Behrman asked Max if it were true that although Shaw hadn't an enemy in the world, none of his friends really liked him:

> Well [Max said], he had a powerful brain ... but he was a cold man. It's true I never had anything but kindness from him. Though I had written, in the *Saturday*, several sharply critical articles about him, it was Shaw who, in the absence of Frank Harris – Harris was on holiday, or whatever, in Athens – approved Runciman's slipping me in, rather, to the post of drama critic. Shaw was not vindictive. There was no element of vindictiveness in him. This is an admirable quality. In his case, it may have emanated ... from his absolute conviction ... that there was no one living who was worthy of his animosity. ... He was a coarse man.

---

* Many people find Madame Tussaud's distasteful, but Max claimed the place made him positively sick. These "cadaverous and ignoble dolls," regarded by some as so lifelike, have less verisimilitude than any fine art: "Life, save only through conventions, is inimitable. The more closely it be aped, the more futile and unreal its copy. ... The unreality of everything [in Tussaud's] oppressed me, in brain and body, with an indescribable lassitude. I felt dimly that the place was evil, everything in it evil. Life was a sacred thing – why had it been profaned here, for so many years? Whence came this hateful craft? With what tools, in what workshop, who, for whose pleasure, fashioned these obscene images? ... It flashed upon me that, as I watched them, they were stealing my life from me, making me one of their own kind."

Max thought Shaw arrogant, offering as an example the lines from *Maxims for Revolutionists,* "He who can, does. He who cannot, teaches":

> The arrogance of it.... He himself so manifestly *can*! Of course it is simply untrue. Many teachers have done moving and delightful things – Lewis Carroll, and A. E. Housman, for example. But even those who haven't – if they teach well, if they inspirit the young, they are perhaps more valuable than those who have done the moving and delightful things. But then G.B.S. had been talking rot for more than fifty years. Will anyone ever write a book on the vast amount of nonsense uttered with such brilliance and panache by G.B.S.?

What are we to make of this ambivalence about the works, the fault-finding with the man, calling him self-centred and inhuman? Why should Max have caricatured him so often? (One explanation is that he simply thought him a good subject for caricature: "He has a temperance beverage face," Max told Florence Kahn. And Max thought it hilarious that Rodin was doing a bust of him "for Mrs Shaw and posterity. It is difficult to imagine that tremulous beard in marble – rigidly fluttering its way down the ages.") What are we to think of the extreme lengths he went to doctor photographs, "improving" them so as to make Shaw look like a leering devil and a pig? Well, one interpretation, and I adapt it from Lawrence Danson, argues that in the days of which we speak there were two pairs of great self-publicists, artists who "made their personalities inseparable from their work." First came Whistler and Wilde; then Shaw and Beerbohm, the second generation, so to speak, whose "iconic signatures" – "G.B.S." and "Max" – betokened the identification of their work with their personalities. With Wilde and Whistler gone, G.B.S. and Max had the field pretty much to themselves. Max, himself a self-confessed personality, kept praising Shaw as a personality: Shaw is "the most distinct personality in current literature," and, again, "As a teacher, as a propagandist, Mr Shaw is no good at all, even in his own generation. But as a personality, he is immortal." G.B.S. and Max behaved in different ways: Shaw loud and outrageous and shocking, the misbehaving Irish outsider; Max quiet and mild and caustic, the correct English gentleman. Still, as specialists in irony and as self-created personae they could be seen as competitors. Where might these considerations be leading? Well – and here comes the inner man stuff – yes, Max's antipathy towards Shaw may have come partly from a vague sense of Shaw as his principal rival. But even while conceding this much, I am inclined to retract it. Or at least to say that it represents little more than a commonsensical possible reading of the facts. But I must not keep qualifying or my one concession to this kind of thing will find itself reduced to nothing. Let it stand that Max's ambivalence towards Shaw and his works may have come from an unacknowledged, indeed unrecognized wariness about his one and, oh, so successful rival. Max would have called this nonsense, and insisted that his real rival was Lytton Strachey. But competition from Strachey came only after 1918, when *Eminent Victorians* appeared. Thus, *Stet.* And yes, I realize that in attributing possible unconscious jealous rivalry to Max I am doing exactly what I found fault with Richard Ellmann for doing in regard to Max's "unconscious excitement" about the prospect of the removal of Wilde from the London scene. The difference is that I do not really believe it.

Whatever the cause, Max underrated Shaw. He probably overrated Lytton Strachey.

CHAPTER TEN

Yet Again

During the time that Max was drama critic for the *Saturday Review,* 1898–1910, when he had been under the obligation to write so many reviews, most of his friends thought he was wasting his time. But as year followed year, he himself came to think otherwise:

> I believe that the obligation to write every week a fugitive article for a largish public is no bad thing for a writer inclined, as I was, to "preciosity." I believe that my way of writing became more chaste, through journalism, and stronger.

As early as 1898 he had seen his writing as calming down and his caricatures also as changing somewhat – but let him tell it, in a letter of that year to Henry Arthur Jones:

> As to the difference between my writings and my drawings, I myself have often been puzzled by it. But I think that in the past few years the two dissimilar "sisters" of whom you speak have really been growing a little more like each other. My drawing has been growing a little more delicate and artful, and losing something of its pristine boldness and savagery; whilst my writing, though it never will be savage or bold, is easier in style, less ornate, than it used to be. At least I think so.

The real change in style is evident to us in his next collection of essays, *Yet Again*, published in 1909. For regular play reviewing did not mean a cessation of occasional personal essays in various publications: in the *Saturday Review* itself, but also in the *Pall Mall Magazine*, the *New Liberal Review*, the *Cornhill*, *Traveller*, and half a dozen others. As had become his custom, he reprinted in hard cover less than half of what he had written for the magazines. We have already had a taste of this later style, in the material quoted from "Whistler's Writing." Here's the opening of another later piece called "The Humour of the Public":

They often tell me that So-and-so has no sense of humour. Lack of this sense is everywhere held to be a horrid disgrace, nullifying any number of delightful qualities. Perhaps the most effective means of disparaging an enemy is to lay stress on his integrity, his erudition, his amiability, his courage, the fineness of his head, the grace of his figure, his strength of purpose, which has overleaped all obstacles, his goodness to his parents, the kind word that he has for everyone, his musical voice, his freedom from aught that in human nature is base; and then to say what a pity it is that he has no sense of humour. ... And what could match for deadliness the imputation of being without sense of humour? To convict a man of that lack is to strike him with one blow to a level with the beasts of the field – to kick him, once and for all, outside the human pale. What is it that mainly distinguishes us from the brute creation? That we walk erect? Some brutes are bipeds. That we do not slay one another? We do. That we build houses? So do they. That we remember and reason? So, again, do they. That we converse? They are chatterboxes, whose lingo we are not sharp enough to master. On no possible point of superiority can we preen ourselves save this: that we laugh, and that they, with one notable exception, cannot. They (so, at least, we assert) have no sense of humour. We have. Away with any one of us who hasn't!

To determine the humour of the public, Max investigates a week's run of the comic papers and comes up with a list of themes, exactly coinciding with themes common in the old music halls: Mothers-in-law, Hen-pecked husbands, Twins, Old maids, and on down to Bad cheese and "Shooting the moon" (leaving a lodging house without paying), among others. He looks for some unifying principle.

Mothers-in-law. Why should the public roar, as roar it does, at the mere mention of that relationship? There is nothing intrinsically absurd in the notion of a woman with a married daughter. It is probable that she will sympathise with her daughter in any quarrel that may arise between husband and wife. It is probable, also, that she will, as a mother, demand for her daughter more unselfish devotion than the daughter herself expects. But this does not make her ridiculous. The public laughs not at her, surely. It always respects a tyrant. It laughs at the implied concept of the oppressed son-in-law, who has to wage unequal warfare against two women. It is amused by the notion of his embarrassment. It is amused by suffering. This explanation covers, of course, the second item on my list – *Hen-pecked husbands*. It also covers the third and fourth items.

And so on, with amusement at "Bad cheese" alone defying analysis and remaining a mystery.

Here's another sample from *Yet Again* of the easier, less ornate style, an essay headed "Seeing People Off":

> I am not good at it. To do it well seems to me one of the most difficult things in the world, and probably seems so to you, too.
>
> To see a friend off from Waterloo to Vauxhall were easy enough. But we are never called on to perform that small feat. It is only when a friend is going on a longish journey, and will be absent for a longish time, that we turn up at the railway station. The dearer the friend, and the longer the journey, and the longer the likely absence, the earlier do we turn up, and the more lamentably do we fail. Our failure is in exact ratio to the seriousness of the occasion, and to the depth of our feeling.
>
> In a room, or even on a door-step, we can make the farewell quite worthily. We can express in our faces the genuine sorrow we feel. Nor do words fail us. There is no awkwardness, no restraint, on either side. The thread of our intimacy has not been snapped. The leave-taking is an ideal one. Why not, then, leave the leave-taking at that? Always, departing friends implore us not to bother to come to the railway station next morning. Always, we are deaf to their entreaties, knowing them to be not quite sincere. The departing friends would think it very odd of us if we took them at their word. Besides, they really do want to see us again. And that wish is heartily reciprocated. We duly turn up. And then, oh then, the gulf yawns! We stretch our arms vainly across it. We have utterly lost touch. We have nothing to say. We gaze at each other as dumb animals gaze at human beings. We "make conversation" – and *such* conversation! We know that these are the friends from whom we parted overnight. They know we have not altered. Yet, on the surface, everything is different; and the tension is such that we only long for the guard to blow his whistle and put an end to the farce.

That's just the opening. Frivolous subjects? Well, and thank God for it, not everybody can be writing about big, so-called important issues: population, genes, semantics, sex, death. Surely there is value in anything that makes us laugh, that makes us understand ourselves more. A shrewdness of observation coupled with common sense can amount to a kind of wisdom. Good sense about trivialities, Max once said, is better than nonsense about things that matter. He also said that only the insane take themselves quite seriously. Moreover, these essays, however light, are not frivolous, either in subject or treatment. But my point in this brief chapter is the development of style. In the passages quoted you see immediately the contrast with the earlier writing: a quieter tone, a less brassy irony, a little less youthful cleverness; and no obsolete, rare, or even big words, no foreign-language phrases, no tricky syntax – just simple, straightforward prose. Max thought his *Saturday* reviewing had much to do with the change. I myself still think he simply outgrew his earlier, much-influenced-by-Oscar-Wilde manner.

CHAPTER ELEVEN

Hosts and Guests

From the mid-1890s to 1910 – the Edwardian era – Max had what might be called a third career. He was a writer, a caricaturist, but also, in his own words, a personality. As such he enjoyed a large and varied social life. He was a presentable young man, a bachelor, he had a name, he was a respected critic, essayist, and caricaturist, he was amusing and amusable; he was a good talker and a good listener; his clothes were so special as to make a subject for conversation. His manners were perfect. All this made him immensely popular as a guest. He had his small circle of close friends, but he had scores and scores of other friends and hundreds and hundreds of acquaintances. They ranged from spicy theatre and newspaper people to the leaders of Edwardian high society. Lord David Cecil, himself a product of the aristocratic world, says that Max gradually got invitations of a "more glorious kind" (if there is any portion of this book where I must depend on my predecessor, it is here):

> We read of him [Cecil writes] lunching and dining with the musical Lady Maud Warrender, the gorgeous Lady Féo Sturt, with Mrs George Keppel, racy friend [mistress, actually] of King Edward VII himself, and with Lady Elcho and Mrs Grenfell, afterwards Lady Desborough. These last two were conspicuous and fascinating representatives of the set called "The Souls" which, more than any other, was considered to combine the attractions of elegance, charm and intellect. Among its male members were Arthur Balfour, George Wyndham, Lord Curzon and Maurice Baring. Lady Desborough was also the most celebrated hostess of the age. ... His frequenting London society ... was an inspiration to his talent. His imagination had always been stimulated by the spectacle of the great world. ... Now in these great houses he was able to meet and talk to men as eminent as Gladstone had been in his boyhood: Rosebery and Balfour, Curzon and Haldane, Wyndham and Randolph Churchill's sensational son, Winston. Others besides statesmen engaged Max's attention: financial magnates like Mr Benjamin Cohen, men about town like Lord Grimthorpe, *bon viveurs*

like Harry Chaplin, sportsmen like Lord de Gray. And there was an exotic little group of distinguished foreign diplomats that appealed strongly to his sense of the picturesque: the Austrian Count Mensdorff, the Russian Count Benckendorff, the Portuguese Marquis de Soveral [closest confidant of King Edward]. All these habitués of the Edwardian social scene came as fresh grist to Max's mill.

He was a frequent weekend guest at country houses, and in his semi-autobiographical tale "Hilary Maltby and Stephen Braxton" (in *Seven Men*, 1919) he makes fun of his insecurities among the wealthy and famous. Again, David Cecil is a sure guide: the story's Keeb Hall is Taplow; the Duchess of Hertfordshire is Lady Desborough; Lady Thisbe Crowborough is (probably) Lady Helen Vincent; and Lady Rodfitten is the Marchioness of Londonderry. Balfour appears as himself. Maltby's crude rival Braxton may be modelled on Yeats. Hilary Maltby is partly Max himself, who joked that he had towards these great people a (Thackerayan) "mere disinterested flunkeyism" and that they really did not further his career. But insomuch as he was able to go home and caricature them, these society folk did help considerably.

Max's friend Reggie Turner has supplied us with a portrait of Max at the height of his London period, the much-in-demand social butterfly who knew everybody. Tucked away in one of Turner's many unsuccessful novels (*Davray's Affairs*, 1906) is a description of one "Hans Branders." Reggie forewarned Max of what he had done, and Max wrote back that he had already "instructed" his solicitor. Turner's description of Hans/Max was, for all its hero-worship, not uncritical:

Hans Branders was by no means averse from playing a part in the comedy of life himself, but he was quite as pleased to watch the comedy going on, and his eyes were keener than most people's. His eyes, which were the best part of his face, were given to troubling men and women alike. When he looked at women it was difficult to say whether they were being used for love-making, or for prying into the heart of the person on whom they gazed; and when they fell on men, especially men who had a good opinion of themselves, they seemed to be lighting, in kindly fashion, on a weak point. . . . The eyes, big blue eyes surrounded by long lashes, seemed glimmering with amusement. Everyone who knew Hans Branders – and everyone either knew him or wanted to know him – called him Hans. He signed his articles "Hans," he signed his caricatures "Hans," and his friends and acquaintances called him "Hans." The name possessed a portmanteau of meaning. On different occasions it expressed intimacy, dignity, affection, or social recognition. His great success in life was due far more to his personality than to his achievements. He did not, as a matter of fact, do very much compared to other producers, but everything that he did was first-class, everything was distinguished; very seldom, though it had happened, was Hans to be caught tripping in judgment or in execution. And when that did happen, his sturdy refusal to recognise his weakness caused others to forget it, or to think they must have been mistaken. People said he was one of the most interesting and engaging figures in London life, and, like so many other distinguished Englishmen, he was English neither by blood nor temperament. His popularity was amazing. He was not a sportsman, nor a Bohemian; as a very young man superficial people had pronounced him effeminate, but sportsmen, artists, fools and wise men, and women of all ages and conditions, had a real affection for him. He never made any apparent effort to push his work, or to make a friend. ... In dress he inclined to an eccentricity of old-fashioned fashion, and street urchins sometimes looked on him with a wonder that might easily have developed into a grin or an exclamation: but people did not easily take a liberty with Hans. The secret of his popularity – for it did not spring from those obvi-ous causes which give the victory to the good-looking, good-humoured fellow – was himself; that personality which influenced people who met him. He had not the curly locks and fresh complexion which win so many hearts; he was not a man who would good-naturedly stand any amount of chaff; he was not given to making himself useful, or putting himself out for other people; and for all his amiability, he was sometimes imperturbable to the verge of irritation. There was a strain of cruelty in him, not harshness nor brutality, but cruelty simple and isolated. But there was no malice in him, no pettiness, and he had the kindest of hearts. Two qualities, bad and unpleasant in mediocre men, vanity and selfishness, were in him as in all great personalities, however they may be disguised, or unseen by the crowd; and he did not attempt, as fortunately do most smaller and weaker men, to conceal them. Finally, he had that quality in common with nearly all great men – he had a great appreciation of all people and all things, big and little. There was nothing and no one he could not draw satisfaction from. Where meaner people condemned, he smiled or was silent; where narrower people were blind, he saw the light. Such was Hans.

So Max, according to his closest friend, had a side to him that was vain and selfish and, nice phrase, "imperturbable to the verge of irritation." And also a strain of cruelty, not harshness or brutality, but "cruelty simple and isolated" that may go a long way in explaining Max the satirist, parodist and, especially, caricaturist.

Max himself offers a partial self-portrait in a late essay that develops the distinction between Hosts and Guests:

> I would go even so far as to say that the difference is more than merely circumstantial and particular. I seem to discern also a temperamental and general difference. You ask me to dine with you in a restaurant, I say I shall be delighted, you order the meal, I praise it, you pay for it, I have the pleasant sensation of not paying for it; and it is well that each of us should have a label according to the part he plays in this transaction. But the two labels are applicable in a larger and more philosophic way. In every human being one or the other of these two instincts is predominant: the active or positive instinct to offer hospitality, the negative or passive instinct to accept it. And either of these instincts is so significant of character that one might well say that mankind is divisible into two great classes: hosts and guests.
>
> I have already (see third sentence of foregoing paragraph) somewhat prepared you for the shock of a confession which candour now forces from me. I am one of the guests. You are, however, so shocked that you will read no more of me? Bravo! Your refusal indicates that you have not a guestish soul. . . . I believe guests to be as numerous, really, as hosts. It may be that even you, if you examine yourself dispassionately, will find that you are one of them.

It's a longish essay, ranging broadly over hospitable habits and guest habits of people from the cave days to the present. Our interest is biographic so I quote Max on his own state of "guestship":

> Boys . . . are all of them potential guests. It is only as they grow up that some of them harden into hosts. It is likely enough that if I, when I grew up, had been rich, my natural bent for guestship would have been diverted, and I too have become a (sort of) host. And perhaps I should have passed muster. I suppose I did pass muster whenever, in the course of my long residence in London, I did entertain friends. But the memory of those occasions is not dear to me – especially not the memory of those that were in

the more distinguished restaurants. Somewhere in the back of my brain, while I tried to lead the conversation brightly, was always the haunting fear that I had not brought enough money in my pocket. I never let this fear master me. I never said to any one "Will you have a liqueur?" – always "What liqueur will you have?" But I postponed as far as possible the evil moment of asking for the bill. When I had, in the proper casual tone (I hope and believe), at length asked for it, I wished always it were not brought to me *folded* on a plate, as though the amount were so hideously high that I alone must be privy to it. So soon as it was laid beside me, I wanted to know the worst at once. But I pretended to be so occupied in talk that I was unaware of the bill's presence; and I was careful to be always in the middle of a sentence when I raised the upper fold and took my not (I hope) frozen glance. In point of fact the amount was always much less than I had feared. Pessimism does win us great happy moments.

At inexpensive Soho restaurants (such as the Vingtième where Max had his memorable lunch with Enoch Soames), " 'It's cheap' was the only paean that in Soho's bad moments ever occurred to me, and this of course I did not utter. And *was* it so cheap, after all? Soho induces a certain optimism. A bill there was always larger than I had thought it would be." At his club, the Savile (to which he was elected in 1899), he had the "luxury" of signing for the bill and not worrying about having enough money on him:

> Offering hospitality in my club, I was inwardly calm. But even there I did not glow (though my face and manner, I hoped, glowed). If my guest was by nature a guest, I managed to forget somewhat that I myself was a guest by nature. But if, as now and then happened, my guest was a true and habitual host, I did feel that we were in an absurdly false relation.

Even when technically a host, Max remained, fundamentally, a guest. The closest he came to hostship was on the frequent Sunday afternoons when his mother – herself a true host – would provide lunch for Max and his friends, first at 19 Hyde Park Place and then at 48 Upper Berkeley Street. The latter place, one guest wrote, "... was a shabby, friendly little house with a life-worn air. Every bit of furniture looked as if it had grown up with the family, it had such a Georgian atmosphere." Regulars included Will Rothenstein, Reggie Turner, Robbie Ross, Charles Conder, Somerset Maugham, William Nicholson. The meal was always exactly the same: roast beef, Yorkshire pudding, and apple dumpling with cream. Max would carve the roast. But for the most part he ate out, practically every night of his life. It wore him down. Asked in later life why he left London, he replied, "How many people were there in London? Eight million? Nine Million? Well – I knew them *all*."

CHAPTER TWELVE

Max in Love

We have brought Max's career up to 1910. Now it remains to go back and pick up his emotional life, his love life, of the previous seventeen years. The delay until now may seem the wrong emphasis in a biography, but not, I think, in this one. It could be that I have put off for as long as possible the distasteful task of intruding upon and speculating about his private life. Yes, he has been dead for nearly half a century. But, at bottom, what has that to do with it? Fifty years ought not to take away the obligation to honour someone's much-desired privacy. On the other hand, there is no hope for it. So many of Max's letters have been published, and so much written about his emotional life, that I must follow suit. But I should like to go on record as saying that I do not share the modern biographer's felt need to learn all he can of his subject's sex life. Myself, I don't believe it is important in most cases. In Max's case I don't think it matters at all.

During these years Max was "involved" in varying degrees with five women: Cissie Loftus, Mrs Ada Leverson, Grace Conover, Constance Collier, and Florence Kahn.

Cissie (or Cissey) Loftus. The daughter of an actress, she made her début, aged fifteen, in July 1893, at the Oxford Music Hall. Dubbed "the mimetic wonder," Cissie Loftus captured a large following by imitating the songs of popular singers. Max wrote that the whole town went mad about her; she was, he said, the real thing, much to be contrasted with "clever malaperts" like Marie Lloyd who only burlesqued innocence and girlishness with "experienced pouts and smiles under the sun-bonnet." Himself a music-hall devotee, Max was utterly beguiled by Cissie. Some think it was all a joke carried on in letters to Reggie Turner: Max was describing a counterfeit obsession to entertain and perhaps to prompt some little jealousy in the male friend he most liked. I don't see this as an adequate explanation. The infatuation is *partly* a joke, and in his very first mentionings of her to Reggie he is plainly clowning:

Oh God – how I wish myself wholly free and able to lay vast riches at her feet and marry and live with her unhappily ever after. . . . Shall I go to the Tivoli again tonight, I wonder? I can hardly bear to think of her being anywhere at all without my seeing her.

He tells Turner that he goes to sleep clutching a newspaper photo of Cissie. A few days later he writes:

Picture her moving always between the walls of some nunnery – wearing at first the veil of the Novitiate and dying long after either of us . . . Sister Cecilia. It would be lovelier almost than if we married – unless she were to die in childbirth. I cannot imagine anything lovelier than that. Think of one year's happiness – always at its height: then a sudden great grief that will sanctify the rest of one's life, though it grows less day by day: a grief growing fainter, instead of a joy, as would happen if she had not died. Happy the man whose young wife dies in childbirth! His pain is not degraded by the knowledge of how good the gods have been to him.

Max has his eye on a revolver in the window of a gun shop in Bond Street: "Not that I suppose I shall ever use it, but, as I am always saying, the feeling that you may at any moment solve the whole problem (simple division by death) is certainly a consolation." He thinks more of Cissie than anything else; he finds it "very very charming to feel really in love." He wants Reggie, his "first confidant," to admire her. Soon, he claims that his love for Cissie is troubling his conscience: he has spent his time in idleness, a fairly happy life he had supposed, until Cissie Loftus. Now, because of her, it appears a "distorted" career: "I am no longer contented – and she is only the end of the old life to me I am afraid, not the beginning of a new one. I haven't the vitality for that." Of course this is fooling.

But it need hardly be remarked how frivolity can have its serious underpinnings, especially when it is long lived (and the bit about low vitality sounds unfeigned). Max faithfully attends her performances, he manages to get an interview with her, he draws her picture for *The Sketch*, he actually goes down and hangs about the neighbourhood where she lives with her mother at Herne Hill. Turner is bombarded, sometimes daily, with letters about Cissie. For Max she is the Lady Cecilia, the Infanta, the Small Saint, Mistress Mere, White Girl, the Shy Child, the Blessed Damozel. At one point he doesn't know which is more beautiful – his Lady Love or the specially bound copy of Wilde's *Intentions* that Reggie has sent him. A month or so into the involvement, Max also writes to his new friend, Will Rothenstein:

> I am in love. . . . I must see you rave about her; you would hardly know me now. . . . Oh my dear Will I am so happy and good. . . . I should love to marry her. I am so good and changed.

But Reggie Turner remains the principal recipient of Max's lovelorn confidings. And two months later it is ". . . all over. I hate Cissie Loftus now." The infatuation soon revives, temporarily, but a year later she only is a tender memory: "I live very much in the past already." In 1896 she provided the original for Jenny Mere, the heroine in *The Happy Hypocrite*, Max's best-known fairy tale.

Mrs Ada Leverson. Cissie Loftus was so remote as to be almost a dream, a source of fantasy, a good model for the saintly heroine of a fairy tale. Max's next infatuation was with someone very different: whereas Cissie Loftus was a girl, Ada Leverson was very much a woman. She was married (to the son of a wealthy diamond merchant) and a mother; she was ten years Max's senior; she was a wit, a journalist (for *Punch* and other magazines), parodist, and aspiring novelist (she would publish six London society novels between 1908 and 1916). Many prominent writers and artists frequented her London salon. Grant Richards called Ada "the Egeria of the whole 'nineties movement, the woman who provoked wit in others, whose intelligence helped so much to leaven the dullness of her period." Wilde, who gave her the label Sphinx, called her "the wittiest woman in the world."

Max, who was drawn into Ada's circle in the summer of 1894, seems to have had with her an affair of the heart that was in part a joke, in part strongly felt on both sides. Her marriage was not particularly happy; neither she nor her husband Ernest was monogamous (the marriage would fail altogether in 1902). Her affections went out to men who, one way or another, presented no real danger of demanding a lasting commitment. With George Moore, for example, she could have a passing, discreet, though truly sexual affair; with Wilde, or Robert Ross – who quipped that "she almost persuadeth me to be a mulierast" – Ada could have open and deep fondness without anybody raising an eyebrow. With Max, the lines were less clear cut, and we don't know the precise nature of their involvement. But we do know that his many letters to her of 1894–95, all addressed to "My dearest Mrs Leverson" and all undated, invariably contain romantic sentiments such as "I feel a terrible *longing* to see you – It is awful to be so dependent on any body" or "I should love to come to lunch on Saturday. ... There is nobody half so charming to talk to as you – I hope you do not get sick of seeing me."

From Rouen, where he was holidaying with Reggie Turner, Max writes:

> Thanks *most* immensely for your letter, it is most dear and delightful of you not to have forgotten that I exist. You may imagine that I think of little here but of you and of your London. To-night you are going to the Haymarket and will see poor Herbert in that dreadful play. I would give Heaven and Earth to be going with you. I wonder what you will wear? Your gray and rose-colour? ... It is awfully sweet of you to miss me – I can't tell you what a horrible difference it makes to the whole of my life – to be away from you.

Again from Rouen: "I *am* so longing to see you – you can't *think* how much. ... I long to see [her recent article in *Punch*] and everything that has anything to do with you – You are all that is delightful to me." A few days later, he writes that her letters and telegrams to Rouen "have made my stay here just tolerable."

From Broadstairs, where he and his family were taking a holiday, and from where Ada herself had just returned to London, he writes: "You will have a lot of people probably on Saturday? And I do so want to see you all alone. ... I was never so happy in any place as here when you were also here."

From Oxford, where he and Reggie were staying at the Clarendon Hotel (for Bosie's sake, though Max would have preferred "the dear little Mitre – the cynosure of the town"), he tells her, "Tomorrow I think I shall return – as I miss you fearfully despite Oxford and its excitements. I hope you are missing me."

In January 1895, just before sailing with Herbert to America, where he was supposed to help with Herbert's correspondence during a six-week tour, Max tells her: "So many thanks for your sweet letter. ... I shall always be thinking of you and how delightful you are, the whole time in America." Having arrived in New York, he writes, "Do you still miss me? I miss you and think of you more than ever." Again, answering a letter from her:

> But what absurd and affected nonsense you talk about my being likely to forget you. You know you are the most charming & irresistibly delightful person on the face of the earth and will always seem so to me.

Max keeps Mrs Leverson up to date on his meetings with women:

> I have not fallen in love with anybody. Last night, in one of the entr'acts I renewed the acquaintance of Cissie Loftus, the bride of Justin McCarthy – but no faint echo of my love returned to me. She looked very pretty, nevertheless. Nor am I in love with Una Cockerell [an actress in Herbert's Company]. She is very nice.

And from Chicago:

> I have seen Miss Cockerell, a good deal. She is very stupid and sweet – I fear I shall never be in love with her, but I like her very much – also a Miss Conover, an Irish girl, also the Sisters Hanbury [Lily and Hilda, also actresses in Herbert's Company]. So there is no lack of female society.

These early letters are signed "Max and Baby" or "Baby Beerbohm," evidently a nickname she had given him. One could read the love passages as jokes, but somehow they seem more than that. It is clear, although her side of the correspondence has not survived, that Ada wrote to him in kind. Her biographer thinks she may have tried to seduce him. I think it unlikely. But we do not know. Still, that their relationship had real "romance" for Max is undeniable.

After Max returned to London, newly attached to the aforesaid Miss Conover, he and Ada remained steadfast though clearly less ardent friends. Dozens of later letters to her (undated but many addressed from 48 Upper Berkeley Street, where the Beerbohm family moved in 1898) and signed "Affectionately yours Max" – no longer "Baby" – show him exchanging gossip,* family news (Ada became close to all the Beerbohms), accepting or, because of his hectic social schedule, regretfully postponing invitations to lunch or dinner. He encourages her writing and thanks her for the privilege of reading a "most brilliant and delightful" novel of hers in manuscript. In 1916 he tells her how pleased he is that she likes "Enoch Soames" so much, "... but I don't at all agree with your estimate of me as a writer: I merely

---

* At a later date, impossible to tie down today, he writes: "I happened to meet at dinner tonight Bosie Douglas – hadn't seen him for years – was amazed to find that he hadn't changed one little bit. I gazed at him across the gulf that separates the 19th from the 20th century, and plucked wonderingly at my long grey beard while he passed a petulant hand through his rebellious golden curls: not curls really: the hair is straight enough; but it *looks* curly across the gulf."

admit that I do write very carefully and well." It is evident that Ada Leverson continued always as one of his special friends. I suspect that references to their early attachment were among the "certain youthful extravagances" that Max had excised from his letters to Reggie Turner.

Grace "Kilseen" Conover. The "Miss Conover" mentioned in passing in Max's letter to Mrs Leverson was, like Mrs Leverson, much more real and substantial than the fantasized Cissie Loftus; but her being young and unmarried made her a more suitable object of his affection. Max's involvement with Grace Conover was both real and somehow unreal. She was an actress in his brother's touring company. Reggie, as usual, is the recipient of the news:

> I am (not a word to dear Mrs Leverson) in love with a certain Miss Conover ... a dark Irish girl of twenty, very blunt and rude, who hates affectation and rather likes me. We only know each other during this tour and have seen a good deal of each other. On the car from N. York to Chicago we sat together all the time. I made her cry on the first afternoon by telling her circumstantially that she was known at the Garrick as "Kill-Scene Conover" – and immediately fell in love with her. There were two sleeping cars, one entirely for the actors and the other for actors and actresses, who slept in berths partitioned off by effectual curtains that were perpetually being withdrawn to let people pass. Miss Conover looked extremely pretty in her night-gown and gave me an apple from her hamper. ... Here in Chicago I see Miss Conover perpetually and have asked her to be my wife, but as we have always been on terms of chaff, she is only just beginning to realise that I am in earnest – which perhaps I am not – who knows? I took her to a theatre last night and in the cab home we held hands all the way. I have her photograph in my little green case now. I really am very much in love with her and she will be very much in love with me, I think, soon. Do be sympathetic.

A year later, considering himself uneasily engaged to Kilseen, he writes daily to her while she is away. Max's family did not particularly like the idea of her as a mate for their darling Max. For long stretches she took lunch and dinner at Upper Berkeley Street, and Mrs Beerbohm grew somewhat tired of her. Max's sister Constance, who managed the family finances, felt that Kilseen's continual presence put a strain on their meagre budget and showed "extremely bad taste." But nothing, Constance lamented, could be done,

"Mamma worships Max so. She has never once been able to tell him she doesn't want Miss C. to dine." The Beerbohm women thought Kilseen "common." Sister-in-law Maud Tree was more outspoken and said something in Max's presence that roused him to unaccustomed anger (we cannot discover what it was, though I believe, given Maud's snobbishness, that it had to do with Kilseen's low social status). He wrote to Maud saying that "your extraordinary lapse of good-feeling, good-taste and so forth this evening makes it impossible for me to have any further friendship with you." The rift did not last, but it shows Max in earnest about Kilseen and what he considered a point of honour. Whatever the family's misgivings about Kilseen as a wife for Max, they were pleased that his having a girlfriend, a fiancée, "diverted" him from "an unfortunate set – dangerous friends," i.e. the Wilde set. Indeed, Constance wrote that Kilseen herself had actually "had the courage to tell him that the *rumour* of his being friendly with them and intimate with them was misunderstood by outsiders, and harming him." Still, Constance cannot repress her dislike for Kilseen: "I won't say any more about her – I don't want her! And I should be grieved for Max to marry her."

During the following years Max and Kilseen were both plainly unhappy about their situation. One observer claimed to have watched them from the other side of a restaurant during one of their weekly meals together: Max spoke animatedly when going over the menu and ordering but then lapsed into silence, and Kilseen never spoke at all. Another observer is said to have overheard Kilseen asking "When shall we be married?" to which Max replied, "Whenever you like, my dear, whenever you like. But *you* must make all the arrangements." Reggie Turner took it upon himself to be kind to Max's fiancée; he asks after her in his letters and he sends her presents. Robbie Ross and Will Rothenstein, though staunch friends of Max, sympathized with Kilseen. In 1899 Ross reported to Will, "Max looks more unmarried than ever and poor Kilseen does not look particularly engaged. I feel so deeply for her." In 1901 Ross invited Kilseen to lunch, where he spoke kindly to her on "a difficult subject." She wrote thanking him for his efforts, but said that even discussing it made her feel "mean" towards Max: "But all the argument on earth cannot undo the last six years. All I ask of Max's friends is not to judge him too unkindly, and they can go on thinking me 'a fool' ... I am paying for going by my heart's instincts"; she doesn't want to be considered a "martyr"; she hopes things will be settled one way or the other, "But if I can care for Max and believe in him, don't make me unhappier by being unkind about him." Things were not settled: she cared too much for him to break it off, and he had not the will to do so himself. The dubious engagement lingered on for eight years. In a manner bewildering even to himself he had got engaged, and he considered himself honour bound to her. But he was not seriously in love with her and would not push forward to marriage itself. His treatment of Kilseen was something he was to regret and feel guilty about for a long time; it was the only truly unworthy thing he ever did. And if it didn't sound so ridiculous, I would say he couldn't help himself.

Constance Collier. She was the daughter of touring players and at twenty-four still a "chorus girl" (her words) at the Gaiety Theatre. Then, in 1902, Herbert chose her to star in his production of *Ulysses*, a verse drama by Stephen Phillips. Suddenly the tall, statuesque, "dark" (half Portuguese) Constance Collier became Herbert's leading lady; she was even rumoured to be having an affair with him. One authority describes her as "very handsome in the stately, showy style admired by the Edwardians, with flashing dark eyes, magnificent shoulders, and a classical profile ... a fully fledged public personality, complete with a histrionic manner, a rich-toned languid mode of speaking and any amount of warm flamboyant temperament." She sounds exactly what Max would not be looking for. Constance and Max had met through Herbert, and in 1903 Max arranged for her to come to Dieppe where he was taking his annual holiday. During these August days in his favourite vacation spot, surrounded by his great friends Reggie Turner, Walter Sickert, and William Nicholson, Max fell in love with Constance. It was a holiday romance; and into their very separate old age they kept fond memories of Dieppe, the meals they had taken at Maison Lefèvre, the hotel Max and his friends frequented, the drinks at a café facing the sea, and lunch at a nearby inland restaurant where Max, Sickert, and Nicholson scribbled sketches on the tablecloth; how they placed small bets at the casino; how they had gone to a French comedy, of which Constance understood not a word (while the audience laughed, Max "translated" what was happening on stage into a heartbreaking tragedy, bringing her to tears, for which she forgave him). They cherished also a photograph, a snapshot taken of Max and Constance sitting at a café on the terrace: she wearing a "beribboned, flowered, floppy straw hat and a light summer dress. A parasol is slung over her shoulder. Max is wearing a white flannel suit, with a flower in the buttonhole;

his straw hat is in front of him on the table, and his hand is resting on the head of his walking stick." They were so enthralled with each other that they leapt to thoughts of marriage; they even visited the little English church at Dieppe where the wedding was to take place. The whole thing seems highly implausible, given what we know of the two of them, but there you have it.

Max had first to return to London and break with Kilseen. She seems to have taken the news with some relief. "We didn't suit each other at all," Max recalled many years later. "I felt relieved when we broke off the engagement after I had fallen in love with Constance Collier."*

To Reggie Max wrote in December 1903:

Please don't breathe to Bobbie [Ross] or anyone about my engagement to Constance. ... The position of fiancée to Max Beerbohm is rather a ridiculous position, after poor Miss Conover's experience, and I don't want Constance to be placed in it publicly. So we mean to be married quite suddenly (as far as the public is concerned). If anyone asks about Miss Conover and me, then you can say that we have agreed to dissolve our engagement, and if anyone asks whether Miss Collier has anything to do with it, of course say "no." But don't *volunteer* the information.

With Constance the engagement was short-lived. We can readily believe that Max's family disapproved of this betrothal almost as much as they had of the one with Kilseen. Constance lacked, they felt, "refinement." But their opposition would have mattered little to Max. It was Constance herself who broke off the match. After four months Max was writing again to Reggie, this time with "a rather sad and beastly piece of news":

Constance and I are not going to be married after all. ... last Saturday I had a letter from her saying she had been so wretched and had not known how to tell me that she felt it would never do, after all, for us to marry – neither of us being the sort of people for the serious responsibilities of life. It was a very sweet letter indeed, and *of course* I don't blame her the very least. Indeed, long ago I had always been telling her that it would be

---

* Kilseen left the stage, and when Max met her a few years later, he wrote to yet his third fiancée, "Tonight I have been dining with Miss Conover ... and was so pleased to find her seeming happy and well – so much happier and better than in the old days – and also prospering now in her dress-making business – and thus lightening my conscience; for I did not treat her well – though I remember you had a theory that I was not really to be blamed."

madness from the commonsense point of view for her to marry me. I thought I was right then; I think she is right now. But of course it is sad – being without her, breaking off so many ties of love.

A few days later he tells Reggie that he does not think he will go to Dieppe this year, much as he loves the place: "For it meant to me Constance, more than anything else. And I don't think I could stay in it this summer. I couldn't quite bear that little place on the terrace where they make the electric light, and where we used to sit together at night, and the English church where she wanted to marry me 'next Tuesday,' and the dining-room at Lefèvre's. . . . All this sounds very 'literary' and sentimentalistic, but it is real enough to me."

Constance had fallen in love with another man. Fifty years later her friend Samuel Behrman, himself a man of the theatre, asked her teasingly how she could have broken off an engagement with so exquisite a man as Max: "Well, you know, Herbert sent me on tour. The leading man was very tall and handsome. We got to Manchester, and – well, you know how it is on tour." Constance went on to a celebrated career on the stage and in the movies. She made nearly forty film appearances, beginning with D. W. Griffith's *Intolerance* in 1916 and including *Stage Door*, 1937, and *The Perils of Pauline*, 1947. She was also acting coach for such luminaries as John Barrymore, Colleen Moore, and Audrey Hepburn. This probably explains Hepburn's interest in playing Zuleika Dobson because Constance, till her dying day, believed, quite impossibly, that she had been the original for Zuleika. Max's novel had been begun long before he met her.

CHAPTER THIRTEEN

The Mystery

I am nervous about what comes next. Florence Kahn – Max's courting of, marriage to, and life with – is the strangest part of his story. So here we go again, in a not unwitting exercise of *praeteritia,* saying the very thing you claim you are not going to say. Of course I could put down the simple facts and let it go at that: when they met, when they married, and how many years they lived as husband and wife. There would be comfort in this, in keeping my resolve to stay, for the most part, out of Max's private life, to address his public career, his writings and drawings. But it can't be, the fat is in the fire. Max's love life, as I have said, has been so thoroughly documented and so much speculated upon as to make silence on the subject impossible. Moreover, I find myself especially uneasy because W. H. Auden took even the unadventurous and non-speculating biographer David Cecil to task for publishing too much about Max and Florence; specifically Auden thought Cecil printed too much of Max's correspondence with her, even though it contained nothing sensational. Why do I allow Auden's remonstrance, made in a review forty years ago, to trouble me? My tendency to put great store in eminent persons' opinions when these agree with or collide with my own is perhaps a defect in my nature. I cannot help it. When Virginia Woolf says Max is the prince of essayists, that she cannot imagine what it would be like to write as he does, I am impressed. (I am equally impressed when she says we believe in Trollope's characters the way we believe in our weekly bills.) When Edmund Wilson says Max is "the greatest caricaturist of the kind – that is, portrayer of personalities – in the history of art," I pay attention. I pay attention even when Bernard Berenson calls Max "the English Goya." Accordingly I must ask myself what Auden (to say nothing of Max himself) would have thought of the rest of this chapter because I have to explore a lot further than did Cecil. In 1988 Rupert Hart-Davis, editor of a selection of Max's letters, put forth a theory about Max's sexuality that must either be argued down or agreed with. Whereas Cecil thinks Max a mild, "gentle amorist," a man of low vitality but in other respects heterosexual, and whereas others think him a secret, or even unknowing, homosexual, Hart-Davis thinks him asexual.

Enter Florence Kahn, the great oddity in Max's life, the jarring note, the unexplainable dimension. She's important, arguably the most important person in his life, if someone coming into the life of a thirty-two-year-old can, so tardily, warrant that distinction. There survive more than a thousand of Max's letters to her, most of them from the six years preceding their marriage, a time when they were frequently apart. During these separations he wrote to her at least twice a week, sometimes daily. The amazing thing is that often enough these letters are sentimental, even saccharine. In spite of an occasional infusion of teasing or playfulness, they are utterly unlike anything we would expect from Max. And the love passages are not at all ironic; they are straightforward, earnest, romantic. I am afraid his admirers, Auden among them, are unhappy with their publication not merely because this seems a violation of his privacy, but because they deem the letters themselves unworthy of Max.

Somehow we are uneasy with bare emotion of this kind coming from him. We expect distance, detachment, coolness, wit. He was a writer who ordinarily could not dash off a note declining a dinner invitation without some display of humour or charm, and here he is writing conventional (if sometimes beautiful) love letters. It's embarrassing, especially embarrassing (and this is probably crucial) because the object of all this devotion seems, to most of us outsiders in posterity, undeserving of all this attention. More importantly, his friends and contemporaries felt the same way. They, in a word, did not like her; and they thought her especially ill-matched with Max. They found her nervous, shy, timid, retiring, humourless, moralizing, idealizing, prudish, frequently sad and depressed, and anti-social. He was playful, she was serious; he loved joking, she disapproved of jokes; he enjoyed being with people, she was reclusive; he, except for his old-world gentlemanly code was above moralistic judgements; she would leave the room in tears at the mention of the word "adultery." And yet Max clearly saw her as his perfect mate. What are we to make of this match? The record is as extensive as it is baffling. Of course arguments can be made to show that she suited him nicely: that she was intelligent; that she would help him get away from hobnobbing with the famous and talented, he having grown tired of playing the charming bachelor guest; that she loved Italy and the sea almost as much as he did and was willing to forsake all and live with him on slender means on the Italian Riviera; that she was a good housekeeper and an excellent cook (only shallow people will make little of this last). To these arguments must be added the strongest consideration of all: Max, who was loved, adored, and waited upon by his mother and sisters all his life, needed a woman always to look after him. I cannot imagine Max Beerbohm ever making a cup of tea for himself. And here was a woman who, as it turned out, could take excellent care of him, look after him painstakingly and gracefully. He in turn would give her absolute and unswerving devotion. Marshalling these considerations, you can come up with a sound though unromantic basis for their long and apparently very successful marriage. But the record shows an enormously strong and long-lasting romantic foundation as well. To say that she "appealed to the strain in Max that had imagined Jenny Mere," the innocent and unworldly heroine of *The Happy Hypocrite*, is true, but hardly enough to explain their relationship.

Who was she? Florence Kahn was the daughter of a Jewish family in the city of Memphis, Tennessee. Her father, Louis Kahn, owned the largest dry goods business in their part of the world and was an amateur Shakespeare scholar. Louis and Pauline Kahn had eight children, seven boys and Florence, their fourth child, born in 1876. (That made her four years younger than Max.) The Kahn children were all intelligent, and all musically gifted. Florence played the piano. Two brothers became professional musicians, one became a civil engineer; another was in real estate, another a surgeon, another an editor and writer. "The Kahns had ninety percent of the brains in Tennessee," a friend wrote, "and Florence was all brains." Her affluent family sent her to private school, to dancing lessons, to finishing school, and, supporting her desire for the stage, allowed her to attend drama school in New York. She made her way, gradually but not spectacularly, on the American stage, touring much of the country. For a brief while in 1900 she was leading lady to Richard Mansfield, America's foremost actor. But her early promise was not followed by success, and more frequently than not she was looking for engagements. In March 1904 she appeared in New York as Rebecca West in Ibsen's *Rosmersholm* with calamitous results. The play closed quickly, and the *New York Times* singled her out for most of the blame: "She 'acted' always; not for a moment was she a live woman, least of all an Ibsen heroine. She waved across the stage and coiled upon the furniture, and when the crisis of passion ran highest she looked foolish and bleated." In June of the same year she travelled to London, hoping for work there, bringing with her a letter of introduction to Max.

He called on her at her hotel and was immediately taken with, indeed smitten by, this auburn-haired, slim, frail, Pre-Raphaelite figure of a woman. She was rather old-fashioned in her ways, trustful, innocent, idealistic. He took her to dinner, to the theatre, for walks on Hampstead Heath, to tea at Jack Straw's Castle, and to meet his mother and family at Upper Berkeley Street (pronounced "Barkley," he warned her). And, of course, he wrote to her. So let's have a look at a selection of the letters, the publication of which so much annoyed W. H. Auden.

Max has scarcely met her when he writes how he longs to see her "... you yourself, with no footlights between us – you yourself with all your dear little graces and virtues, and moods of happiness and sadness – so utterly unlike all the other people I have known – not necessarily finer, but more differently fine than they from the rest of humanity." He even tries to kiss her, after which attempt he writes, "I don't think I have done anything that I need repent of to *you*. Except perhaps that I *ought* to have deceived you into supposing that I had no desire to kiss you. My fault has been my excess of honesty ..." A second attempt at affection brought her to tears and another defence from him:

> I wonder if you are disliking me very much – me who broke my promise so disgracefully – me who actually made you cry? but me who was really and truly sorry and quite full of blame for myself? It was quite too absurd of you to pretend to blame *yourself* in the least little way. *You* behave so very well and haughtily. It is quite a lesson in deportment to be with you. ... In any case, will you come here and dine on Wednesday evening? My mother is so anxious to see you again. ... I do so hate the recollection of seeing you crying all to yourself on that sofa this afternoon. There was no reason why you should cry, though, *was* there? It isn't *your* fault that I am a rude person and mal élevé. And in spite of my faults I am really very nice, and it is just as well that you met me. You cannot imagine how glad I am that *I* met *you*.

When she goes with friends to Berlin, he tells her, "Mind you have a happy time in Berlin – and don't live up to *too* many dear little self-made standards of what must and what must *not* be done. There is no need for you to make rules for yourself – still less to keep them. For you couldn't do anything that wasn't sweet and dear, however hard you tried." Once, when she confided in him how a particular lamp inspired deep thoughts in her, he replies:

I suppose you will think I am laughing at you for telling me about the lamp. That is because you don't understand me. I love what you told me about the lamp, and the way you told it; and that is the reason why I am also amused. . . . *One teases only what one loves.* One travesties only what is worth travestying. So there! Dear little thing, I can see you standing with your hands folded behind your back, and with *such* a serious face, speculating on the inner workings of the lamp, and making your poetry around it. And I can't see any one else behaving in that way. And that is the reason why I like you better than anyone.

He teases her about America ("that country of which I always so cordially acknowledge the size") and her aversion to blood sports and her loyal republicanism (he promises not to mention "dead pheasants or monarchy or any other such subject"). He shocks her by saying he couldn't really appreciate Shakespeare. He tells her she is an

omniscient creature; and I despair of taking you by surprise. It is quite a new sensation for me – writing to someone who is my superior in literary knowledge – and rather frightening and oppressive. I think I always have been a little frightened by you, dear, and always shall be – for you are so much cleverer than I, and than the rest, *and* so much better.

He manages to take his annual Dieppe holiday after all, his recovery from Constance Collier quite complete; he even writes to tell Florence that he had been there the year before with his "second fiancée." He sends her a photograph of himself. He tells her he loves merry-go-rounds, "Have you such things in America? I am very fond of them, I have had many nice rides this year, renewing my youth. It is quite sad how young I can feel, at a pinch. I who might be the father of a large family, am always quite capable of behaving like a schoolboy, and only afterwards do I detect the impropriety." He recounts his latest practical joke: depositing many empty champagne bottles in the bedroom of a sleeping chauffeur, putting the man's watch back two hours, and similar "lamentable" tricks. She writes back that such youthful high spirits could act as a safety valve; he replies that this is no excuse: "I am *not* young, and my spirits are *not* high." He tells her he "detests" his "routine of gadding about in London." On 24 August he writes that this is "the fifth birthday I have had in this dear little place. . . . It is the first birthday I have had since I knew the dear little friend – and therefore a special birthday for

me ... Max aetat: 32." He is pleased with having encouraged her to read
Henry James: "I *am* so delighted that you delighted in 'The Portrait of a
Lady.' Do read some others: *any* of H. J.'s early period you would revel in.
... I take a real pleasure in having discovered something both worth reading
and unread by you."

When they are again in London, Max writes:

> I am not such a *very* dreadful person. I did hold your hand, I admit. But,
> dear, why shouldn't you let me hold your hand? Surely mutual sympathy
> may be allowed to have its outward manifestation. Surely that is very right
> and natural. But of I course I *will try* not to do it, if you feel afraid of it.

This crisis past, he sees her frequently; they resume their dinners and visits to
the theatre and dining with his family. He takes her to see Oxford. When she
returns to the States, having had no luck securing work on the English stage,
he pursues her in letters: "I miss you very much, as you may imagine – and
it seems horrid to have to write 'U.S.A.' on the envelope." She has been serving as first reader for him: "I wish you were here to listen to what I have written, in the chair upstairs, and to be asked whether you love it or loathe it, and
to have to be cross-questioned very much before you will put approval into
words." Again, "When you like a thing, I feel sure it *is* good." He rehearses
their "unforgettable summer" and singles out their visit to Oxford, "I suppose because that is the one place I saw you in outside London, and so my
seeing you there made the deeper dint in my brain and heart. And because
Oxford is as unlike any other place as you are unlike any other person." He
misses her terribly: "Dear, I wish you were still here. I feel lonely without
you."

But he is nowhere near to proposing marriage to Florence, and he never
uses the word "love." He is acutely aware, given "poor Kilseen's" experience
of nearly eight years of frustration and Constance Collier's quick discarding
of him, what a ridiculous figure he cut as an engaged man. The reasons for
this were plentiful. He didn't have enough money to marry; and more
importantly, he would never have the push to make enough money to marry.
In the letter to Reggie telling of the end of his engagement to Constance
Collier, he had said:

> It *is* a pity I was not born either rich or the sort of solid man who could be
> trusted and who could trust himself to make his way solidly in the world.

1. Max Beerbohm. Aged ten or eleven. Orme Square schoolboy.

2. Max. Aged fourteen or fifteen, at Charterhouse. " . . . my delight at having been at Charterhouse was far greater than had been my delight in being there."

3. Will Rothenstein and Max Beerbohm. At Oxford, 1893. Both are twenty-one. "I was a modest good-humoured boy," Max wrote. "It was Oxford that made me insufferable."

4. *Oscar Wilde*. 1894. "He has deteriorated very much in appearance," Max told a friend in April 1893, "his cheeks being quite a dark purple and fat to a fault"; "He looked like one whose soul had swooned in sin and revived vulgar." After Wilde's trial Max realized how cruel his early caricatures of him had been.

5. *Mr Aubrey Beardsley.* [1896.] Max said of Beardsley, who died at twenty-five, that he had remained always "rather remote, rather detached from ordinary conditions, a kind of independent spectator. . . . This kind of aloofness has been noted in all great artists. Their power isolates them. It is because they stand at a little distance that they can see so much. No man ever *saw* more than Beardsley."

6. Max Beerbohm. *Ca.* 1893.

7. *Mr Julius Beerbohm.* Max's half-brother and inspiration as dandy: "so cool and calm and elegant . . . Julius never raised his deep voice, and never put any expression into it, and his straw-coloured hair lay around his head as smoothly as satin. Julius had always a gardenia or Parma violets, and his hat was dazzling, and his linen was washed in Paris. Also, he had a moustache."

8. *(facing page) Genus Beerbohmiense. Species Herbertica Arborealis, Species Maximiliana.* Max with his big brother, actor-manager Herbert Beerbohm Tree. Herbert was very much Max's opposite: a great deal bigger, with carrot-coloured hair, flamboyant, vital, untidy, restless, histrionic, extroverted; a man of huge energies and ambitions and a "sanguine radiance."

Mr. Rudyard Kipling
takes a bloomin'
day aht, on the
Blasted 'Eath, with
Britannia, 'is gurl.

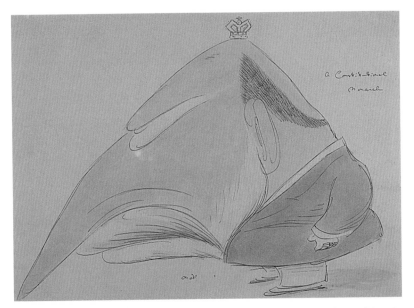

10. *A Constitutional Monarch*. King Edward VII, Max's favourite target, here subjected to a more-than-usual "monstrous" distortion.

11. *Illustrating the force of ancient habit*. 1903. "King Edward's Visit to the Convent of Dom Successio. King Edward: 'Enfin, Madame: faites monter la première à gauche.' [So, Madame, let me see the first on the left.]" The caricature celebrates the King's highly successful tour of Europe and his reputation for womanizing.

9. *(facing page) Mr Rudyard Kipling takes a bloomin' day aht, on the Blasted 'Eath, along with Britannia, 'is gurl*. 1904. For Max Kipling was an "apocalyptic bounder who can do such fine things but mostly prefers to stand (on tip-toe and stridently) for all that is cheap and nasty."

12. *Mr Whistler.* "Tiny – Noah's Ark – flat-brimmed hat – band almost to top – coat just not touching the ground – black gloves – magnificent eyes – exquisite hands, long and lithe – short palms."

13. *Mr. Swinburne. June 1899.* "The divine singer" in the year Max met him. Swinburne, Max explained, was in posture, like certain trees, a "leaner-backward."

14. *Mr Reginald Turner.* 1907. "The dearest of all my dear friends."

15. *Un revers* [On Second Thought]. 1909. Essayist: "'They call me the inimitable, and the incomparable, and the sprightly and whimsical . . . I wonder if I *am*.'" Max, a consummate dandy, drew himself more often than any other subject, and always in formal wear of some kind. Here, even at his writing table, he will concede nothing to informality except the slippers on his feet.

16. Zuleika Dobson. Private copy frontispiece, 1911. "Her eyes were a trifle large, and their lashes longer than they need have been."

17. Florence Kahn Beerbohm. Drawn by Max "from the life," on the terrace of the Villino Chiaro, 1913.

18. Florence. Snapshot, taken by Max at the Villino, 1913.

19. *Quis Custodiet Ipsum Custodem?* [Who will guard the guard himself?]. 1916. Theodore Watts: "Mr Caine, a word with you! Shields and I have been talking matters over, and we are agreed that this evening and henceforth you *must* not and *shall* not read any more of your literary efforts to our friend. They are too – what shall I say? – too luridly arresting and are the allies of insomnia." A drawing from *Rossetti and His Circle*. Rossetti's guardians quarrel over their hero. Paintings of Jane Morris adorn the walls of 16 Cheyne Walk, Chelsea.

20. George Bernard Shaw. Max, a friend but not an intimate, said his admiration for Shaw's genius was marred by a "dissent from almost any view that he holds on anything."

21. *London in November, and Mr Henry James in London. Ca.* 1907. ". . . It was, therefore, not without something of a shock that he, in this to him so very congenial atmosphere, now perceived that a vision of the hand which he had, at a venture, held up within an inch or so of his eyes was, with an almost awful clarity being adumbrated . . ." From James's "middle and later" writings – here parodied – Max got "the finest of all literary joy."

22. Fresco from the Villino Chiaro. 1922. (*Left to right*) King Edward VII, Marquis de Soveral, Joseph Chamberlain, Henry James, Lord Rosebery, Reggie Turner, A. W. Pinero, Will Rothenstein, George Moore, Rudyard Kipling, Lord Burnham, and Winston Churchill.

23. *Some Persons of "the Nineties."* 1925. (*Left to right*) Richard Le Gallienne, Walter Sickert, Arthur Symons, George Moore, Henry Harland, John Davidson, Charles Conder, Oscar Wilde, Will Rothenstein, Max Beerbohm, W. B. Yeats, Aubrey Beardsley, and Enoch Soames.

24. *Mr Lytton Strachey.* 1931. This caricature of Strachey (whom Max deemed "a perfect master of English prose") was drawn about the time Max decided his caricatures were becoming likenesses: "I seemed to have mislaid my gift for dispraise. Pity crept in. So I gave up caricaturing."

25. The Villino Chiaro, Max's home, 1910–56. View from the coast road, looking towards Rapallo.

26. Elisabeth Jungmann. Max's devoted friend and chatelaine of the Villino Chiaro, 1951–56, whom he married on his deathbed.

27. Max Beerbohm. In his eighties he told Cecil Beaton, "No gentleman should be photographed after he's reached the age of eighty." This photograph by Douglas Glass was taken when Max was seventy-five.

Of course I am a success in a way, and may continue to be so for some time; but that is in virtue of certain qualities in my defects: it is in virtue of a sort of nimble fantastic irresponsibility; for solid worldly success this is no good at all. And I now, for the first time clearly, see myself as on the whole a failure. I have never coveted the *solid* quality until now, when I find that without it, I cannot get, and don't deserve, Constance.

Or Florence Kahn. His involvements with women caused him to look, however fleetingly, inside himself. He did not do so often, but Florence, in her letters from America, had pressed him on the question of whether he was "happy." Somewhat surprisingly, he took her question seriously. He has "nothing to complain of on the score of happiness." But, he continues,

> I don't think I ever am or shall be happy in the full sense, as some people are. As I think I told you, I can only stand life when it is made pleasant for me. Usually it *is* made pleasant for me. I have really been rather pampered than otherwise. So I have been all right, on the whole. But I do not like life when it does not offer me something nice every day. And if it ever offered me something *not* nice I should feel myself very much aggrieved. A *happy* person, it seems to me, is the sort of person who requires no aids to happiness – who can grapple with life on any terms. And I never shall be that sort of person. That is all I have to complain of. And it is little enough in comparison with average grounds for complaint. So *there*, dear, I have told you as fully as I could – at tedious length, I am afraid.

Max's letters of the next few years, while remaining affectionate, are somewhat cooler than the very first ones. In fact, during the summer of 1907 he was mildly infatuated with a woman of an altogether different stripe. He was sitting for the sculptor Kathleen Bruce, an independent-minded, high-spirited young woman who had made a name for herself in artistic circles in London and Paris. (Her statuette of Max is in the Senior Common Room at Merton College, Oxford.) The two became involved in a lively but never serious flirtation. In June Kathleen was taken ill with appendicitis. Max wrote to her solicitously about getting the peacock feathers out of her room: "There are heaps of other kinds of feathers, just as pretty. Have some of them instead. I can't, of course, justify my distrust of feathers. But, if it comes to that, what *can* one justify? There is no such thing as pure reason. At least we mortal creatures have never hit on it. We have to depend on superstitions, some of which *seem* reasonable, whilst others . . . but here I am arguing about what can't be argued about, instead of merely begging you to destroy those beastly feathers." Again he writes, saying that she would be fine but for the peacock feathers and telling her that the "patern" on her wallpaper is really spelt with two *t*'s. A third letter tells of Max throwing her peacock feathers into the Thames; he sends her Butler's *Way of All Flesh* because Shaw raved about it, and one of his own great favourites, James's *Aspern Papers,* along with *The Happy Hypocrite.* She liked the fairy tale, and this pleased Max: "It is the only *popular* thing I have ever written: I might be quite rich now if I had continued in that vein. But the vein left me." When Max went on holiday to Dieppe, he wrote to her of playing La Boule in the casino. The infatuation died out quickly, and the following year Max sent her congratulations on her engagement to Robert Scott, who a few years later would perish during his famous voyage to the South Pole.

Max then became fascinated, briefly, by yet another extraordinary woman, the about-to-be-divorced Irish-American Baroness von Hutten, a writer of popular novels. Max, with his great friend William Nicholson, was visiting her and her husband at their villa at Portofino (just around the bay from Rapallo). The entire group seems to have had a gay old time, Max surprising himself with his talent in a game of writing "shocking" and scandalous sonnets: "I have to tear them up," he wrote to a friend, "and watch them well on their way to the sea before I can regard myself as fit to mix in decent society!" That Max and the Baroness were very much attracted to each other he himself would later admit. She went so far as to contend she could have married him at the time, an absurd claim, but worth noting. Of their parting, she wrote, "The darling wept." Theirs was the most short-lived of his flirtations.

Meanwhile, back in America, Florence's acting career was going nowhere. She was considered for the part of Cleopatra, and for the title role in *Salomé,* both of which seemed unlikely parts for someone of her make-up and temperament. She got neither role; but apparently she would have hesitated about the Salomé out of fear that people might assume that she herself might behave like Salomé. Max assured her no one would so assume. She returned to London, and their dinners and theatregoing resumed; she met Reggie Turner, who feared she did not like him. She did not; she never much took to Max's friends.

Having again retreated to the States, she did get an engagement, as Mrs Elvsted in *Hedda Gabler* (Florence was a great Ibsen devotee). Max told her that Mrs Elvsted "surely is the normal and well grounded *human* person; definitely a foil to the hysterical and inhuman Hedda." A month later she left the company to attend her mother's funeral in Memphis. She never again appeared on the American stage. She received a legacy of $100 per month, a helpful amount of money in 1907.

The letters flow on. Max reports on his social rounds:

I have been "going out" a good deal during the past two months. I do agree with your criticism of the party you went to – the futility of talking to a succession of people – "giving" a few moments to one after another – mostly strangers or mere acquaintants – with a new topic for each. No, not a new topic. There is, in all kinds of society here, at present, only one topic – Mr Bernard Shaw. And as few people know him personally, and are very keen to know all about him personally, the topic is brought to bear on me with especially high pressure. I am quite "tired" of him – and am tired of London altogether.

On another occasion he recounts how he has to order a false moustache for a costume dinner party: "I absolutely refuse to take the trouble to get myself up as a cardinal, or a Bedouin Arab, or Edward I, or George Washington, or anything of that sort. Why didn't I refuse to go at all – why I should let myself in for even a false moustache – I really do not know. My old weakness – 'living in the moment' – the moment when it is easier to say *yes* than *no*." He tells her that he went to "the usual New Year's Eve party at the Gosses." Also,

I met the Princess of Wales the other night, and had a longish talk with her – or rather *to* her; for the system is that *she* starts a topic, and then expects *you* to dilate till you are out of breath; and then after a pause she starts another topic for you. She began on caricatures. I went on as long as I could. Then, after a pause, she started me on the weather. And so on. That sort of thing is more amusing afterwards than at the actual time of the performance!

Again,

I am very well as (unberufen [touch wood]) I always am – but rather bored with all the things that distract me from boredom – rather bored by the net-work of lunches and dinners without which my life would be rather a blank. This is just the full "season" for me – and I wriggle and grumble, but in a sort of a way, I suppose, I like it; only, I should like better some animating single purpose in life which would enable me to spurn it all from me.

The closest he came to a single animating purpose was his caricaturing, and this was intermittent. He tells Florence: "My bout of caricature still is on me, I am glad to say; and I do revel in the obsession, and hope not to lose it yet awhile. What an odd thing ... that this mania for drawing should suddenly descend on me after months in which I had no desire to draw a single stroke and then should pass away, and absent itself from me for some mysterious interval." Another time he bursts out, "I have been drawing a great many caricatures – and oh, how I rejoice in them! They are what I was put into the world to do." A series of letters to Florence document his involvement with Alfred Harmsworth – later Lord Northcliffe – who had recently acquired the magazine *Vanity Fair*. Harmsworth, Max tells Florence, "is very keen on my things, rather frightened by them, anxious to publish a lot of them, convinced that I am a lazy artistic person who won't work for him, and so on, and so on." Another letter tells her that Harmsworth "has always had a great platonic admiration of my caricatures; but of course the moment I let him *have* some definite caricatures for pub-lication, he is frightened out of his wits, and wants me to do something quite different – wants pretty portraits, I suppose, which any schoolgirl could do much better than I, and for much less remuneration. So I am going to see the great man, and find out how far he is willing to sacrifice his predilections. It will end, I expect, by my not doing any caricatures for V.F. I should rather like to do them; but it won't be worth my while to stultify myself." What Harmsworth wants, Max tells Florence in his next letter, "is caricature that will be taken as a pleasing picture by the subject of it. An omelette with no eggs broken, in fact. He is afraid of libel actions – which is a quite groundless fear, as I try to make him understand – though he ought to understand such matters better than I." Max apologizes for writing so much about "a subject which can't be a very interesting one to you. But it is so to me, because I believe as intensely in my caricatures as I am indif-ferent to my writing; and I should love to have a really good medium (like

V.F.) for giving them out. So forgive all this temporary egoism!" Remarkable sentiments, these – even if they come at a time when Max was increasingly exasperated by his weekly *Saturday Review* deadlines that left him little time or energy for other writing. Harmsworth eventually accepted half a dozen caricatures.

Florence came again to London and managed to secure the role – the very one that had proved so disastrous earlier in New York – of Rebecca West in *Rosmersholm*. This was in February 1908 for a week's run at the small, unfashionable Terry's Theatre. Max attended faithfully, bought tickets for friends and family, wrote urging Shaw to come and see her act, "a true tragedian with a quite extraordinary beauty of style. Do go and see . . ." And of course he reviewed her in the *Saturday*. While the article was in proof Max wrote to her that it was hard to do justice to a friend, though he hopes his "enthusiasm" will show: "I have managed to credit you with force and emotion, intellect, sense of beauty, and so on. . . . It would have been more aggressively flaring if I had never met you." Just how he could have "flared" more on her behalf is unclear. He raved about the whole production: here we have "a masterpiece . . . played nobly"; and after praising the other actors, he writes,

> It is difficult to write about Miss Florence Kahn's impersonation of Rebecca, for it is never easy to analyse the merits of great acting. . . . The part [of Rebecca] is a very subtle and difficult one, a convoluted one, needing an intellect to grasp it, and extreme skill to express it. . . . Miss Kahn betrays the fact that she has a voice of great power and resonance, and a face that will eloquently express the soul. . . . There is not on the English stage any actress, except Miss Lana Ashwell, who could have made the scene of Rebecca's confession in the third act so moving, so thrilling, as it was made by Miss Kahn.

She is as graceful and as natural as Mrs Campbell; she gives us a Rebecca doing things "just as a real woman in a real room would do such things," while all the time reminding us that Rebecca is a woman "who has passed through tortures of the soul." Max never wrote anything more enthusiastic in his twelve years of theatre reviewing. If we did not know him better we might label the review fulsome or even dishonest in its hyperbole, but I have no doubt that he sincerely believed and meant every word. He was a great debunker but an absolutely enthusiastic praiser.*

Amid the many letters of 1908 comes one that may or may not explain an awful lot about Max Beerbohm. Undated but written some time in mid-November, it reads, in part:

> I mustn't be selfish [in regard to her returning home]. And indeed in our great friendship I do think more of you than of myself. And I constantly reproach myself with what has so often been evident: that I tend to make you unhappy. It rather seems that making people unhappy is my métier. I like you better than any person in the world. But the other sort of caring is beyond me. I realise quite surely now that I shall never be able to care in that way for any one. It is a defect in my nature. It can't be remedied. Dear, you have brought *so much* happiness to me. I can't bear to think of being the cause of unhappiness to you. It is difficult to express myself.

Here one must speculate on another's speculation. Rupert Hart-Davis maintains that this letter is saying that if they were to be married, the marriage would not be consummated. Max, Hart-Davis says, was "a natural celibate" who probably never had a sexual experience of any kind. Hart-Davis further suggests that Florence, whom he judges as "undersexed" as Max, "accepted his confession with relief." What is there to be said for this interpretation? To begin with, Hart-Davis is not one to hatch or espouse crackpot ideas; he is a solid and level-headed authority on Max and Wilde and their respective eras. Hart-Davis doesn't try to elaborate his position

---

* A curious incident would happen in March 1909: Max and Will Rothenstein were visiting the London home of Mrs Grace Chadbourne, where Rothenstein jokingly said that Max was a very "corruptible" critic. Next morning, Max told Florence, "I wrote him a long and deadly letter, packed with rankling home-truths. And he, poor friend, seems to have been horribly upset. And my rejoinder (to which I suppose there will be a reply today) was of a gentler and friendlier kind. It is such a rare feeling for me – anger; and I didn't like it at all, and was so glad when I had got rid of it by venting it!" Will's letter (Max's he apparently destroyed) said how "staggered" he was: Max's words seemed to evince "a real dislike to me ... I am so upset & grieved & humbled. ... It seems so tragic and unreal to me that you should ever have written me a letter of this kind"; the "corruptible critic" remark, Will explained, had been innocently intended as "crude chaff"; it went back to an old (1903) joke between them about Max himself regarding as a lark his reviewing in the *Saturday* an exhibition of the New English Art Club. The two men made it up. But Max's rare, almost unexampled loss of temper and his unreasonable anger are surprising. His attachment to Florence may have made him willing to risk one of his oldest and dearest friendships.

beyond quoting Beerbohm Tree as saying that Max possessed "more brain than heart, and an entire absence of passion" – and then remarking that Tree was wrong about Max's heart. Hart-Davis knew all there was to know of the record, consisting chiefly of Max's own letters, showing some seventeen years of infatuations, flirtations, pursuits, engagements (the engagements alone add up to ten years). With the same record before us today, no one would deny that Max felt a deep and romantic urge towards women. In a very real sense women were necessary to him, and not just because he needed someone to look after him. Should we make the leap from this fairly uncontested stance and go on to embrace the "natural celibate" reading? Was theirs to be a companionate marriage, a *mariage blanc*? Here is a clear case, if ever there was one, of every reader for himself or herself. I for one agree with Hart-Davis. I think his choice of words, "natural celibate," unfortunate, for "celibate" often means an unmarried person. "Physically chaste," while clumsy, might be more accurate here. Like Hart-Davis, I hasten to add that I may very well be wrong. I have no additional evidence to offer, nor any means of supporting Hart-Davis's position unless I were to say that Max's repugnance to physical exertion and exercise may be relevant here. He himself wrote in an essay that he never took a walk unless he had to – though I have since learned that he took walks into town in Rapallo. I cannot imagine him swimming, though he did refer to sea bathing during his Italian years. He boasted that he had never been on a horse. This much is uncontested.

Max's actual proposal, hard upon this letter, was made in person, and as Florence remained in London, the epistolary record is spotty. But the letters do become immediately much more intimate: "Very dear little friend" changes to "*Darling* love" and the simple "Max" at the close becomes some variation on "Your own loving Max." Florence, we can infer, hesitates. She may have been wondering about the (putatively) peculiar nature of Max's proposal; or she could simply have been questioning whether she wanted to marry at all. Marriage would mean the end of her career, for she believed that actresses on marrying ought to quit the stage; she knew too that marriage would mean living in Italy on a very modest income. Max gently presses his case. He asks, "Did my idea seem to you very preposterous? It does seem rather so to me – from your point of view. It would seem so to me if I were you – I suppose. But if it doesn't seem so to you, as being yourself, – why then, dear, all is well. I am perfectly certain about my own feelings. I know *I* should be happy, if *you* were. You are very much more to me than any one else in the world, and always will be ..." In the next letter, he writes,

> Darling, don't try to decide quickly. Think it over *and think only for your-self.* That is also the only way of thinking for *me.* For if you were happy I should be happy in exact proportion. ... It would be no good at all to marry me just in kindness – for my sake, as it were. For I should very soon find *that* out, and should be miserable at your unhappiness. So take time to think, dear.

In early December Florence gives a hesitant yes. Max writes, "I wonder if you will change your mind about our plan. I know I shan't. But it seems to me so very much more attractive for me than it can be for you. Meanwhile I am 'glad.' Till tomorrow, sweet." She must then have reassured him, for he next writes, "Dear sweet, I feel so much happier than I have felt for a long time. A sort of feeling of peace – of being able to look into the future, hand in hand with you." And so they were engaged.

The letters continue, and trail Florence back to America:

> Darling love.... Today, on the red sofa in my room – on the bolster of it – I found Baedeker's "Italy" just where you had left it one day when you have been reading it lying down; and it did so remind me of you – not that any reminder is needed! – reminded me of all the times you had spent there, protesting that the time was wasted if you were not reading; and reminded me of all the times we shall spend together in the place named on the book's cover. Dear darling, how lovely it will be, won't it? I feel so happy in the thought of it, in the thought of you. I love you so much, dear, and think of you all the time.

In July he writes,

> I ... am glad my "season" is almost over. I am not at all beginning to feel sentimental about England, and London, and dinners, as things of the past; only a feeling of good riddance; though without animosity.

In August he takes his last holiday at Dieppe, where he has a room facing the sea:

> We must live in sight of the sea together, as we both approve of it and its ways. ... and, my darling, I do so live for that time and long for it – just that and nothing else. And all my love to you.

He writes again, assuring her that he will not miss London and all his great friends:

> You will be the whole population of my globe. We shall be brilliant for each other, wherever we are.

Other letters follow:

> I don't think I shall try to "teach" you to want to see people – so long as you are happy with *me*. I shan't want to see people at all: though so much of my time has been spent that way.

> Darling, I do look forward so much to the future. It is a thing I have never done before – and it seems almost too good to be true. I have always lived so much in the present moment, *faute de mieux*, with a vague dread of the future to spoil the fun. And now it is all quite changed, thank you very much.

> . . . to me your presence is all sufficient . . . I love you for yourself.

> Darling love, I long to see you, and it will be so lovely, won't it? And we shall be so happy.

Still she worries that he will miss his friends and his social life. He counters:

> I don't think I have a really gregarious nature at all: wherever I am, I am always detached, however genial my surface – never really mingling in the thing. So there won't be any act of *detaching* myself when I leave it all behind – will there?

He assures her, with ample candour, that he is not "fascinated" with Baroness von Hutten:

> I am in the position of *having* been somewhat fascinated two years ago. The safest of all positions! Dear darling love, how unnecessary for me to say these things. You know how I feel.

She must not be depressed:

> Let us be *happy* – and let me be forgiven for the defects of my qualities. Nobody is perfect except (I DO believe) you. . . . I count myself very lucky in having met in you both the person I love best and the best person that is to be conceived.

He resumes working on *Zuleika Dobson* – begun and put aside as far back as 1898 – and reports his progress to her faithfully; he sends sections for her approval:

> Tell me *truly* won't you? Say, with your usual bluntness, that it's damned nonsense, if you think so. But I don't think you will. Darling I think of you all the time I write it, and at all other times.

Again,

> There isn't any opinion but yours that I should dream of soliciting – but yours I do value so much, and want to have.

Sometimes his humour breaks through:

> You don't endorse my "epithet for Tolstoi." I called him an "inspired ass." Which epithet do you mean? I think he is rather inspired – but perhaps he isn't!

He asks that she show him how to wrap a book in a brown parcel for the post:

> I am so hopeless: I can *write* a book; but the packing business is beyond me.

He is forever concerned with her health, urging her to bundle up, to keep warm, to take care of herself. Rarely does he mention his own health:

> I am very well, though I have a slight cold: nothing to bother myself about – and I shouldn't bother myself if it *was* anything to bother about: that is one of my few virtues: I fuss about other people – at least, about *some* other people – but about myself never.

Even a visit from abroad by Reggie seems dull:

> All that happens to me happens inside my heart, and is all about *you.*

Max tells no one of his intentions until April 1910, a month before the event, and then he tells only his mother and sisters, and, alone among his friends, Reggie Turner. To him Max writes:

> Florence is the one woman with whom I can be always and wholly happy, and the woman apart from whom I could not be happy. I count myself extraordinarily fortunate in having, after my various driftings and pleasantries and narrow escapes, had Florence vouchsafed to me. To me she represents the achievement of happiness, happiness for good and all.

They shall not have much money, he tells Reggie, but – Reggie is sworn to secrecy – Ernest Brown of Leicester Galleries has given him an advance against a future exhibition. George Alexander has also given him an advance, £100, for a one-act play.* The move to Italy, Max informs Reggie, will enable him to give up drama criticism and "do a good deal of work." He closes: "Dearest Reg, dearest of all my friends, I am sure you will be glad for my happiness."

To his family the news that at long last Max was really to be married was not especially welcome. His mother tried to accept Florence, but it was difficult going; moreover, she didn't relish losing her son, and having him go off to Italy. Of his three sisters, Dora was friendliest towards Florence, but, being in the convent, was rather out of the picture. Agnes made an effort to like her. Constance did not at all like her. The Trees thought her "downright tiresome." Reggie, keeping his own counsel, was friendly always to his friend's chosen. He fired back a letter of congratulations, sent a "staggering cheque" as a wedding present, and agreed to let himself be "hauled" out of Paris for the ceremony. Max wrote back that he was "overwhelmed" by the gift. As for Reggie's promise to come as witness, "Without your presence the marriage would seem hardly valid."

Max and Florence were married on 4 May 1910. Two carriages conveyed the wedding party to the Paddington Registry in Harrow Street, Max, his mother, his sister Constance, and Reggie in the first, Florence and his sister Agnes in the second. Mrs Beerbohm and Reggie were the witnesses. All returned to Upper Berkeley Street for a wedding cake, which arrived late. These sparse facts are all we know of the day itself. We cannot credit one set of particulars because they came years after the event and from that imaginative and inveterate liar, Frank Harris. In 1923 he published an account of the wedding supposedly given to him at the time by Max's sister Agnes (Mrs Neville):

* *A Social Success* is a Wildean farce about a London bachelor who, because of his "confounded easy-going amiability and general niceness" and his inability to say no to lunch and dinner invitations, is so popular in society that he will do anything – including cheating at cards – to get out of society. Card-sharping aside, the character embodies Max's almost desperate longing to quit the London scene. The play was eventually produced by Alexander in 1913, at the Palace Theatre, to fairly good reviews.

"Oh, yes," Mrs Neville began, "Max was married, you can take it from me, legally married in church even, to a very charming and very pretty girl ... Max went through the ceremony beautifully, as such a dandy would, omitting nothing, not even the first kiss of the blushing bride. I could not help telling him how proud of him I was, and now, I said, as we were all leaving the church and the bride was getting into the carriage, I must say 'Good-bye, dear Max.' Suddenly his marvellous self-possession broke down; frantically he seized me by the arm: 'You're not going to leave me *alone* with her,' he cried. And when I replied: 'Indeed I am!' he looked at me reproachfully, muttering 'It's hardly decent!'"

On learning this, Max, with unwonted energy, immediately left Italy for London, consulted his lawyer, got the publisher to agree to remove the offending passage from future copies of the book, and had inserted in the *TLS* a letter expressing his "deep annoyance" at this "entirely untrue" anecdote, which was "palpably false" in itself and in its attribution to his sister. Why have I bothered to reprint it? For one thing, no matter how false, the story reveals how odd some of Max's friends thought it that he should marry Florence or, for that matter, that he should marry anyone.

His marriage took the press and all of his friends completely by surprise. It became news only after he had departed the scene. He liked to joke that he left London because knowing everybody there was too much for him. But late in life, he told Samuel Behrman, "I wanted to be alone with Florence."

CHAPTER FOURTEEN

A Married Couple

Max married and was, in effect, gone for good. The pair honeymooned at Chesham, then at Hythe; in June they crossed the Channel and stopped briefly in Paris, where Max spotted Edmond Rostand and watched from outside a shop where Rostand was selecting ties with "immense anxiety and gesticulation and 'patter.'" He did not speak to Rostand; Max and Florence wanted to be alone. They travelled to Italy. Max reported their progress to Reggie: they were in Santa Margarita, a small resort town located on the bay of Tigullio between Rapallo and Portofino. Here Max saw E. F. Benson "in a blue flannel blazer and white canvas shirt and tennis shoes," but kept out of sight himself. Their hotel was "bang on to" the sea, and he and Florence bathed – "three strokes." Max tells Reggie,

> Florence (you will be glad to hear) continues to justify the confidence I have reposed in her; and altogether she is – there is no other word for it – divine, and seems all the time like a thing too good to be true, and I doubt whether I shall ever become used to being with her.

They went next to Rapallo, a place he at first found not as "sympathetic" as Santa Margarita, and "very *hotel-y*," but still pretty, and here they found a house high up above the town. Max sent home for furniture (causing his sister Constance to lament to Robbie Ross, "I knew it! ... that she, not being English, would not be the means of bringing him back. ... I will try to be pleased he married her!"). To Reggie Max described his new home:

> It is on the road between here and Zoagli – about a twenty-five minute walk *up*, and twenty *down*. On one side of the road is the cliff, very olive-ish, going sheer down to the sea. On the other side of the road is the cliff again, going up into the sky; and our place is on this side. The ground floor is high, having been built by the landlord as a garage, and except as a garage could be of no use to anyone but to us, to whom it is used as a sort of pedestal, rising up above the road and giving us a good view across to the

sea. ... We don't want to have motors living under us, so we have taken the garage with the flat ... and Florence says it will be useful for keeping an ice chest in; so that is all right. The flat above has four rooms on the sea-side – and on the other side a bathroom and a dressing room and a kitchen; all small, but just about the right size. And the roof itself is built as a terrace, with a balustrade all around, and a heavenly view out to sea. And in the middle of the terrace stands a small room, which will be my "study." And behind the terrace – on the side remote from the sea – is the garden; a small and rough garden up the side of the cliff. ... and we have a fig tree, and a vine, and an orange-tree and an almond-tree, and a lemon-tree. There are also tomatoes. ... Florence and I think the place is really delightful (it is brand-new, by the way: plaster hardly dry).

This was Villino Chiaro, and it was to be their home for the rest of their lives. They never wanted anything more grand. (In 1922, after some successful caricature exhibitions, they were able to buy the house outright; and in 1932 they would buy a small adjoining cottage, the "Casetta," described by Max as a "hovel" which Florence managed to transform into "commodious" rooms.) From the first they could scarcely credit their luck. Here was everything they were looking for: the sun, the sea, privacy, a place where the natives were friendly and helpful but also left them alone. Florence had taken up Italian in preparation for coming to Italy and became a fluent speaker. Max never bothered to learn Italian. In fact, it was said that he never as much as held a lira in his hand.

When Max had been married six months, when he was half a year into what he called his "rest cure from dining-out in London," he finally got around to answering Will Rothenstein's congratulatory letter. Rothenstein had said that marriage would bring Max closer to himself and his wife, "for you no longer will be surrounded by that peculiar & elusive distinction the bachelor holds in the married household." Max wrote:

I didn't at all agree with what you said about the "distinction" which unmarried men had in your eyes (e.g. Tonks, etc). In *my* eyes, at least, they are positively vulgar; and lamentable, also, and incomprehensible. And every day and all day I am thankful not to be one of them – though I cannot imagine that I ever would have ceased to be one of them but for the blessed dispensation by which Florence came into my life. She is even more an angel than I had ever guessed, absolutely perfect in everything and adorable. And I am as happy as the day is long. And I think *she* is, too. And it is a great joy for us to be together in a very beautiful place, quite alone.

But, as usual, Reggie hears more than anyone:

It is no news merely to say that I am consciously happy during sixteen hours out of the daily twenty-four, and unconsciously happy during the other eight; and yet that is the only news I have. What goes to constitute that happiness would make a poor recital. Absolutely nothing "happens." Florence and I "see" nobody: there is no one to see – except a good many German tourists who all look exactly alike. There are Italian peasants and tradesmen, to whom I say "*Buon Giorno*" with a singularly pure accent; but I haven't conversed with a single human being except Florence since we left England. . . . The sun shines, and the sea shines under it, and I eat a good deal twice a day, and the camellias are just beginning to bloom, and the oranges and lemons are ripe, and I do a great deal of work, and everything goes on from day to day with a heavenly sameness of peace and happiness.

Once married, whenever Max was separated from Florence, he wrote to her faithfully every day. Having returned briefly to London in 1911 to prepare an exhibition, he writes:

Perfect darling, it is so lovely to think of being with you again. When I say perfect darling I mean to imply perfection in the literal sense . . . because you *are* perfect. And I send all my love and all my thoughts, and I am your own, Max.

When he writes again from London in 1914, nothing has changed:

Goodnight my dear darling love. I am living in the prospect of seeing you. I can't imagine that anything lovelier could happen to anyone than my seeing you and being with you again.

After ten years of marriage Max, in town for the publication of *Seven Men*, is still addressing Florence as "Darling sweet love" and continuing in the same vein:

I am immensely pleased and touched, darling, by what you say of my stories. They would never have been written but for you. I should probably still be doing dramatic criticism! . . . Darling love, I hope you will be happy with me. I love you all the world. Your own Max.

Some people may think the lovingness and uxoriousness more than enough to counter the "undersexed" argument. Myself, I think they show that, without physical sex, romance can be sustained indefinitely.

Their devotion to each other was complete. She gave him all the care he needed, and he would have been lost without her. In 1934, at a luncheon party, Florence fainted. Max, for once flurried, knelt beside her: "Please don't leave me, you can't be so unkind. Please, please come back." She did have some occasional longing for her old passion, the stage, and in this Max encouraged her. In 1931, having been married more than twenty years, she was invited to act in a Pirandello play, *The Life You Gave Me*, performed by a small repertory company at Huddersfield in Yorkshire. She got decent notices, but no more parts until 1935 when she appeared as Ase in *Peer Gynt* in a brief engagement at the Old Vic. (In that production, William Devlin, a young actor, had been shaking with nerves in the wings, seemingly unable to go on. Florence slapped him across the face and pushed him on to the stage.) In February 1936 she was given the part of the Duchess of Gloucester in the Oxford Union Dramatic Society's production of *Richard II*, directed by John Gielgud. The play ran for one week. Max of course attended loyally. Between performances he wrote to her – still addressing her as "Darling sweet love" – "You must be pleased with your Duchess and with all the deep and genuine affection for her. You couldn't possibly be better than you were last night. You were in complete control of your feelings, without the slightest loss of *her* emotions. Very lovely and perfect." Other people were less enthusiastic: older critics respectfully approved; younger ones thought her comically mannered. We are told that she had a gesture for every line: at the mention of her heart she would point to her heart; at the mention of a spear, she would throw an imaginary weapon; it was a style of acting from the 1890s. She was, as Max had dubbed himself, "an interesting link with the past." This *Richard II* part would be her last stage appearance. However, she made one movie, the 1936 Gaumont British production of *The Secret Agent*. The film, based on the novel *Ashenden* by Somerset Maugham and directed by Alfred Hitchcock, starred John Gielgud, Peter Lorre, Madeleine Carroll, and Robert Young. Florence had a supporting but important role, playing an elderly German woman, the wife of a man suspected of being a German spy. You can see her on video! She does the German accent and the German itself excellently (Florence spoke German). She is thin and angular, with a long face and prominent nose, and looks very much like an older version of Max's drawing of her (plate 17).

It's safe to say that married life was happier for Max than for Florence. This was so partly because of Florence's make-up. She was not of a naturally cheerful disposition; hers was a rather melancholy nature, and she suffered from bouts of depression (his state of mind was continuously cheerful). Then too, it must have been tiresome to be always identified as Max's wife. As an actress, she had occasionally been the centre of attention, but now, almost never. People wanted to see and hear, or even just to meet, Max Beerbohm, and a steady stream of visitors, old friends and anxious new admirers, came year after year to the Villino as though to a place of pilgrimage. It was a difficult arrangement. Florence was, as even her latter-day apologist Catherine Lyon Mix admits, "reserved, aloof, and difficult to know." She was likely to be ill at ease in the presence of Max's clever friends; sometimes she didn't understand or didn't like his jokes; she disapproved of some of his drawings; she was not happy about his adorning their house with fresco caricatures (see plate 22).

During the Second World War, when the Beerbohms were staying with the Sydney Schiffs in Abinger, Surrey, Mrs Schiff (a younger sister of Ada Leverson) scrutinized Florence and thought her self-dramatizing, theatrical, self-deceiving, and moralistic. When a servant girl was found to be pregnant with an illegitimate child, Florence could not bring herself to see the girl again. Some of Max's "improvements" to newspapers caused her to turn away saying they were too horrible. The old complaint that she interrupted Max when he was talking grew apace with her years. On one occasion she left the table when he insisted on opening a second bottle of wine with his guests. And once, when for another visitor Max started to draw a caricature of some Oxford friend, Florence seized the paper and tore it up, apparently thinking the conversation too flippant or trivial. But at the Villino, their normally quiet life suited her perfectly, and she took pride in the house and the garden. The person who saw most of the Beerbohms at Rapallo was Max's old friend Gordon Craig, who – to Florence's displeasure – had a home nearby. Asked if it was a happy marriage, Craig said, "Of course it was. Max was such a dear fellow. He had been a good son; and good sons make good husbands. Any woman would have been happy with him." Max loved Florence, in spite of her frailties and failings, her dejected moods, her puritanical views, her lack of humour. Until the end, his letters to her are unfailingly loving and tender, as in what was almost his very last to her, written on 3 September 1947: "Darling sweet love … I wish I were … with you. I always wish I were wherever you are! Take care of your dear self. Your own loving Max." To us, Florence may sound like a person we wouldn't want to spend five minutes with. On the other hand, who are we to judge her? No accounting for tastes. Max Beerbohm and Florence Kahn were a strange couple.

CHAPTER FIFTEEN

An Oxford Love Story

Max's escape to Italy in 1910 brought to fruition, in October of the following year, his long-in-the-making novel, *Zuleika Dobson*. The book had been started way back in 1898 and then laid aside. He thought about the novel for years, fiddled with it, and then in 1908, about the time of his engagement to Florence, he returned to it steadily, though of course he had many distractions: his reviewing for the *Saturday*, his caricatures, his hectic social life. But he plugged away at the book, giving Florence sections to read as he went along. Once settled in Rapallo, and after the caricatures and arrangements for his first Leicester Galleries exhibition were completed, he returned to the book full-tilt, finished it, and painstakingly saw it through the press. Publisher William Heinemann allowed him to control the physical format of the book, its boxy, squarish shape, the brown binding, the cream-coloured paper, the typeface, the wide margins: "If the binders and paper-makers don't play me false," Max wrote to Will Rothenstein, "the book will [at least] *look* nice: not like a beastly *novel*, more like a book of essays, self-respecting and sober and ample." An intimidating fanatic about the details of his books, he carried on endless battles with publishers and printers over the particulars. For covers and jackets, for example, he insisted on small lettering and opposed any vertical lettering (he got the title "Rossetti and his Circle" printed horizontally on the very thin spine of that volume of twenty-three drawings). When he said that he would care more about a misplaced comma than if Britain were to lose her empire, he meant it.

This fussiness was part of his campaign to make his books as perfect – perfect to his tastes – as he could. A large work of art, he said, could succeed in spite of carelessness and faults, but a trifle, even a trifle as lengthy as *Zuleika Dobson*, had to be perfect. He was an unflappable person, for the most part, but misprints and unauthorized alterations in his books came as close as anything to driving him crazy. When *Zuleika Dobson* was finally published, he found, in spite of all his efforts, much to complain of in the printed text, and he fired off via his publisher what he himself called a "furious" (and now-missing) letter to the printers, Ballantyne. Charles McCall, managing director of this eminent firm, answered that three misprints among 90,000 words (and therefore 89,997 words "printed correctly") was as good as one could hope for, and that the "infinitesimal defects" of alignment and spacing that Max griped about could have been eliminated only by special handling that would have raised the printing costs by as much as 300 per cent. Max replied that he seemed "to take the craft of printing rather more solemnly" than did the printers. There ought to be *no* misprinted words: if printers were to excuse their errors by pointing to a balance of words printed correctly, they might in future congratulate themselves on printing 45,001 of 90,000 words correctly. He also contested the spelling the printer imposed on his word "inexpellible":

> As to ... Messrs Ballantyne's impressive invocation of half-a-dozen dictionaries and "the custom of 120 years" against me: I know very well how the word is spelt in dictionaries, and I further assume that Messrs Ballantyne's proof-readers have instructions (also 120 years old) to correct *in proof* any obvious mis-spelling and to query *in proof* any doubtful spelling. Of *Zuleika Dobson* I have had two proofs, and in neither of them was "inexpellible" queried. Had it been so, I should have written *stet*, and (as my nature is keen and communicative in such matters) have explained that for good reasons of Latinity "inexpell*a*ble" is as vile a word as would be "inelig*a*ble" or "inaud*a*ble."

As for his broad complaint of untidy typography, "those letters bobbing up, those letters slipping down, and other defects over which I had to expend so much time in correcting the proofs, and which have not wholly been purged away from the published edition," he must of course now accept Ballantyne's explanation that "a slight inequality in the alignment to this particular fount" was to blame; he could, however, at least implore the printer "to seal up this particular fount (which is evidently our old friend the *fons et origo malorum*) for ever and ever."*

---

* His fastidiousness about the physical aspects of his books existed side by side with an indifference, once they were published, to owning the actual books. He regarded the mania for first editions " – even mine – " as a kind of madness: "And let me waive modesty for once," he wrote to a collector, "and say that mine are rather more worth-while than most others in as much as I have always selected my own type, bindings, margins, labels, etc., and have led the

But whatever his annoyance with printer's founts and spellings, the publication of *Zuleika Dobson* brought him deep satisfaction. It was his most sustained and ambitious work. After thirteen years he had reason to celebrate. The press was for the most part enthusiastic: the book was called everything from diverting and entertaining to coruscating and inimitable; it was extolled as "the perfect Oxford novel" and "the wittiest and most amusing of extravaganzas." Some reviewers, among them C. M. Francis in the (New York) *Bookman*, thought the designation of *Zuleika Dobson* as "Max's masterpiece" to be "very unfair" to his previous writings: *Zuleika* is good, but not that good, and for all its sustained irony, mock heroics, and clever parodies, the book when "read continuously … becomes monotonous." I think this a reasonably fair criticism. Max himself, in his fashion, relished certain of the more outlandish reviews. Into his own copy he pasted carefully clipped lines from the *Birmingham Daily Post*: "Max Beerbohm can draw, he cannot write" and "He plays with words, not considering their meaning," and "This, indeed, is imagination run riot," the last two referring apparently to Chapter XII where Max insists that Oxford would not be "menaced" by the deaths of all the undergraduates. Max loved literal-minded people – they provided so much fun. He also pasted into this copy, at the end, words from the *Western Daily Post* calling *Zuleika Dobson* "a powerful example of a healthy modern novel."

Healthy or not, *Zuleika Dobson*, it's safe to say, is a very peculiar book, one that people have trouble describing or even finding a category for. It's usually labelled a satire. But of what? Of the literary *femme fatale*? Of the New Woman? Of the new novel? Of Oxford University? Of undergraduate life? Of aestheticism? Of athleticism? Of dandyism? Of the herd instinct? All of these? Moreover, if *satire* is the right word, and I am not at all sure that it is, we ought quickly to note that this satire is of the gentle, affectionate kind. As such it is rather unlike the commonly accepted notion of satire, which is often seen as rooted in anger or dislike. The writer of *Zuleika* is neither angry nor unhappy; he is not critical of anything; he intends no reform; he plainly

---

publisher a dog's life by my pernickety insistence on having everything come out according to my own ideas. Mistaken ideas, for the most part, perhaps. But still, the author's. And because they were his I do rather like the look of a first edition of mine when I come across one. And someday, perhaps, if ever I am very rich, and quite mad (but at large), I shall butt into the market and try to rival your collection."

delights in the persons and phenomena he "satirizes." Max loved Oxford, the place as well as the University; he relished its traditions and foibles and sillinesses. He is not annoyed, much less angered, by the boat races in Eights' Week. And of course he himself remained always an aesthete of sorts and pre-eminently a dandy; and he was, in his own curious and strange way, hopelessly romantic about women. So *Zuleika* is again a case of mocking what one loves, though mocking is too strong a word here (and more appropriately describes his practice in drawing caricatures). Best for us to fall back on the broad category of the comic novel.

When addressing the question himself, Max, in a prefatory note to a later edition and in the usual unhelpful fashion of authors, wrote that the book was "just a fantasy" but added that "all fantasy should have a solid basis in reality." Thus, side by side with fantastic elements – everything from Max's appointment by Clio, the Muse of History, as historian of Zuleika's calamitous visit, to Zuleika's prodigious sexual magnetism and the mass suicide of all the undergraduates – we find plenty of reality in the book. Oxford itself is real enough and most of the characters have their real side, even Zuleika herself and the hero, the preternaturally talented Duke of Dorset. But the fantastic predominates. When Reggie Turner found parts of the novel too sad, when, as he put it, "the exquisite reality of some of [the Katie Batch scenes] occasionally make the exquisite fantasy of the tragedy too poignant," Max was surprised. "It never occurred to me," he wrote back, "that ... I was giving to the characters anything in the nature of a *real*, as opposed to fantastical-humourous, reality." Not real reality but fantastical-humorous reality. Another real presence in the book is Max himself as narrator, present, as we say with an accepted hyperbole, in every sentence of his narration. He manages, rather more so than even Thackeray's narrator does in *Vanity Fair*, to be always centre stage while telling his story. Remove Max and the book dwindles to nothing, a fact that explains the many failures to make stage plays, musicals, or movies of the novel, by such interested parties as, among others, Wolcott Gibbs, S. N. Behrman, George and Ira Gershwin, and Audrey Hepburn.

Zuleika Dobson is, as the subtitle indicates, "An Oxford Love Story," although a weird one: Zuleika's attractions are such that all males find her irresistible, but, as she is incapable of loving anyone who loves her, all the undergraduates, following the lead of the Duke of Dorset, commit suicide. However, a plot summary of this novel is much more useless than most plot summaries. Better to convey something of the flavour of the book through quoting a few lines. What did Zuleika look like, this young woman who through her wondrous sexual allure has become the toast of two hemispheres?

> Zuleika was not strictly beautiful. Her eyes were a trifle large, and their lashes longer than they need have been. An anarchy of small curls was her chevelure, a dark upland of misrule, every hair asserting its rights over a not discreditable brow. For the rest, her features were not at all original. They seemed to have been derived rather from a gallimaufry of familiar models. From Madame la Marquise de Saint-Ouen came the shapely tilt of the nose. The mouth was a mere replica of Cupid's bow, lacquered scarlet and strung with the littlest pearls. No apple-tree, no wall of peaches, had not been robbed, nor any Tyrian rose-garden, for the glory of Miss Dobson's cheeks. Her neck was imitation-marble. Her hands and feet were of very mean proportions. She had no waist to speak of.

This passage earned Max a certain critical renown when William Empson, in his highly influential *Seven Types of Ambiguity* (1930), used it to exemplify his sixth type of ambiguity, or contradiction. His lengthy discussion is provocative: How *large*, for example, was the *trifle*? Are we to be charmed or appalled? Empson closes his analysis, "I hope I need not apologise, after this example, for including Mr Beerbohm among the poets."

Max's descripton of Zuleika provides me with an occasion to mention his illustrations to his fiction. He disliked illustrated novels. In a theatre review he once wrote, "If I cannot see the characters in a novel, they are not worth seeing. If I can see them, then any other's man's definite presentment of them seems to be an act of impertinence to myself and impiety to the author." Privately, he wrote to his mother, "I hate illustrations to books, as a general principle; and I had a special clause in my contract with Heinemann, by which he agreed not to publish at any time an illustrated editon [of *Zuleika Dobson*] 'without the author's permission.'" But, and always after they had first appeared in print, he drew all his own fictional characters. Of Zuleika he drew half a dozen formal caricatures and made her the subject of one of the frescos he painted in his house. For a new edition of the novel in 1947 he provided Heinemann with a little colour drawing as frontispiece. More importantly, back in 1911, in the two months following the novel's first publication, he drew and pasted into a private copy eighty illustrations, most of them in colour, for his private use, to entertain friends and to "dazzle" Heinemann.

But he stuck to his resolve and would not allow the publisher to have this copy. In what I can only hope was not "an act of impiety to the author" I assisted in bringing out a facsimile edition in colour reproducing the eighty drawings as *The Illustrated Zuleika Dobson* (1985). What did Zuleika look like? It's instructive to compare the descriptive text, above, with Max's graphic images of her, especially with the early frontispiece, reproduced as plate 16. One false step here would be fatal. We wouldn't want a "realistic" or photographic representation of the woman who launched a thousand suicides. This 1911 frontispiece (where she looks a lot *younger* than in the 1947 version) seems nicely to embody and to complement the words of the text. Take a look for yourself. Eyes a trifle large, lashes longer than needed, brow not discreditable. Even granted that first-rate illustrated fiction is rare, and best limited to the comic (Mr Pickwick, not the fallen Little Em'ly), *The Illustrated Zuleika Dobson* will pass muster with most people. But not all. There are those who don't want even Max's drawings of her; they like to be left alone with the text.

Illustrated or not, *Zuleika Dobson* has a devoted following. It is, among the ten books of prose Max published, the one that has been most continuously reprinted, the one title that people who know next to nothing about him are vaguely aware of. It was a book that until recently most university students in Great Britain knew. Far less so in the US. Some twenty years ago at one distinguished urban university, "Zuleika Dobson" was listed as one of fifty random and "trivial" literary identifications that formed part of the Ph.D. qualifying exam. Not one student got it right. In England, certainly at Oxbridge, no student would have failed to identify it.

We are still up against the problem of how to describe *Zuleika Dobson*. I've heard it called a "Wildean" novel. But Wilde had long since departed as a major model for Max's prose. And it would be wrong to say the book is Thackerayan. Of course Wilde and Thackeray and Meredith are *in* there as influences. I grant you *Zuleika Dobson* is unlike the relaxed, straightforward, graceful prose of the later essays; it is something of a throwback to his earlier writing, self-consciously and deliberately artful, brimming with allusions either playful or learned or fictitious. But it is also rather different from his essays on cosmetics and dandyism and George IV. The *tone* is different, unlike the youthful, "smart," paradox-laden essays of his *Yellow Book* period. Incidentally, *Zuleika Dobson* can't be called "quintessential" Max because it is rather unlike his other writings; at the same time it is unmistakably his in that we cannot imagine anyone else writing it.

Shall we settle for "comic fantasy"? E. M. Forster called *Zuleika* "the most consistent achievement of fantasy in our time." What kind of comic fantasy? Admirers say sparkling; debunkers say precious. The best single-sentence criticism? Various critics have written that *Zuleika Dobson* is to the English novel what *The Rape of the Lock* is to English poetry. But the century mark has just passed and Pope's poem and Max's novel are pushed back a century, so to speak, become more rarefied, more and more a special and limited taste. Nothing can be done about the slippage. Of course there is the occasional surprising development in these matters. In 1998 a board of judges (nine men and one woman, A. S. Byatt) for the Modern Library (Random House publishers) selected a list of the "100 best" English language novels of the twentieth century and ranked *Zuleika Dobson* 59th. There was the expected hue and cry in the press about masterpieces left out and worthless stuff included. It's not that I thought the list terribly good. And what would Max have thought of *Lolita* coming in fourth? The whole notion of "ranking" by number is a mug's game, especially as the judges themselves did not rank their choices (except for the top five); the order resulted from a compilation by the Modern Library editors, according to the number of times a novel appeared on the judges' lists. They ranked *Ulysses* number one, and nobody complained though so few have got through the book. (Joyce wrote four books, *Dubliners*, *Portrait of the Artist as a Young Man*, *Ulysses*, and *Finnegans Wake*, and I am sure that Max would have estimated their excellence in precisely that descending order.) Still, ranking is fun if you do well in the ranking, and there is *Zuleika Dobson*, resting just below Edith Wharton's *The Age of Innocence* and above *Of Human Bondage*, *Heart of Darkness*, *House of Mirth*, *A Farewell to Arms*, *Scoop*, *Kim* (!), *A Room with a View*, *Brideshead Revisited*, *Lord Jim*, and *The Old Wives' Tale*, to name only those by Max's contemporaries and, always excepting Kipling, friends. Some people, as reported in the press – including, sadly, one of the judges, William Styron – had the temerity to single out *Zuleika Dobson* as one of the list's many errors, even a blatant one, "a toothless pretender" (along with Tarkington's *The Magnificent Ambersons*, the latter having squeaked in as number 100). You could also argue how surprising it was that the jury had Max in there at all, that they got this one right.

CHAPTER SIXTEEN

A Dreadful Talent

In October 1912, two years into Max's Rapallo "retirement," he published *A Christmas Garland*. The book was a singular achievement, singular in the sense that nothing else quite like it exists. There are better comic novels than *Zuleika Dobson*; there are probably ghostly comic short stories equal to those in *Seven Men*, though I for one am unfamiliar with them; and there have been many excellent collections of personal essays. But there is no book of parodies in English comparable to *A Christmas Garland*. The closest may be Thackeray, once again (but no one these these days reads his *Novels by Eminent Hands* or even the novelists Thackeray parodied). One phenomenon that makes Max's parodies so distinctive is his ability not merely to imitate both the manner and the matter of his parodied authors but also to remain himself discernibly present in the parodies. Some remarks of Filson Young, in a review of *A Christmas Garland* on its first appearance, may be helpful here. After saying that Max has "not so much copied his models as extended them," Young insists that Max's "delicate exaggerations" reveal not only weaknesses but "forces" in his victims' writings:

> It is as though, instead of elaborately describing the clothes worn by his subjects, Max had himself put on each suit in turn, strutted or lounged awhile in the manner of each, and spoken thoughts like theirs in a telling imitation of their tones. And behind these solemn parodies of Kipling, Henry James, Wells, Meredith and so forth lurks the shadow of Max himself, making it quite plain to you in what estimation each is held and mocking with a merciful humour the mannerisms of them all.

This, it seems to me, is just right. Behind the burlesques of James and Meredith, however amusing, however cruel, you find admiration, even reverence; behind the parody of Wells, you detect disagreement, distaste; behind the parody of Benson, you sense bemusement; behind the parody of Kipling, you get the feeling of genuine dislike. All are the result of what Max called his "rather dreadful little talent" for parody.

I am well aware that formal parody (as different from a kind of broad allusiveness) is a "problematic" genre and not everybody's favourite. You can discount Max's kind of parody for various reasons: it is derivative and accordingly can be seen as a second-hand if not second-rate, some say parasitic, undertaking; and it has behind it, or so many people think, a hostile or at least unfriendly impulse, which can be unpleasant. Then, too, in many cases parody becomes quickly dated: when no one knows or cares about the writers being parodied, the whole point is lost. Moreover, some readers find – a less frequent problem – that parody "spoils" their favourite authors. Finally, in Max's case, his strategy of uniting his seventeen sketches by a Christmas theme is off-putting for some people (even though the Christmas connection is often quite oblique).

But I don't think parody should be so readily depreciated. It has, after all, a noble lineage going back at least to Aristophanes. As to the objection from hostility, I am not convinced. (The hostility argument works somewhat better with caricature than it does with literary parody.) Max admired most of the writings he parodied; he positively adored the prose of Henry James; and he placed Meredith, Bennett, and Galsworthy in the first rank of writers of his time. As he never tired of saying, he mocked what he loved. In fact he really disliked the work of only four of his seventeen authors: he considered Shaw and Kipling "geniuses" who prostituted their talents; he thought Wells's style undistinguished, and he regarded A. C. Benson as utterly banal. All the others he prized, in spite of reservations, especially about what used to be called the "content" of their writings – Hilaire Belloc's Roman Catholic braggadocio ("Mr Belloc knows God's point of view"), for example, or Hardy's pessimism (an overemphasis on "the Bad, the Ugly, and the False"). So the hostile impulse argument falls to the ground, for the most part; and, even in cases where it is valid, who cares? A little hostility, visited on the deserving mediocre and even on the honoured great, is not misplaced. The one writer whose work he truly detested on all counts, Hall Caine, is not among the authors parodied.

The other problem with parody, the necessity of knowing the author parodied, is inescapable. While many people are conversant with James, Shaw, Hardy, Conrad, and Kipling, few people today actually read, or read much of, Meredith, Wells, Bennett, or Galsworthy; and most people know nothing at all of A. C. Benson, G. S. Street, or Maurice Hewlett. No doubt about it, parodies of lesser knowns and unknowns are nowhere near as enjoyable as those of writers we know. But, at times, even those of obscure writers can be palatable in their comic implications. Let's look at the George Moore parody.

Moore came from a well-to-do Irish family, the Moores of Moore Park, County Mayo (they claimed descent from St Thomas More). He was once widely known as a writer (the "English Zola") and as an eccentric and was the author of *A Modern Lover, A Mummer's Wife, Esther Waters*, other novels, plays, essays, criticism, and, as Max put it, "many autobiographies." The *Christmas Garland* parody reflects in its few pages much of what Max found intriguing in Moore: the enthusiasms, the meandering thought, the lack of logic, the factual gaffes, the constant and frank admiration for women, the all-absorbing love of things French (picked up during a decade-long residence in Paris during his twenties), his championing of the French Impressionist painters, the innocent, uninstructed, unselfconscious appropriation of other writers' material, the disillusionment with the Irish language as a vehicle for literature. (I grant that giving even this much background is cheating.) Max's parody, a critical essay called "Dickens," begins, not of course with Dickens, but with "I had often wondered why when people talked to me of Tintoretto I always found myself thinking of Turgéneff . . . for at first sight nothing can be more far apart than the Slav mind and the Flemish." Arriving eventually at his subject, Moore asserts boldly, "There never was a writer except Dickens," even though, distracted by his worship of Balzac, Zola, Yeats, "*et tous ces autres*," he has so far read but one chapter in Dickens, the Dingley Dell Christmas scene from *Pickwick Papers*:

> Christmas – I see it now – is the only moment in which men and women are really alive, are really worth writing about. At other seasons they do not exist for the purpose of art. I spit on all seasons except Christmas.

And Dickens's Mr Wardell is "better than all Balzac's figures rolled into one. . . . Balzac wrote many books. . . . One knows that he used to write for fifteen hours at a stretch, gulping down coffee all the while. But it does not follow that the coffee was good, nor does it follow that what he wrote was good. The *Comédie Humaine* is all chicory." But the discussion of Dickens's Christmas chapter inevitably settles down to a flight of fancy about Arabella: "only Manet could have stated the slope of the thighs of the girl"; and presently, "Strange thoughts of her surge up vaguely in me as I watch her – thoughts that I cannot express in English. . . . Elle est plus vieille que les roches . . ." – seven lines in French lifted word for word from Pater (another Moore enthusiasm), the famous lines about the Mona Lisa from *Renaissance Studies*. But the plagiarized apotheosis is interrupted by the exclamation that he cannot express his thoughts even in French because, like all European languages, French is a "stale language," though "the stalest of them all is Erse." There follows a sudden decision to go to Mexico, "buy a Mexican grammar," and there await the new artistic dawn.

Let's move to Henry James, whom everyone is supposed to know. James was Max's favourite novelist, in spite of the fact that Max sometimes complained, like everyone else, of the difficulties of James's later, more convoluted style. The parody of that late style, "The Mote in the Middle Distance," an account of two children, Keith and Eva Tantalus, debating whether to "peer" into their Christmas stockings, has attained classic status and must be the most anthologized parody in the language. Any passage taken at random is redolent of the Master. Listen to the opening lines:

> It was with the sense of a, for him, very memorable something that he peered now into the immediate future, and tried, not without compunction, to take that period up where he had, prospectively, left it. But just where the deuce *had* he left it? The consciousness of dubiety was, for our friend, not, this morning, quite yet clean-cut enough to outline the figures on what she had called his "horizon," between which and himself the twilight was indeed of a quality somewhat intimidating. He had run up, in the course of time, against a good number of "teasers;" and the function of teasing them back – of, as it were, giving them, every now and then, "what for" – was in him so much a habit that he would have been at a loss had there been, on the face of it, nothing to lose. Oh, he always had offered rewards, of course – had ever so liberally pasted the windows of his soul with staring appeals, minute descriptions, promises that knew no bounds. But the actual recovery of the article – the business of drawing and crossing the cheque, blotched though this were with tears of joy – had blankly appeared to him rather in the light of a sacrilege, casting, he sometimes felt, a palpable chill on the fervour of the next quest. It was just this fervour that was threatened as, raising himself on his elbow, he stared at the foot of his bed. ...

Critic John Felstiner, seeing Keith and Eva as a burlesque of Merton Densher and Kate Croy in the final scene of *The Wings of the Dove*, discovers here all of James' late style: "the broken sentences, roundabout simplicities, syntactical quibbles, colloquialisms made genteel by inverted commas, italics for delicate intonation, stunning double negatives, accumulated homely adjectives, abruptly placed, vague adverbs, banal metaphors worried and reworried, the narrator's unsettling glances into the future and his intimacy with 'our friend' Keith, the exasperating, magnified scruples, and, at last, the vibrant moral renunciation by Keith and Eva – 'One doesn't violate the shrine – pick the pearl from the shell!' "

What did Henry James think of the parody? We know that James, a friend but not an intimate of Max's, asked Edmund Gosse to tell Max that he read it with "wonder and delight"; he called *A Christmas Garland* "the most intelligent [book] that has been produced in England for many a long day"; James thought the parodies so good that none of the writers satirized in *A Christmas Garland* could now write "without incurring the reproach of somewhat ineffectively imitating" Max. James expressed the same views to Sydney Waterlow, calling the book "a little masterpiece," and, although deploring the cruelty of some of the attacks, declared himself delighted with the parody of himself, saying that now whenever he wrote he felt he was "parodying himself." High praise.

James was not the only one who enjoyed his own parody. Galsworthy was much taken with Max's treatment of "scents" in the parody "Endeavour"; and he found it uncanny that the husband and wife in the story, members of the Feathered Friends League, crusaders against the feeding of wild birds by private "doles" and thus meddling in what ought to be done collectively by the State, have a terrible moment of doubt as to whether their reforming labours are doing any good. But the husband argues that their very uncertainty makes their efforts nobler – "Because it takes more out of us." Galsworthy, an inveterate activist reformer in nearly every liberal cause – woman's suffrage, minimum wages, and, especially, the treatment of animals – evidently decided that the sentence "Because it takes more out of us" perfectly bespoke his own mind, and he wrote and asked Max where he got it. Max answered, "I think I may claim that I 'divined' it. I don't think it is in any of your books; and I don't think you ever said it to me: you would have adjudged me too frivolous for such a confidence. I must have read it in your eyes – particularly in the unmonocled eye!" Galsworthy wrote back that he regarded Max as the West's "nearest approach to the Yogi."

Edmund Gosse was happy to be parodied; the author of nearly a hundred books (one of which survives, *Father and Son*, an autobiographical account

of his childhood and youth with a fanatically Calvinistic parent), he specialized in the "anecdotal history" of authors in which he posed as an innocent go-between among the famous. This gave Max the idea for "A
Recollection" in which Gosse, on a visit to Venice, comes across his idol,
Henrik Ibsen, whom he championed and translated.* As Gosse's friend
Robert Browning was also in Venice, Gosse introduces the two great men
to each other. Their meeting, on Christmas Day 1878, is nearly cata-
strophic. Neither had heard of the other, and when Ibsen says that no
woman can be a great poet, Gosse has to save the situation by babbling a
mistranslation: "Imagination reels at the effect this would have had on the
recipient of 'Sonnets from the Portuguese.'" Gosse's only complaint about
the parody was that "I ... will never be able to draw another portrait without calling down upon me the sneer, 'Not half so amusing as your dinner
with Ibsen and Browning!'"

Joseph Conrad was also pleased with his parody. Public acceptance had
come slowly to him, and in 1923 he wrote, "I have lived long enough to see
[his story "The Lagoon"] most agreeably guyed by Mr Max Beerbohm ...
where I found myself in very good company. I was immensely gratified. I
began to believe in my public existence."

Shaw, we may presume, enjoyed his. He never dodged attention, and he
was also a very good sport.

The only persons on record as disturbed by the parodies of themselves were
A. C. Benson and, of course, Kipling. Arthur Christopher Benson, Master of
Magdalene College, Cambridge, and man of letters, is today the least remembered of Max's subjects. Benson's most popular works were sentimental, self-
indulgent, meandering essays; an apt word for them would surely be *harmless*,
something Max captures in his title, "Out of Harm's Way." In his essays and
in the parody Benson seems a kind of apostle of the self-evident; moreover, if
at any time he makes a statement of the slightest force, he immediately qual-
ifies it. The reviewer for the *Spectator* in 1912 judged the Benson parody the
best piece in *A Christmas Garland*. Times change. (Max drew only one caricature of Benson, and it has disappeared, but its caption survives: "Mr Arthur
Christopher Benson vowing eternal fidelity to the obvious.") It's also easy to

---

* William Archer, Gosse's rival in introducing Ibsen to English audiences, challenged his trans-
lations, giving as evidence Gosse's rendering of a passage Archer knew to mean "distinguished
himself on the battlefield" as "always voted right at elections."

see why Kipling was offended. "P.C., X, 36" features a crude policeman arresting and kicking Santa Claus, whom he has caught emerging from a chimney, while the Kiplingesque narrator – nastier, more sadistic than the policeman – dances about the two shrieking, "Frog's-march him! For the love of heaven, frog's-march him!" It is the cruellest thing Max ever wrote.

The original reviewers of *A Christmas Garland* could not agree on which of the parodies were the most successful. But they concurred, with marvellous unanimity, that Max had not merely captured the styles or "externals" of his subjects, but had unbared "their brains and hearts"; he "not only *sounds* like them but actually comes to *look* like them"; he seemed to have obtained "temporary loans of their very minds"; he has "caught the very colour and cast of their minds, and from . . . their attitude to life and letters, he has worked outwards to the perfect jest." Each reader will have a favourite parody, a choice dictated, most likely, by how well he or she knows that author. For Jamesians it will be "The Mote." For disciples of Wells, it will be "Perkins and Mankind." For Kipling admirers, though, it will not be "P.C., X, 36."

Let's try a little quiz (answers overleaf*). See if, from the opening line or two, you can divine the writer being parodied:

1.

> In the heart of insular Cosmos, remote by some scores of leagues of Hodge-trod arable or pastoral, not more than a snuff-pinch for gaping tourist nostrils accustomed to inhalation of prairie winds, but enough for perspective, from those marginal sands, trident-scraped, we are to fancy, by a helmeted Dame Abstract familiarly profiled on discs of current bronze – price of a loaf for humbler maws disdainful of Gallic side-dishes for the titillation of choicer palates – stands Clashthought Park, a house of some pretension, mentioned at Runnymede, with the spreading exception of wings given to it in later times by Daedalean masters not to be baulked of billiards or traps for Terpsichore, and owned for unbroken generations by a healthy line of procreant Clashthoughts, to the undoing of collateral branches eager for the birth of a female.

Hint: He has been called the only English novelist who needs to be translated into English. David Garnett said that another line from the same parody, "Suspicion slid down the banisters of her mind, trailing a blue ribbon," amounted to the final word on his style. G. M. Trevelyan claimed in 1952 that this parody was "still the cleverest . . . in all literature."

2.

> This has been composed from a scenario thrust on me by some one else. My philosophy of life saves me from sense of responsibility for any of my writings; but I venture to hold myself specially irresponsible for this one.

Hint: These two lines constitute in their entirety an author's note at the beginning of a Sequel to his poem. Note the misused word? T. S. Eliot said this man's prose style touched the sublime without passing through the stage of good.

No hints on the next three:

3.

> When a public man lays his hand on his heart and declares that his conduct needs no apology, the audience hastens to put up its umbrellas against the particularly severe downpour of apologies in store for it. I won't give the customary warning. My conduct shrieks aloud for apology, and you are in for a thorough drenching.
>
> Flatly, I stole this play. . . . The reason lies in that bland, unalterable resolve to shirk honest work, by which you recognize the artist as surely as you recognise the leopard by his spots. In so far as I am an artist, I am a loafer.

4.

> The hut in which slept the white man was on a clearing between the forest and the river. Silence, the silence murmurous and unquiet of a tropical night, brooded over the hut that, baked through by the sun, sweated a vapour beneath the cynical light of the stars.

5.

> I had spent Christmas Eve at the Club listening to a grand pow-wow between certain of the choicer sons of Adam.

As for parody spoiling a writer for certain readers, this is a risk that I think we can afford to take.

* 1. Meredith; 2. Hardy; 3. Shaw; 4. Conrad; 5. Kipling.

CHAPTER SEVENTEEN

Inspired Lunacy

In a famous anecdote, possibly even true, James Joyce, when asked what he did during the Great War, replied, "I wrote *Ulysses*." Max Beerbohm could have replied, I drew *Rossetti and His Circle*. At the beginning of the war, August 1914, he stayed on in Rapallo in hopes of a short duration. Italy was of course an ally. The war brought out a sense of patriotism in Max that almost surprises us. To Reggie he wrote, "What a world! What a period we have been born into! It is all very epical and all that; but the horror and sadness and absurdity of it! ... Dear England has behaved with all the fineness one expects of her ... the *spirit* of England is beautiful. Ever since I have lived away from England I have been growing more and more fond and proud of England as an *idea*. As such, there never has been or will be anything to touch her." He felt, as do many artists, especially comic artists, at a loss as to what to do during time of war. He wrote to Brown and Phillips and cancelled an exhibition scheduled for April: "My caricatures, exhibited while England is in the throes of a life-and-death struggle, would not merely fall flat: they would be an offence against decency. ... Imagine a nation being called on, in the midst of a whole world's tragedy of suffering and horror, to enjoy my little jokes about Mr Hall Caine and Sir Gilbert Parker and Mr Bonar Law and Mr Sidney Webb and other people whose foibles, in time of peace, are very good fun, but whose very existence is forgotten in time of war. The idea is inconceivable." Even for many months after peace is eventually declared, he tells Brown, his drawings will have to be kept locked up in a drawer. (He would not have another exhibition until 1921.) When it became apparent that peace would not come quickly, Max and Florence, in the spring of 1915, returned to England. He wanted, he said, to be in England during her hour of need; he wanted to be "where English is spoken and English thoughts and feelings expressed." Once there, he even volunteered for clerical war work. He was turned down. And he himself turned down the suggestion that he draw war propaganda cartoons: whatever his sympathies and his new-found patriotism, he would not work at anything he was not cut out for.

Over the next few years Max and Florence lived at Will Rothenstein's farm at Far Oakridge, Gloucestershire. At first they stayed in the Rothensteins' house, then in a cottage nearby, although they came over to the house for lunch and dinner every day. (Rothenstein's wife Alice was the daughter of W. J. Knewsteb, Rossetti's painting assistant in his early Cheyne Walk days.) Rothenstein recalled that Max never had any "country clothes" but came always nattily dressed, wearing spats and gloves and carrying an elegant walking cane. At his cottage, Max worked assiduously at both writing and drawing by turning away from the depressing current scene to the "recent past." He explained, "Somehow one doesn't feel sentimental about a period in which oneself has footed it. It is the period that one *didn't* quite know, the period just before oneself, the period of which in earliest days one knew the actual survivors, that lays a really strong hold on one's heart. The magic of the past for me begins at the 'eighties and stretches as far as the 'sixties." For Max, the key figure of this period was Dante Gabriel Rossetti, who shone, Max wrote, "with the ambiguous light of a red torch somewhere in a dense fog." And Rossetti was always surrounded by interesting, talented, people – artists, writers, models, mistresses, adventurers, hangers-on. They included Millais, Hunt, Burne-Jones, Whistler, Morris, Ruskin, Browning, Tennyson, Swinburne, Carlyle, Christina Rossetti, Elizabeth Siddal, Fanny Cornforth, Jane Morris, and two dozen more. The whole lot struck him as eccentric, their peculiarities constituting what he called a "silver thread of lunacy running through the rich golden fabric of 16 Cheyne Walk." In all he produced twenty-three Rossetti drawings, done in a style slightly less distorting than the already softened and less "savage" manner that had become customary with him. These drawings were also distinctive in having more detailed backgrounds and more complete colouring than any of his other work; and they would come to constitute, for many people, his highest accomplishment in caricature.

How to describe the feelings *Rossetti and His Circle*, this "reconstruction of a period," arouses in its enthusiasts? Here is a somewhat convoluted formula: for people familiar with Rossetti's life and work and knowing something of his friends and satellites, there is no more enlightening or entertaining complement to the works and to the memoirs and biographies than this collection of caricatures. I doubt that any artistic coterie has ever been favoured with the equivalent of Max's book. It is true that Max's temperament and the very nature of his mocking-what-one-loves caricature demanded that he skirt the tragic and the unseemly in Rossetti's career: he must avoid, for example, the suicide of his wife, or his eventual alienation from almost all of his earlier friends. But everything else is here. Sexual commentary is understandably muted and subtle, but animated: Rossetti's compulsive "interest" in women; Fanny Cornforth's ambiguous position as "housekeeper," model, and mistress; his passion for Jane Morris, wife of one of his best friends, whose presence is insinuated only in stylized paintings hanging on the walls at 16 Cheyne Walk; Swinburne's sado-masochism; Ruskin's undeveloped sexuality. The rest is more straightforward: Rossetti's decade-long "courtship" of Lizzie Siddal; Millais's departure from his early Pre-Raphaelite painting; the fiasco of Rossetti's Oxford Union murals (painted on a scarcely dry plaster with the result that what Ruskin called "the finest piece of colour in the world" pretty much disappeared); Coventry Patmore (the "Angel in the House" poet) preaching domesticity to the drearily married Rossetti and Lizzie; Morris and Burne-Jones settled on their colossally decorated settle in Red Lion Square; Ruskin being forced to meet Fanny Cornforth; "Jimmy" Whistler explaining blue china to a doubtful Carlyle; Swinburne reading his sensational "Anactoria" to Rossetti and his brother; Rossetti pleading with his sister not to dress like a pew opener; and much more. There are people who claim – and they may well be right – that some of the scenes depicted are apocryphal: that the young John Morley did not introduce J. S. Mill to Rossetti in hope of having the artist supply colour illustrations to Mill's *Subjection of Women*; that Mrs Tennyson did not ask the sculptor Thomas Woolner, as he was modelling his famous bust of Tennyson, when he would begin on the halo. The literal truth of incident here is unimportant. Max is getting at, as they say, poetic truth. One of Rossetti's nieces wrote of *Rossetti and His Circle* that "no person living within [the Pre-Raphaelite] circle had given so accurate a picture of its physical and spiritual composition."

Plenty of background material to the individual drawings of *Rossetti and His Circle* is available, but without the drawings to hand, it's of little use. I'll limit myself to supplementing the one Rossetti caricature that is reproduced here, as plate 19. The title "Quis Custodiet Ipsum Custodem?" is adapted from Juvenal: "Who will guard the guard himself?" The time is 1881, a year before Rossetti's death. The two faithful guardians over the ailing painter/poet are Theodore Watts, solicitor-turned-critic and custodian also of Swinburne; and Frederick Shields, painter and close friend. The guardian they are guarding against is none other than Hall Caine. Two years earlier, while apprenticed to a Liverpool architect, he had written to Rossetti, telling of a lecture in which he had defended him. Encouraged by friendly letters from Rossetti, Caine visited Cheyne Walk in 1880, and by 1881 he was invited to live in the house as a companion and secretary. For his services he received bed and board and the thrill of entry into Rossetti's life. Watts and Shields, constant for some years in attendance on their hero, have their doubts about newcomer Caine. Watts is telling him, "You *must* not and *shall* not read any more of your literary efforts to our friend. They are too – what shall I say? – too luridly arresting, and are the allies of insomnia." Caine's "luridly arresting" novels were of a later date. But immediately after Rossetti's death Caine rushed into print with his *Recollections of Dante Gabriel Rossetti*, a self-serving book Max detested. Caine went on to become a fabulously successful novelist and playwright, whom Max persecuted in articles and caricatures. (He was hardly alone in his feelings about Hall Caine. Oscar Wilde said that in some gatherings you could get a laugh simply by saying out loud the two words "Hall Caine.")

The round mirror on Rossetti's wall next to the "arresting" Rossetti paintings of Jane Morris is part of the record. When Treffry Dunn, Rossetti's painting assistant, first visited Cheyne Walk and was ushered into the sitting room, "mirrors of all shapes, sizes and designs, lined the walls, so that whichever way I gazed I saw myself looking at myself." William Michael Rossetti wrote that his brother "had a particular liking for convex round-shaped mirrors." Max, on reading these two witnesses, had been heartened, indeed inspired. For he himself owned a convex mirror, originally purchased by his father at the Paris Exhibition of 1867; it was a part of Max's life from his nursery days until his death. As a boy this mirror fascinated him: "I began to think of all it had seen since my father bought it ... and when I reached the age of twenty-one – the age of reminiscence, of *seasoned* reminiscence – I began to see this mirror as a collaborator, with memories of its own, a *temps perdu* of its own. I began to write a novel about it, an autobiographical novel called *The Mirror of the Past.*"

Max started writing this book, his second novel, in the months immediately prior to his return to England in 1915. *The Mirror*, like all his fictions, was a blend of fantasy and fact. It is the story of Sylvester Herringham, who had lived for many years near Rossetti in Cheyne Walk, Chelsea. In 1896 Herringham meets Max and shows him a most remarkable mirror. This convex mirror had been "transformed" in 1889 by Herringham, an amateur scientist, so that it reflects images of what took place in his drawing room years ago. By the time Max meets Herringham, the mirror is showing, in reverse chronological order, goings-on in 1882. The next year it will reflect 1881, and so on. Max visits Herringham regularly, for some fifteen years, watching Herringham's "Monday Evenings" and listening to the old man's tales of Rossetti and his friends. Herringham dies in 1909, leaving the mirror to Max. When Max moves to Italy, he takes the mirror with him and continues to watch its revelations.

Eventually, Max gave up on the novel. "Scientific" fiction, he decided, was not his forte, and the thing got "too complicated." It may well be that *Rossetti and His Circle* substituted for the novel. Certainly the Rossetti caricatures and the unfinished novel derive from the same stimulus. The drawings could have been illustrations to the novel, which itself seems an incomplete prose version of *Rossetti and His Circle*. In his 1922 prefatory Note to *Rossetti and His Circle* Max acknowledges that he never set eyes on Rossetti or most of his friends, and that the few he did meet he saw only in their old age. Hence, Max continues, he fell back on old drawings, paintings, and photographs; he has also read about Rossetti and his friends in various memoirs and biographies. But these were not his only sources: "I have had another and surer aid, of the most curious kind imaginable. And some day I will tell you all about it, if you would care to hear." Max's "surer aid" was Herringham's mirror. (In 1955, one year before his death, Max salvaged some of the material from *The Mirror of the Past* – the messy manuscript had been stored in his "garage" at the Villino – for a radio broadcast called "Hethway Speaking." Here, changing Herringham's name to Hethway and discarding the device of the mirror, he related some of the stories Herringham had told him about Rossetti and his friends.)

Herringham may be a "fictional" character, but his judgements and his stories about Rossetti and his friends are sound, based in fact, completely in character, hardly more fictional than the memoirs of actual members of the circle. Herringham's views are usually Max's. The contrast Herringham drew between Carlyle and Ruskin is typical Max: teaching or preaching geniuses always have messages "characteristic of the messengers," of whom two kinds are discernible, "the vain ones who want us to be just like themselves; and the modest ones who would have us be just what they are not. ... Mr Carlyle, for all his faults of temper, was one of the modest kind, and Mr Ruskin – generous and usually angelic though he was – was one of the vain. Mr Carlyle, being eloquent, and a peasant, and always ailing, desiderated a race of strong silent aristocrats; and dear Mr Ruskin despaired of a world in which not everybody admired Giotto and Turner and Miss Kate Greenaway as much as he." Similarly Herringham's words on Tennyson and Browning sound altogether like Max:

> They were as unlike their own work as they were unlike each other. . . . The smoother Tennyson's verse became, the more rugged and tangled was he to look at. The more tangled and rugged Browning made his poetry, the more surely would anyone meeting him for the first time have taken him for a banker, or a fashionable physician. The greater the exactions he made, as he grew older, on the intellect and the patience of his readers, the easier was it to understand what he said – and even to foretell what he *would* say – at a dinner-table. And Tennyson's manners – ah, they were the very least of all adapted to courtly circles at the very time when he had finally purged his art of anything that might conceivably vex the ghost of the Prince Consort.

This has been a rather long gloss on a single Rossetti drawing. My effort has been, not to explain the joke, but to show how these drawings are richer when seen in their very considerable contexts.

As things turned out, Max was exhibited during the war, but not by his own doing. The Rossetti drawings were purchased by Mrs Charles Hunter, widow of an immensely wealthy coal magnate and hostess to many artists and writers. In November 1917 she lent fifteen of the drawings to the Grosvenor Gallery for its Modern Loan Exhibition. Of course the Rossetti drawings were not his usual comic commentary on living men, the kind of thing he had judged almost indecent during time of war. All his subjects (except for Edmund Gosse, John Morley, and Hall Caine) were historical figures, long dead. The Grosvenor Exhibition was an important showing of modern art, and included English and American painters whom Max loved to caricature: Steer, Conder, Sickert, Augustus John, Sargent, Whistler, Tonks; but also Blanche, Degas, Rodin, Fantin-Latour, Corot. Max must have been pleased at being the only caricaturist in the company.

In September 1921, the Leicester Galleries, which had acquired the drawings, exhibited all twenty-three, along with drawings and paintings by the Pre-Raphaelites and others, whereupon they were purchased for 800 guineas by Hugh Walpole, an insatiable collector of art.* In 1923 Walpole lent the series to the Tate Gallery for an exhibition called "Paintings and Drawings of the 1860 Period." While the Pre-Raphaelites could hardly have been said to be in vogue at the time, the exhibition, which included 334 works by Rossetti, Millais, Burne-Jones, Arthur Hughes, Elizabeth Siddal, Holman Hunt, Frederick Sandys, George Boyce, and others, got good press. As in the Grosvenor Gallery and Leicester Galleries exhibitions earlier, Max was again the only caricaturist to be represented.

The series was published as *Rossetti and His Circle* by William Heinemann in September 1922. It was more properly a book than Max's other collections of caricatures because of its unity of theme, its story-line, and the indispensable legends. *The Times* said, "Each [drawing] is worth a whole volume of sermons on ideals in art and life." Herbert Gorman in the *New York Times* wrote, optimistically, "Here is the final criticism of the Pre-Raphaelite Brotherhood."

---

*In 1938, Walpole told John Rothenstein, Director of the Tate, that after his death Rothenstein could select for the Tate fourteen paintings from Walpole's collection. What about Max's twenty-three Rossetti drawings, already on loan to the Gallery? "Oh, count them as one item," said Walpole. And thus the *Rossetti and His Circle* caricatures (along with oils by Renoir, Forain, Steer, Sickert, John, Tissot, Ford Madox Brown, drawings by Blake and John, and a watercolour by Cézanne) became, in 1941, the property of the nation.

CHAPTER EIGHTEEN

Memories

On 3 June 1997 there gathered in the great Reading Room of the British Museum some one hundred people, masquerading as scholars but in fact devotees of Max Beerbohm. For decades people had promised themselves they would be in the British Museum on that day. I was privileged to be there myself. We were anxiously awaiting the appearance or, among the doubters, the non-appearance, of the 1890s decadent poet Enoch Soames. It was exactly a hundred years since Soames had made his fatal pact. The reading world had known of the date's significance since 1916, when Max's account of Soames was first published in the *Century* magazine. No short piece in the language – I shall not call it a story, for Max always said it was a "Memory" – has ever created such expectancy and curiosity. In early 1997 articles appeared in *The Times*, the *Evening Standard*, the *Daily Telegraph*, the *TLS*, and the *Sunday Times* about the possible appearance of Enoch Soames. The forgathered crowd were not exactly disappointed, though reactions were mixed. It is all very complicated.

But this, as the biographers say, is to anticipate. The British Museum event is eighty years ahead of where we were in Max's life, the years of the First World War. Justifiable as it is to make *Rossetti and His Circle* the crowning accomplishment of these years, an equally compelling argument can be made for the prose at this time, most notably *Seven Men* (1919). This book comprises autobiographical reminiscences about six different men,* including Soames, all of them seen interacting with Max, the seventh man of the title. We are given depictions of Max himself in various roles and places. In "Enoch Soames" we find his 1890s bohemian *Yellow Book* period; in "A. V. Laider" we have Max a convalescent at an English seaside inn; in "James Pethel" we touch his August holiday world at Dieppe; in "Hilary Maltby and

---

* A later edition (1950) was called *Seven Men and Two Others* because it included an additional chapter "Felix Argallo and Walter Ledgett"(written 1927).

Stephen Braxton" we see him as visitor to the country houses of the rich and powerful; in "Savonarola Brown" we revisit his days as drama critic.

These memoirs – with the possible exception of "Enoch Soames" – cannot be summarized to any advantage. I know I said the same thing of *Zuleika Dobson,* but it is even more true of these tales. Take "A. V. Laider," for example. It does present a rather agreeable example of what is supposed to be an English trait, part of the so-called national character, a peculiarity that was a definite feature of Max's own personality, namely the desire for privacy, the keeping of strangers at arm's length. In this "Memory," Max tells how, staying at a seaside hostel in February, recovering from influenza, he keeps to himself, as does the one other guest in the place, the A. V. Laider of the title. Max is gratified to find that the man "evidently wasn't going to spoil the fun by engaging me in conversation. . . . a decently unsociable man, anxious to be left alone." If, in the dining room, their eyes met, the two men would instantly avert their gaze:

> Anywhere but in England it would be impossible for two solitary men, reduced by influenza, to spend five or six days in the same hostel and not exchange a single word. This is one of the charms of England. Had Laider and I been born and bred in any other land we should have become acquainted before the end of our first evening in the small smoking-room, and found ourselves irrevocably committed to go on talking to each other throughout the rest of the visit. We might, it is true, have happened to like each other more than any one we had ever met. This off-chance may have occurred to us both. But it counted for nothing as against the certain surrender of quietude and liberty. We slightly bowed to each other as we entered or left the dining-room or smoking-room, and as we met on the widespread sands or in the shop that had a small and faded circulating library. That was all. Our mutual aloofness was a positive bond between us.

Then on the last evening, quite by unexpected circumstance, when Laider realizes he is reading a magazine Max had brought into the smoking-room, and, with neither party to blame, the "ice was broken" and the two men actually talk. This is the setting. What is it *about?* Well, they begin speaking about a correspondence raging in the weekly periodical that had occasioned their speaking to each other. Faith and Reason was the subject, and Max especially liked the latest entry, from "A Melbourne Man," dismissing all previous correspondents as groping in the dark and settling the whole controversy with a sharp flash: "Reason is faith, faith reason – that is all we know on earth and all we need to know." How nice, Max tells Laider, to "read anything that meant nothing whatsoever." Laider takes the letter more seriously, and their conversation moves on to belief in palmistry. But the story is not really about faith and reason or palmistry or story telling or improvisation or conscience or will-power or the difficulty of getting at what really happened. Rather it provides an occasion for Max's late, effortless prose style to play around these themes. Here, if anywhere, content is style, style content – and that is all we need to know.

"Enoch Soames" is, after *Zuleika Dobson*, the most popular item in the Beerbohm canon; some people, myself included, think it likely to outlast *Zuleika*. The story-line of "Enoch Soames" has an interest in its own right. The opening is as follows:

> When a book about the literature of the eighteen-nineties was given by Mr Holbrook Jackson to the world, I looked eagerly in the index for SOAMES, ENOCH. I feared he would not be there. He was not there. But everybody else was. Many writers whom I had quite forgotten, or remembered but faintly, lived again for me, they and their work, in Mr Holbrook Jackson's pages. The book was as thorough as it was brilliantly written. And thus the omission found by me was an all the deadlier record of poor Soames' failure to impress himself on his decade.

Here we have a real person, Max Beerbohm, writing in his own name, looking in the index of a real book, Holbrook Jackson's *The Eighteen Nineties* (1913), and finding that, actually, Soames is not there. He is not there. I have checked, of course. So Max, filling in the gap in the record, sets down his own recollections of Soames, a little-known, frustrated, unappreciated, pretentious poet of those bygone days, a self-styled Catholic diabolist decadent. Max, Oxford undergraduate, first meets him – where else? – at the Café Royal, through the offices of – whom else? – Will Rothenstein, in October 1893:

> [Soames] was a stooping, shambling person, rather tall, very pale, with longish and brownish hair. He had a thin vague beard – or rather, he had a chin on which a large number of hairs weakly curled and clustered to cover its retreat. He was an odd-looking person; but in the 'nineties odd apparitions were more frequent, I think, than they are now. The young

writers of that era – and I was sure this man was a writer – strove earnestly to be distinct in aspect. This man had striven unsuccessfully. He wore a soft black hat of clerical kind but of Bohemian intention, and a grey water-proof cape which, perhaps because it was waterproof, failed to be roman-tic. I decided that "dim" was the *mot juste* for him.

But this Soames had written a book! *Negations* it was called. "Not to buy a book," Max says, "of which I had met the author face to face would have been for me in those days an impossible act of self-denial," and on returning to Oxford he bought a copy. He was never able to say what it was about. The preface, with lines such as "Life is web, and therein nor warp nor woof is, but web only" offered no hint. In the book itself there was a story about a midinette apparently about to murder a mannequin; and a dialogue – "lack-ing, I rather felt, in 'snap' " – between Pan and St Ursula. Was the fault with Soames or with Max? He gives Soames the benefit of the doubt. After all, Max had read Mallarmé's *L'Après-midi d'un Faune* "without extracting a glimmer of meaning." A little later, Max buys Soames's next book, a slim volume of poetry called *Fungoids*, a title suggestive of "strange growths, natural and wild; yet exquisite, and many-hued, and full of poisons." Max quotes the poem "To a Young Woman":

> *Thou art, who has not been!*
>   Pale tunes irresolute
>   And traceries of old sounds
>   Blown from a rotted flute
> Mingle with noise of cymbals rouged with rust,
> Nor not strange forms and epicene
>   Lie bleeding in the dust,
>   Being wounded with old wounds. ...
> *Thou has not been nor art!*

Max thought this, in spite of some vagueness, graceful: " 'rouged with rust' seemed to me a fine stroke, and 'nor not' instead of 'and' had a curious felic-ity."

Soames and Max met occasionally, but in a few years Max was in the ascendant. He became the author of two books and had made a name for himself. Soames's books, on the other hand, have failed utterly. Then, in June of 1897, at the little Restaurant du Vingtième in Greek Street, Soho, the two men run into each other and have lunch. It turns out that Soames, his disdain for notoriety all collapsed, is desperate:

"You think I haven't minded."
"Minded what, Soames?"
"Neglect. Failure."
"*Failure?*" I said heartily. ... "Neglect – yes, perhaps; but that's quite another matter ..."

Soames remains inconsolable. Max's suggestion that the world never appreciates the truly new and great artist during his lifetime is unhelpful:

"Posterity! what use is it to *me*? ... A hundred years hence! Think of it! If I could come back to life *then* – just for a few hours – and go to the [British Museum] reading-room and *read*! Or better still: if I could be projected, now, at this moment, into the future, into that reading-room, just for this one afternoon! I'd sell myself body and soul to the devil, for that. Think of the pages and pages in the catalogue 'SOAMES, ENOCH' – endlessly – endless editions, commentaries, prolegomena, biographies ..."

But you know the story. A tall, rather flashily dressed and foreign-looking man introduces himself, and Soames makes his pact with the Devil. A few hours later Soames returns to Max and the restaurant, disconsolate. In the Catalogue he found only the "three little pasted slips he had known so well." Nothing else. Nor was he in the *Dictionary of National Biography* or other encyclopaedias. He did locate a reference to himself in a late twentieth-century authority, one T. K. Nupton, as an imaginary character in a somewhat laboured satire by a writer named Max Beerbohm. The Devil returns and claims Soames, whose last words to Max are, "Try, *try* to make them know that I did exist!"

So who was it we all saw? Whose picture appeared in the *Daily Telegraph* for 4 June 1997? The paper claimed it was an actor named Steve Walden. I almost don't know what to think. I do think the most sensible of all the newspaper commentaries on Soames in 1997 was a letter to *The Times* pointing out that it would now be possible for the British Library to move out of its old quarters in the British Museum: the problems that had dogged the Library's removal to St Pancras would disappear because Soames, who would have been lost in the new place, had been allowed to keep his appointment.

From time to time someone asks me whether Enoch Soames actually existed. "What do you mean?" I answer. "I mean, did he actually exist, in the

way that, say, Charles Dickens, existed?" "Of course he did, does," I reply.
You ask a silly question. Soames's existence seems real. In bygone times
Catholic philosophers and theologians used to prove all sorts of things, completely to their own satisfaction, by asserting *Contra factum non valet ullum
argumentum.* Against fact no argument has any validity. Well, here we have
all sorts of facts. The British Library mounted a special display of Soamesiana
in its Manuscript Saloon room. There, under glass and under gold lettering,
nicely situated between the Magna Carta and the manuscript of Handel's
Messiah was a copy of *Fungoids* – Elkins Mathews and John Lane, London,
1894. I stood by and witnessed a young Asian woman dutifully taking down
the bibliographical information. Then too there is a solid *Bibliography of
Enoch Soames* (by Mark Samuels Lasner and enthusiastically reviewed in various learned journals). A *Critical Heritage* volume has appeared. Interest in
Soames, or his existence, is limited, understandably. Maybe it's comparable
to being "world-famous in Canada." But Soames is of considerable interest to
students of the decadent London poets of the 1890s; some say he is a com-
posite caricature of decadent poets Ernest Dowson, Victor Plarr, Theodore
Wratislaw, Arthur Symons (his cape chiefly), and W. B. Yeats of his *Celtic
Twilight* period. Yeats is seen lecturing Soames in Max's best-known group
caricature, "Some Persons of 'the Nineties' " (plate 23).

One final point along these lines. I have heard it argued that "Enoch
Soames" is a distinctly "postmodern" text. Postmodernism would have
annoyed Max. We can imagine what he would have thought of the postmodern idea that everything is a text, and the nearly inescapable corollary
that every text is as good as the next; the belief that words are only about
other words, not about things; the certainty that one can be certain about
nothing; the dismissal of aesthetic judgements as elitist; the assertion that
such judgements serve only to reinforce the status quo, that art merely reflects
dominant ideologies, shoring up the current power structures of a society; the
theory that art is simply one of the many "discourses" afloat at a given time
and should be allowed no special standing. Such notions would have distressed him. And if he were told that "Enoch Soames," with its collapsing of
the "binaries" of life/death, present/past, real/ghostly, factual/fictional, was a
precursor of "deconstruction," he would have chuckled and declined the
honour. (Tom Stoppard tells the story that Jacques Lacan once came backstage to congratulate him on writing a "Lacanian" play, Stoppard having
never heard of Lacan.) I think we know pretty much what Max would have

thought, *mutatis mutandis*, about the works of, say, Barthes, Foucault, or Derrida. In his essay "Laughter" (1920) he writes:

M. Bergson, in his well-known essay on this theme says … well, he says many things; but none of these, though I have just read them, do I exactly remember, nor am I sure that in the act of reading I understood any of them. That is the worst of these fashionable philosophers – or rather, the worst of me. Somehow I never manage to read them till they are just going out of fashion, and even then I don't seem able to cope with them. About twelve years ago, when every one suddenly talked to me about Pragmatism and William James, I found myself moved by a dull but irresistible impulse to try Schopenhauer, of whom, years before that, I had heard that he was the easiest reading in the world, and the most exciting and amusing. I wrestled with Schopenhauer for a day or so, in vain. Time passed; M. Bergson appeared "and for his hour was lord of the ascendant"; I tardily tackled William James. I bore in mind, as I approached him, the testimonials that had been lavished on him by all my friends. Alas, I was insensible to his thrillingness. His gaiety did not make me gay. His crystal clarity confused me dreadfully. I could make nothing of William James. And now, in the fullness of time, I have been floored by M. Bergson.

It distresses me, this failure to keep pace with the leaders of thought as they pass into oblivion.

CHAPTER NINETEEN

Crème de la Crème

At this point, I'd like to make some suggestions for those who want to immerse themselves in Max's *oeuvre* or even just discreetly dip into it. We expect a biographer to be a specialist, indeed an expert in his subject, and judgements about that subject's work are as much his responsibility as keeping his facts straight. Here's my short list of Max's finest work.

First, the prose. The decade following Max's marriage and flight to Italy was his most productive in the sense that the four books published during this period are those that have held up best and are his finest work. These include, in chronological order, *Zuleika Dobson*, begun in 1898, published October 1911; *A Christmas Garland*, some old and some newly written material, published October 1912; *Seven Men*, published October 1919; *And Even Now*, published December 1920. The four books represent four kinds of writing: fantasy novel, literary parody, imaginative memoir, and personal essay. And yet, different as they are, these works, including even the parodies, are alike (and therefore comparable) in being unmistakably Max. By this I mean chiefly that the voice, the presiding persona, is so recognizably and consistently his own.

How to "rank" these books? A strong case can be made for putting *And Even Now* at the top of the list because Max is known chiefly as an essayist (it would also make the ranking *neater* – precisely reversing the chronological order.) On the other hand, my vote for Max's masterpiece goes to *Seven Men*. But either way, in these two books you have "the essential Max." Read from *Seven Men*, "A. V. Laider" and, of course, "Enoch Soames"; from *And Even Now* read "No. 2. The Pines" and "A Clergyman" and "Hosts and Guests." That should do it: you will know if you like Max's prose, you will know if you are in the club or not. If you are, so to say, among the enlightened, and wish to continue down the list to *A Christmas Garland*, you would naturally read the parodies of writers you are familiar with – James, Kipling, Conrad, Wells. *Zuleika Dobson*, being a novel, must be read entire. And yes, it could, perhaps, have been somewhat shorter.

The above is hopelessly subjective, but I will press on. In the earlier books of collected essays you find superb pieces. Here are some recommended items from each:

The Works of Max Beerbohm (1896): "The Pervasion of Rouge," "Dandies and Dandies," and "1880."

More (1899): "Actors," "Going Back to School," and "Madame Tussaud's."

Yet Again (1909): "Seeing People Off," "Porro Unum ...," and "The Humour of the Public."

Virtually all his essays were originally published in magazines and newspapers. Max had been, during the fifteen years prior to his marriage and removal to Italy in 1910, "an unexpectedly industrious journalist." But he was, as we have seen, a careful, discriminating, demanding "collector" of himself and evidently decided that many of his writings were not up to the mark: the four books of essays reprint fewer than half of those he wrote.

And there is some fine and lasting stuff in *Around Theatres* (1924) wherein Max reprinted about a third of the nearly 500 drama reviews he wrote for the *Saturday*. (Rupert Hart-Davis eventually published all the reviews, in *More Theatres*, 1969, and *Last Theatres*, 1970.) Among these, the memorial pieces on Ibsen, Irving, and Leno are of most interest today, along with the many reviews dealing with Shaw. I am not very fond of the fairy tales, but, of them, *The Happy Hypocrite* (1896) remains head and shoulders above the others – *The Story of the Small Boy and the Barley Sugar* (1897), *Yai and the Moon* (1897), and, more satiric parable than fairy tale, *The Dreadful Dragon of Hay Hill* (1928). These three stories can be easily avoided by even the most devoted of Maximilians, if only they will make the effort.

The caricatures. Here the task of selecting out the "best" is decidedly more difficult – next to impossible. To start with, choosing a handful from among more than 2,000 drawings is hopeless. There are too many of relatively equal excellence, and there are too many different styles and genres. If you limit yourself to choosing from the ten collections of his caricatures that Max himself published (comprising 341 drawings), your task is, by the simple math of it, simpler, but still questionable. For in addition to the problems just mentioned, must be added the generally poor quality of reproduction in these books and the fact that most of the reproductions are in black and white while most of the originals incorporate colour. Imagine – silly comparison, I know – but what would be your idea of Cézanne or Van Gogh if you knew their work only through small, weak, black and white "plates"? Or, to come closer to home, if you knew Rossetti's Pre-Raphaelite paintings only through washed-out, grey "half tone" reproductions? Even if one grants, and only for the sake of argument, that watercolours usually suffer less than oil paintings from black and white reproduction, the problem persists. Colour, early on, became essential to Max's style. Given this, most people (myself included) bestow pride of place, among the collections Max himself brought together, to *The Poets' Corner* (1904) and *Rossetti and His Circle* (1922). The reproduction in the former, by colour lithography, was the best Max ever had from his publishers. The plates are also generously large (one result has been that dealers often "break" the book and sell the caricatures individually). The *Rossetti* drawings are the most fully and profusely coloured of all Max's work, and although the 1922 colour reproductions are small and slightly too harsh and "brilliant," they are perfectly adequate. But you immediately see the difficulty of comparing these collections with the others: *The Poets' Corner* and *Rossetti and His Circle* stand out largely by virtue of their colour.* But, what if the large *Book of Caricatures* (1907) were in colour? What if *Fifty Caricatures* (1913) or *Things Old and New* (1923) were in colour? And there arises yet another objection to the preference for *The Poets' Corner* and *Rossetti and His Circle* in that they represent a departure from Max's usual mode, which was portraiture of living contemporaries, not re-presentations of long-dead personalities worked up from old drawings and paintings. Then, too, the *Poets' Corner* and *Rossetti* drawings rely on their (sometimes lengthy) legends for much of their wit and point. How are we to weigh these drawings against the hundreds of stunning portraits that have no captions? Are the *Rossetti* drawings, especially, which carry legends *and* an interconnected story-line necessarily, by that very fact, superior? Clearly not. They are different.

One final problem for anyone judging the relative excellence of Max's kind of graphic work remains wholly intractable: caricatures of "actual" people depend more than other works of art on their subjects, specifically on the

---

* I rule out of consideration the two loose folio collections, *The Second Childhood of John Bull* (1911) and *Heroes and Heroines of Bitter Sweet* (1931), the first as truly atypical in dealing with "types" and the second as late, realistic, deliberately sentimental renderings of the Noel Coward characters.

recognizability or, what is frequently the same thing, the eminence of the subject. Painters may do any old man with a hoe or any postal delivery man, but the caricaturist, at least Max's kind of caricaturist, deals with particular, historical persons. And the more visible the person the better: King Edward VII rather than his private financial adviser, Winston Churchill rather than the forgotten back-bencher. No matter how flimsy or indirect our knowledge of what a person looks like, it helps our appreciation of the caricature, and today we are much more likely to be impressed by the caricatures of Thomas Hardy, Oscar Wilde, and Aubrey Beardsley than by those of Maurice Hewlett, William Archer, and Walter Sickert. In that splendid collection, *A Book of Caricatures*, we will be especially attracted to the drawings of Henry James and H. G. Wells and G. B. Shaw, and maybe even of Belloc and Chesterton. But we don't know, for example, who Lord Tweedmouth was, or what he looked like, even though Max judged his caricature of this Liberal politician the best of the forty-eight drawings in the book. We may admire the image, but we don't connect the likeness and we really don't "get" the caricature. The problem lies in the nature of the thing. We are decidedly handicapped when it comes to appreciating or judging nearly 700 of Max's 800 subjects. And some of those whose likenesses we think we are familiar with, even Edward VII's, are known to us chiefly through Max's caricatures. Our grandparents (or *their* parents) had the advantage over us here.

What does anyone do who wants to see Max's caricatures? Ideally, he or she should visit museums and libraries. At the Tate can be seen the Rossetti drawings and others; the Ashmolean Museum in Oxford houses sixty or so memorable drawings (from the Guedalla Collection). The Merton Library Beerbohm Room has a good sampling of caricatures. In the US, the special collection libraries at Princeton, the University of Texas, UCLA, Harvard, and Yale are depositories of numerous Beerbohm caricatures. I shall not say that the one spectacular group portrait (*A Biassed Deputation*, which graced the dust jacket of the Hart-Davis *Catalogue*) merits a trip to the Art Institute of Chicago, but if you happen to be in that great museum, hunt it out. The largest gathering of original caricatures in private hands belongs to the book collector and Beerbohm scholar Mark Samuels Lasner. As for reproductions, you can still find in rare book stores occasional copies of Max's original collections of drawings – and not at exorbitant prices, nothing like those attaching to William Morris Kelmscott books (which Max thought overrated, "not *books* at all") or to Aubrey Beardsley books (which Max thought underrated).

The Rupert Hart-Davis *Catalogue of the Caricatures of Max Beerbohm* (1972) contains 100 well-produced black-and-white plates; but Hart-Davis's decision to include only previously unpublished drawings makes his selection self-limiting and unrepresentative of Max's best-known work. In 1987 Yale University Press brought out a new edition of *Rossetti and His Circle*, photographed from the originals by modern techniques. But short of visiting the museums and libraries where the originals are housed, the best overall book in which to see Max's caricatures, 213 of them, with 80 in colour, covering all Max's periods and styles, is (I'm afraid there is simply no way of getting around this) N. John Hall's *Max Beerbohm Caricatures*, Yale University Press, 1997.

CHAPTER TWENTY

The Golden Drugget

"Drugget" is hardly a common word. Most people, like myself, will have to resort to the dictionary. "A coarse woollen stuff used for floor coverings" is now the chief meaning (the word's "ulterior origin," says the stately *OED*, dismissing any connection with Drogheda in Ireland as "mere wanton conjecture," is unknown). That Max should title a late essay "The Golden Drugget" is evidence that in 1918 he had still the penchant for the quaint or even archaic word. But here such a word is used not comically but poetically. And the essay is poetic, poignant – unusual for him. Its wellsprings were the still-raging Great War and nostalgic memories of his first years in Rapallo. I give here enough of its actual text to convey its feeling because, although all of Max's essays are personal, this one shows a side of him that his comic writings tend to cloak. For *of course* there was a side of him that was nostalgic, and also distressed by the *lacrimae rerum*, the tears of things, and the follies of man, the messy, sorry business that is human nature. War brings these tears to the fore.*

To describe "The Golden Drugget" as Max at his most thoughtful would be to fall into the usual error of believing comedy to be always light-hearted and, by implication at least, shallow. "The Golden Drugget" is not necessarily more thoughtful than his humorous essays, or even more serious (think of Brecht's words that comedy treats the sufferings of mankind more seriously than does tragedy), but it has an emphasis, supplied naturally by the subject matter in hand, that is sombre and pensive. The aesthetic question is whether or not it is sentimental. My first impulse is to deny real sentimentality anywhere in Max: he is ordinarily so resolutely and coolly rational a writer. Still, he had feelings of sadness, and nostalgia too, and nostalgia often walks the line that borders the sentimental. Besides, there is the problem of what we

---

* As does also the death of close friends. Max, in another rare departure from his usual mode, took on this theme in a piece called "William and Mary," written in 1920 shortly after his return to Rapallo and, like the "Golden Drugget," included in *And Even Now*.

mean by the word *sentimental* – anything from thoughtful and tender to weepy and mushy. Call "The Golden Drugget" borderline sentimental if you will. I prefer to characterize it as poignant. But in either case, the tone is steadfastly, though mutedly, hopeful. Notice too, towards the end (the final paragraph is given entire), the decidedly Beerbohmian twist in the unwillingness to test one's cherished beliefs and the decision to remain a spectator. But I had better get on to quoting the essay instead of trying to set the stage and supply glosses. It begins:

> Primitive and essential things have great power to touch the heart of the beholder. I mean such things as a man ploughing a field, or sowing or reaping; a girl filling a pitcher from a spring; a young mother with her child; a fisherman mending his nets; a light from a lonely hut on a dark night.
>
> Things such as these are the best themes for poets and painters, and appeal to aught that there may be of painter or poet in any of us. Strictly, they are not so old as the hills, but they are more significant and eloquent than the hills. Hills will outlast them; but hills glacially surviving the life of man on this planet are of as little account as hills tremulous and hot in ages before the life of man had its beginning. Nature is interesting only because of *us*. And the best symbols of us are such sights as I have just mentioned – sights unalterable by fashion of time or place, sights that in all countries always were and never will not be.

It is irrelevant, Max claims, that new kinds of machinery for more efficient ploughing and reaping have been developed, maybe even some "invention for catching fish by electricity." For while we need poems and pictures about machinery and electricity, such poems cannot touch our hearts deeply, they "cannot stir in us the sense of our kinship with the whole dim past and the whole dim future." The well-lighted façade of the Waldorf Hotel by night is not for the painter or poet as fine a theme, viewed *sub specie aeternitatis*, as that lonely hut with its single light. The essay next moves to a specific image, one "greatly romantic" to Max, an inn from which emanates a golden welcome mat of light. He first offers the time frame:

> These words are written in war time and in England. There are, I hear, "lighting restrictions" even on the far Riviera di Levante. I take it that the Golden Drugget is not outspread nowanights across the high dark coast-road between Rapallo and Zoagli. But the lonely wayside inn is still there,

doubtless; and its narrow door will again stand open, giving out for way-farers its old span of brightness into darkness, when peace comes.

We are told that this inn is "nothing by daylight," just an unassuming little place selling salt and tobacco along with wine and other drink, unimpressive amid surroundings of mountains with their olive trees and cypresses on the one side and the cliff falling sheer to the sea on the other. By day it is an ugly, uninviting, box-like place. Even in the moonlight, it is negligible in this dramatic setting: "But on a thoroughly dark night, when it is manifest as nothing but a strip of yellow light cast across the road from an ever-open door, great always is its magic for me. Is? I mean *was*. But then, I mean also *will be*. And so I cleave to the present tense – the nostalgic present, as grammarians might call it." He recalls walking up in the dark from the town towards his home:

It is on nights when the wind blows its hardest, but makes no rift any-where for a star to peep through, that the Golden Drugget, as I approach it, gladdens my heart the most. The distance between Rapallo and my home up yonder is rather more than two miles. The road curves and zig-zags sharply for the most part; but at the end of the first mile it runs straight for three or four hundred yards; and, as the inn stands at a point midway on this straight course, the Golden Drugget is visible to me long before I come to it. Even by starlight, it is good to see. How much better, if I happen to be out on a black rough night when nothing is visible but this one calm bright thing. ... The continuous shrill wailing of trees' branches writhing unseen but near, and the great hoarse roar of the sea against the rocks far down below, are not cheerful accompaniment for the buffeted pil-grim. He feels that he is engaged in single combat with Nature at her unfriendliest.... But look! that streak, yonder, look! – the Golden Drugget.

There it is, familiar, serene, festal. That the pilgrim knew he would see it in due time does not diminish for him the queer joy of seeing it; nay, this emotion would be far less without the foreknowledge. Some things are best at first sight. Others – and here is one of them – do ever improve by recognition. I remember when first I beheld this steady strip of light, shed forth over a threshold level with the road, it seemed to me conceivably sin-ister. It brought Stevenson to my mind: the clink of doubloons and the clash of cutlasses; and I think I quickened pace as I passed it. But now! – now it inspires in me a sense of deep trust and gratitude; and such awe as I have for it is altogether a loving awe, as for holy ground that should be trod lightly. A drugget of crimson cloth across a London pavement is rather resented by the casual passer-by, as saying to him "Step across me, stranger, but not along me, not in!" and for answer he spurns it with his heel. "Stranger, come in!" is the clear message of the Golden Drugget. "This is but a humble and earthly hostel, yet you will find here a radiant company of angels and archangels." And always I cherish the belief that if I obeyed the summons I should receive fulfilment of the promise. Well, the beliefs that one most cherishes one is least willing to test. I do not go in at that open door. But lingering, but reluctant, is my tread as I pass by it; and I pause to bathe in the light that is as the span of our human life, granted between one great darkness and another.

These lines, with their beautiful scepticism and their unusual seriousness, their delicate way of coming round to that earlier much-desired kinship with the whole dim past and the whole dim future, require no further comment. They are lines that reward slow and repeated reading.

CHAPTER TWENTY-ONE

The Divine Singer

There are so many fine things in *And Even Now*, Max's final book of essays, that I hardly know which to single out. Aside from "The Golden Drugget," this collection boasts, among others, "Hosts and Guests," "Quia Imperfectum," "Going Out for a Walk," "Servants," "A Clergyman," and "The Crime." But doubtless "No. 2. The Pines" enjoys the most renown. Of its kind – an essay both humorous and reverential, recounting a visit to a famous author by a young one – it has no equal, I think, anywhere.

First, Catullus. Today most of us don't know much about Catullus. If you wished to express awe at the prospect of meeting in the flesh some adored avant-garde and racy poet of your younger years, you would probably not deliver yourself of the fancy that it was as if Catullus were alive and living in the suburbs. But for Max, who read the Latin poets with delight, this was precisely how he felt on being invited, in 1899, to meet Algernon Charles Swinburne.

Swinburne, whose poetry of the 1860s shocked most readers but elated others, had been rescued from drink and probably from death by Theodore Watts, who in 1879 took Swinburne into his house in Putney and strictly regulated his life. Watts limited his charge to a slight daily measure of the "wine of the country," English beer. Swinburne was a tiny man with a large head and flaming red hair, so boyish-looking even at thirty as to strike a contemporary as sixteen. Sadly, he suffered from a severe nervous twitching and was subject to epileptic-like fits. He had a quick, indeed brilliant mind and an intense interest in classical literature and Elizabethan and Jacobean plays; he had also a fierce temper, and a complete incapacity for alcohol, of which the smallest amount could inspire him to frenzied poetic flights or paroxysms of rage. He developed a reputation for paganism, sensualism, anti-theism; he admired Baudelaire and De Sade and Blake; he was suspected of a wide range of deviant behaviour, from homosexuality, sadism, and flagellation, to paedophilia, bestiality, and cannibalism. (Only the flagellation is documented.) Some of Swinburne's admirers said, rather unfairly, that Watts also rescued him from poetry; they were hoping in vain for more poems in the manner of

Poems and Ballads. When that work had first appeared in the summer of 1866, a critical storm was let loose against Swinburne for his "nameless shameless abominations" and "putrescent imagination," and for "perversions" that were deemed worse than "blank atheism." His publisher withdrew the book from circulation.

A small handful of poems caused most of the uproar. "Dolores – Our Lady of Pain" treated not the Seven Sorrows of the Virgin Mary but celebrated the seventy-times-seven sins of Dolores and opposed "the lilies and langours of virtue" to the "raptures and roses of vice." Another poem, "Anactoria," described anguished, sadistic lesbian love, beginning, one critic wrote, with an "insane extravagance of passion" – a desire to feed on the blood of the beloved's "scourged white breast" and to drink her "veins as wine"; the poem closed, the same critic wrote, with a "raging blasphemy" – a will to "smite" and "desecrate" God. Occasionally Swinburne's defiant paganism, as in "Hymn to Proserpine," becomes specifically anti-Christian: "Thou hast conquered O pale Galilean; the world has grown grey from thy breath. . . ." Of course these are only high points – or low points – of a few poems among many in the collection. His critics were all the more annoyed in that they could not help but admit Swinburne's enormous poetic talent. The young and rebellious were especially impressed. Max was of the second generation of youths to idolize Swinburne.

At first Max's enthusiasm for Swinburne might strike us as peculiar, until we look more closely. For one thing, as far as Max was concerned, Swinburne's unconventional sexual habits and his private life were his own business. When Edmund Gosse, a good friend of Swinburne's, wrote his *Life* of the poet (published in 1917), he omitted, at the insistence of Swinburne's family, anything unseemly or even unpleasant. Three years later, he put together a "Confidential Paper" documenting Swinburne's alcoholism and predilection for flagellation; he then circulated the paper among a few friends, including Max, asking if they advised him to lodge a copy "for students" with the British Museum. Max answered that the whole "dreary and ghastly and disgusting" business ought to be suppressed altogether: "Why should anyone in posterity *know* that Swinburne did these things?" As Max later explained to Lytton Strachey, the Paper "made Swinburne (whom I revered, and liked) very ridiculous; and I should have preferred the students to be left with a vague notion of mere legendary wickedness."

The poetry itself then. What did Max find enthralling in the early poems? Was it merely the words themselves? Max was, after all, an aesthete, and

Swinburne was one of the original English aesthetes; Max believed in art for its own sake; he wanted (though here he parted from Swinburne, who wrote so much in the cause of Italian independence) no obvious lessons, no propaganda from art; he wanted beauty; and Swinburne's line, with its distinctive blend of assonance, alliteration, rhythm, and rhyme, had for him undeniable beauty. And, in truth, the sheer *music* of Swinburne's poetry does explain much of its enchantment for Max. But not all. You cannot persuasively separate form from substance. Max, although hardly a passionate man, could nevertheless appreciate sexual passion in art; moreover, in his own quiet, non-participatory fashion, Max had been a young man in revolt against much that he saw around him. If it did not sound too grand I would say he was in revolt against the general vulgarity and materialism of his day (phenomena that in his view worsened in the twentieth century); he was in revolt against sexual puritanism, against patriotic and John Bullish cant; and against inane plays and fatuous novels and silly poems. We do not customarily think of Max as having any but the mildest tinge of rebellion in him, but with pen or pencil in hand he was tough-minded and critical. And he was a thorough unbeliever: in God, in immortality, in an afterlife, although (very unlike Swinburne) he was ever courteous to believers and their beliefs. He was fatalistic; he believed that luck played an enormous role in one's life. We know that among his favourite passages from *Poems and Ballads* are these lines from "The Garden of Proserpine" (that they are everyone else's favourites as well, and are predictably found in *Bartlett's* and the *Oxford Book of Quotations* need not detract from Max's taste for this hymn to death as eternal sleep):

> From too much love of living,
>   From hope and fear set free,
> We thank with brief thanksgiving
>   Whatever gods may be
> That no life lives for ever,
> That dead men rise up never;
> That even the weariest river
>   Winds somewhere safe to sea.

Moreover, Swinburne was pre-eminently, gloriously, the poet of the sea (unlike Clement Scott, poet of the seaside), and Max loved the sea, moved near the sea and spent most of his life within sight of it.

Add to these considerations the fact that Swinburne had been friends with
Rossetti, was part of that recent magical past, and you can understand Max's
excitement in 1899 when Theodore Watts (now Watts-Dunton) invited Max
"to come down to Putney and 'have luncheon and meet Swinburne.' Meet
Catullus!":

> On the day appointed "I came as one whose feet half linger." It is but a few
> steps from the railway-station in Putney High Street to No. 2. The Pines.
> I had expected a greater distance to the sanctuary – a walk in which to
> compose my mind and prepare myself for initiation. I laid my hand irres-
> olutely against the gate of the bleak trim front-garden, I withdrew my
> hand, I went away. Out here were all the aspects of common modern life.
> In there was Swinburne. A butcher-boy went by, whistling. He was not
> going to see Swinburne. He could afford to whistle.

Max gathers himself, retraces his steps, knocks, enters:

> But as the front-door closed behind me I had the instant sense of having
> slipped away from the harsh light of the ordinary and contemporary into
> the dimness of an odd, august past. Here, in this dark hall, the past was
> present. Here loomed vivid and vital on the walls those women of Rossetti
> whom I had known but as shades. Familiar to me in small reproductions
> by photogravure, here they *themselves* were, life-sized, "with curled-up lips
> and amorous hair" done in the original warm crayon, all of them intently
> looking down on me while I took off my overcoat – all wondering who was
> this intruder from posterity.

Watts-Dunton welcomes Max but warns him that he won't be able to speak
much with Swinburne, who is "almost stone deaf now." Presently, the introduction is at hand:

> Nor was I disappointed. Swinburne's entry was for me a great moment.
> Here, suddenly visible in the flesh, was the legendary being and divine
> singer. Here he was, shutting the door behind him as might anybody else,
> and advancing, a strange small figure in grey, having an air at once noble
> and roguish, proud and skittish. My name was roared at him. In shaking
> his hand, I bowed low, of course – a bow *de cœur*; and he, in the old aris-
> tocratic manner, bowed equally low, but with such swiftness that we barely
> escaped concussion. You do not usually associate a man of genius, when

you see one, with any social class; and, Swinburne being of an aspect so unrelated as it was to any species of human kind, I wondered the more that almost the first impression he made on me, or would make on anyone, was that of a very great gentleman indeed. Not of an *old* gentleman, either. Sparse and straggling though the grey hair was that fringed the immense pale dome of his head, and venerably haloed though he was for me by his greatness, there was yet about him something – boyish? girlish? childish, rather; something of a beautifully well-bred child. But he had the eyes of a god, and the smile of an elf.

The meal goes forward, Watts-Dunton at the head of the table, Max and Swinburne on either side, with Watts-Dunton talking only to Max while Swinburne says nothing:

> This was the more tantalizing because Swinburne seemed as though he were bubbling over with all sorts of notions. Not that he looked at either of us. He smiled only to himself, and to his plateful of meat, and to the small bottle of Bass's pale ale that stood before him – ultimate allowance of one who had erst clashed cymbals in Naxos. The bottle he eyed often and with enthusiasm, seeming to waver between the rapture of broaching it now and the grandeur of having it to look forward to.

Watts-Dunton plies Max for information about all the latest "movements," and Max, while shouting banalities to him – for Watts-Dunton himself was nearly deaf – keeps glancing at Swinburne:

> Now and again his shining light-grey eyes roved from the table, darting this way and that – across the room, up at the ceiling, out of the window; only never at us. Somehow his aloofness gave no hint of indifference. It seemed to be, rather, a point in good manners – the good manners of a child "sitting up to the table," not "staring," not "asking questions," and reflecting great credit on its invaluable old nurse. The child sat happy in the wealth of its inner life; the child was content not to speak until it were spoken to; but, I felt it did want to be spoken to. And at length, it *was*.

During the apple pie, Watts-Dunton asks Swinburne about his morning's walk, whereupon Swinburne throws back his head and "flutingly *sang* of his experience. The wonders of this morning's wind and sun and clouds were expressed in a flow of words so right and sentences so perfectly balanced that they would have seemed pedantic had they not been clearly as spontaneous as the wordless notes of a bird of song. The frail, sweet voice rose and fell, quickened, in all manner of trills and roulades." He had also seen on the heath that morning "the most BEAUT——iful babbie ever beheld by mortal eyes."

A point of the essay that remains especially vivid recounts how, during one of Max's subsequent visits, Swinburne expressed a wish to show his guest his library:

> Here, as host, among his treasures, Swinburne was more than ever attractive. He was as happy as was any mote of sunshine about him; and the fluttering of his little hands, and feet too, was but as a token of so much felicity. He looked older, it is true, in the strong light. But those years made only more notable his youngness of heart. An illustrious bibliophile among his books? A birthday child, rather, among his toys.

Swinburne flies up and down a mahogany ladder, fetching rare books one by one and presenting them to Max:

> "This, I *think*, will please you!" It did. It had a beautifully engraved title-page and a pleasing scent of old, old leather. It was *editio princeps* of a play by some lesser Elizabethan or Jacobean. "Of course you know it?" my host fluted.
>
> How I wished I could say that I knew it and loved it well! I revealed to him (for by speaking very loudly towards his inclined head I was able to make him hear) that I had not read it. He envied any one who had such a pleasure in store. He darted to the ladder, and came back thrusting gently into my hands another volume of like date: "Of course you know *this*?"
>
> Again I had to confess that I did not, and to show my appreciation of the fount of type, the margins, the binding. He beamed agreement, and fetched another volume. Archly he indicated the title, cooing, "You are a lover, of *this*, I hope?"
>
> I did not pretend to know the particular play, but my tone implied that I had always been *meaning* to read it and had always by some mischance been prevented.... Anon he fetched another volume, and another, always with the same faith that *this* was a favourite of mine. I quibbled, I evaded, I was very enthusiastic and uncomfortable. It was with intense relief that I beheld the title-page of yet another volume which (silently, this time) he

laid before me – *The Country Wench*. "This of course I have read," I heartily shouted.

Swinburne stepped back. "You have? You have read it? Where?" he cried, in evident dismay.

Something was wrong. Had I *not*, I quickly wondered, read this play? "Oh yes," I shouted, "I have read it."

"But when? Where?" entreated Swinburne, adding that he had supposed it to be the sole copy extant.

I floundered. I wildly said I thought I must have read it years ago in the Bodleian.

"Theodore! Do you hear this? It seems they now have a copy of *The Country Wench* in the Bodleian! ... They might have told me," he wailed.

I sacrificed myself on the altar of sympathy. I admitted that I may have been mistaken – must have been – must have confused this play with some other. I dipped into the pages and "No," I shouted, "this I have *never* read."

His equanimity was restored.

Later, while talking with Watts-Dunton, Max recalls "the existence of a play called *The Country Wife*, by – wasn't it Wycherly? I had once read it – or read something about it. ... But this matter I kept to myself. I thought I had appeared fool enough already."

You have not read the essay? I envy any one who has such a pleasure in store.

CHAPTER TWENTY-TWO

An End of Essays

I don't want you to think, on the evidence of "No. 2. The Pines" and, especially, of "The Golden Drugget," that Max had gone soft or altogether outgrown the iconoclasm of his early years. *And Even Now* has its share of irreverence and satire. Take, for example, "Kolniyatsch" (from Colney Hatch, famous London lunatic asylum). The essay is a critique of a Russian writer of that name, much lionized by British intellectuals, a combination, apparently, of Gorky and Dostoevsky:

> Kolniyatsch was born, last of a long line of rag-pickers, in 1886. At the age of nine he had already acquired that passionate alcoholism which was to have so great an influence in the moulding of his character and on the trend of his thought. Otherwise he does not seem to have shown in childhood exceptional promise. It was not before his eighteenth birthday that he murdered his grandmother and was sent to that asylum in which he wrote the poems and plays belonging to what we now call his earlier manner. . . .
>
> Was he a realist or a romantic? He was neither, and he was both. By more than one critic he has been called a pessimist, and it is true that a part of his achievement may be gauged by the lengths to which he carried pessimism – railing and raging, not, in the manner of his tame forerunners, merely at things in general, or at women, or at himself, but lavishing an equally fierce scorn and hatred on children, on trees and flowers and the moon, and indeed on everything that the sentimentalists have endeavoured to force into favour. On the other hand, his burning faith in a personal Devil, his frank delight in earthquakes and pestilences, and his belief that every one but himself will be brought back to life in time to be frozen to death in the next glacial epoch, seem rather to stamp him as an optimist.

But, undoubtedly, most of the essays reprinted in *And Even Now* reflect a cast of mind more relaxed, surely more mellow, less "clever" than that which produced the earlier essays in *Works* (1896) and *More* (1899), with *Yet Again*

(1909) representing an intermediate stage. Listen to a few lines from "A Clergyman," written in 1918, an essay that glosses a brief passage in one of Max's favourite books, Boswell's *Life of Johnson*. First we are given the scene:

Fragmentary, pale, momentary; almost nothing; glimpsed and gone; as it were, a faint human hand thrust up, never to reappear, from beneath the rolling waters of time, he forever haunts my memory and solicits my weak imagination. Nothing is told of him but that once, abruptly, he asked a question, and received an answer.

This was on the afternoon of April 7th, 1778, at Streatham, in the well-appointed house of Mr Thrale. Johnson, on the morning of that day, had entertained Boswell at breakfast in Bolt Court, and invited him to dine at Thrale Hall. The two took a coach and arrived early. It seems that Sir John Pringle had asked Boswell to ask Johnson "what were the best English sermons for style." In the interval before dinner, accordingly, Boswell reeled off the names of several divines whose prose might or might not win commendation.

Max next quotes Boswell's *Life*:

BOSWELL: What I want to know is, what sermons afford the best specimen of English pulpit eloquence.
JOHNSON: We have no sermons addressed to the passions, that are good for anything; if you mean that kind of eloquence.
A CLERGYMAN, whose name I do not recollect: Were not Dodd's sermons addressed to the passions?
JOHNSON: They were nothing sir, be they addressed to what they may.

Then, Max's commentary:

The suddenness of it! Bang! – and the rabbit that had popped from its burrow was no more.

I know not which is the more startling – the début of the unfortunate clergyman, or the instantaneousness of his end. Why hadn't Boswell told us there was a clergyman present? Well, we may be sure that so careful and acute an artist had some good reason. And I suppose the clergyman was left to take us unawares because just so did he take the company. Had we been told he was there, we might have expected that sooner or later he would join in the conversation. He would have had a place in our minds. We may assume that in the minds of the company around Johnson he had no place. He sat forgotten, overlooked; so that his self-assertion startled every one just as on Boswell's page it startles us.

The reader is drawn into Max's imagined version of the man. Perhaps the clergyman was a shy young curate from the neighbouring church; and he may well have spoken in a high, nervous, thin voice:

He sits on the edge of a chair in the background. He has colourless eyes, fixed earnestly, and a face almost as pale as his clerical bands beneath his somewhat receding chin. His forehead is high and narrow, his hair mouse-coloured. His hands are clasped tight before him, the neck standing out sharply. This constriction does not mean that he is steeling himself to speak. He has no positive intention of speaking. Very much, nevertheless, is he wishing in the back of his mind that he *could* say something – something whereat the great Doctor would turn on him and say, after a pause for thought, "Why yes, Sir. That is most justly observed." Or "Sir, this never occurred to me. I thank you" – thereby fixing the observer for ever high in the esteem of all. And now in a flash the chance presents itself. "We have," shouts Johnson, "no sermons addressed to the passions, that are good for anything." I see the curate's frame quiver with sudden impulse, and his mouth fly open, and – no, I can't bear it, I shut my eyes and ears.

A slight theme indeed, but does it not exhibit Max's personality, his sympathies, and his good sense? You will not be able to separate the substance from the style; if you think he is all style, even a wonderful style, you are missing, I think, half the point, or almost half the point. As he himself put it, in 1900, "In essay writing, style is everything. The essayist's aim is to bring himself home to his reader. ... Himself is the thing to be obtruded, and style is only a means to this end. Wherever style is, there too is the author."

These later essays are the work of a man well into his fifth decade and conscious of it; they could not have been written by someone in his twenties. Perhaps the taste for them is older, too. If I were in my twenties, I would probably prefer "Dandies and Dandies" and "The Pervasion of Rouge" to these later efforts. One's tastes change, and so does one's sense of humour. "Laughter" (written in 1920), the final essay in *And Even Now*, engages the question of ageing and laughter. It begins with Max's ironic lament (quoted earlier) about not keeping up with William James and Schopenhauer and, most recently, Bergson, those leaders of modern thought, "as they pass into oblivion." But whatever his inability to make any sense of these philosophers, he is, Max insists, no absolute fool:

> Tell me of a man or woman, a place or an event, real or fictitious: surely you will find me a fairly intelligent listener. . . . Come to me in some griev-ous difficulty: I will talk to you like a father, even like a lawyer. I'll be hanged if I haven't a certain mellow wisdom. But if you are by way of weaving theories as to the nature of things in general, and if you want to try those theories on some one who will luminously confirm or powerfully rend them, I must, with a hang-dog air, warn you that I am not your man. I suffer from a strong suspicion that things in general cannot be accounted for through any formula or set of formulae, and that any one philosophy, howsoever new, is no better than any other. This is in itself a sort of phil-osophy, and I suspect it accordingly; but it has for me the merit of being the only one that I can make head or tail of.

Bergson on laughter, accordingly, provokes in Max not assent or opposition, only a smile; outright laughter is more the province of youth – undignified, uncritical. When nowadays someone rouses him to laughter, he is grateful: "I realize, even after reading M. Bergson on it, how good a thing it is. I am qual-ified to praise it." He goes on to take back any condescension he may have had in writing of music halls in an earlier essay. Part of the problem, he now realizes, lay in himself. He would have enjoyed the fun more had it been pri-vate:

> A public crowd, because of a lack of broad impersonal humanity in me, rather insulates than absorbs me. Amidst the guffaws of a thousand strangers I become unnaturally grave . . . a position that drives me spiritu-ally aloof.

Max asks next whether Shakespeare had not missed a great opportunity when he was finishing the Second Part of *Henry IV*: why had not Falstaff first glowed and then roared with laughter at that "portentous allocution" of Prince Hal? Moreover, not even Falstaff can convulse us as we read Shakespeare's pages. For the thrill of extreme laughter,

> the mirthmaker must be a living man whose jests we hear as they come fresh from his own lips. All I can claim for Falstaff is that he would be able

to convulse us if he were alive and accessible ... to master and dissolve us, to give us the joy of being worn down and tired out with laughter, is a success to be won by no man save in virtue of a rare staying power. Laughter becomes extreme only if it be consecutive. There must be no pauses for recovery. Touch and go humour, however happy, is not enough. The jester must be able to grapple his theme and hang on to it, twisting it this way and that, and making it yield magically all manner of outrageous and precious things, one after another, without pause. He must have invention keeping pace with utterance. He must be inexhaustible. Only he can exhaust us.

Max claims to have known one supreme mirthmaker. He calls him "Comus" (after Milton's god of revelry), a supreme instance of the humorist, an inventive raconteur and mimic who so interprets the human comedy, so broadens that comedy into farce, that "nothing can stop him when he is in the vein. No appeals move him. He goes from strength to strength while his audience is more and more piteously debilitated." Ever the realist, Max has some qualification: "Incomparable laughter-giver, he is himself not much a laugher. He is vintner, not toper. I would therefore not change places with him. I am well content to have been his beneficiary during thirty years, and to be so for as many more as may be given us."

Reggie Turner wrote back saying how wonderful a thing it was "to think that I shall for ever lie snugly hidden in your prose."

With the publication of *And Even Now* Max had done his work as prose writer. A good sampling of his writing has been quoted in this book (and there are, as Thackeray would put it, some "terrific" passages still to come). My effort has been to show rather than analyse his style. I doubt that commentary, learned or otherwise, upon his prose style is of much use. In common parlance, saying a writer has style means he or she writes well, writes, if you will, stylishly, writes with sophistication, with a peculiar individual manner that leaves its mark everywhere on the writing. Max is certainly distinctive, perhaps more recognizably so in his earlier style, the style that owed so much to Oscar Wilde, that revelled in paradox, cleverness, bald irony, and in the occasional outsize, archaic, or even manufactured-on-the-spot word. But for those who care to look closely, the later style, more Thackerayan in tone, more relaxed, easier, clearer, its irony muted and more subtle, is also distinctive.

Common parlance in speaking of style also makes much of the distinction between poetry and prose, usually to the latter's discredit: the very word *prose* (and not just the words *prosaic* or *prosy*) often implies writing inferior to poetry – "mere prose." Max himself, in his early style, once addressed the poetry/prose divide: "... though it is harder to write bad poetry than to write bad prose, beautiful prose is as hardly written as is beautiful poetry. Hardlier, indeed. Prose is the unwieldier instrument." He thought truly great prose rarer than great poetry. He liked the story about Pater advising young Oscar Wilde, who hankered after a prose style, to write poetry for the present: it was, Pater told him, so much easier. And I think Max appreciated the comments of his friend Somerset Maugham on seventeenth-century writers:

> ... to write good prose is an affair of good manners. It is, unlike verse, a civil art. Poetry is baroque. Baroque is tragic, massive and mystical. It is elemental. It demands depth. ... Prose is a rococo art. It needs taste rather than power, decorum rather than inspiration and vigour rather than grandeur.

Of course such assertions can be readily attacked as generalities and simplifications. But the hallmarks of what Maugham considers good prose – precision, ease, sobriety, humour, courtesy, tolerance, horse sense, together with a refusal to risk being boring, and an abhorrence of enthusiasm – are apt descriptors of Max's prose, especially the later prose. I keep betraying my own preference for the later prose. On the other hand, it is just possible that Max himself felt that with the years he was losing his edge; perhaps he regretted that his humour was becoming less quirky, mirthful, iconoclastic, irreverent. Maybe those who prefer the earlier essays have a point. In any case, he believed he had done his share, and, approaching fifty, he left off writing.

CHAPTER TWENTY-THREE

A Terrible Monstrifier

The 1920s, Max's fifties, were perhaps his most serene years; certainly they were uneventful. Life moved along slowly and happily for him and Florence; their pleasure in living calmly at the Villino Chiaro in their beautiful spot above the sea went uninterrupted; no war or threat of war would occasion a return to England as had happened in 1915 and would again happen in the 1930s. The natives paid Max no attention except briefly when word got around that he had written a book on Rossetti, but their interest quickly waned when they learned that it was not about Colonel Giovanni Raffaele Rossetti, an Italian naval hero. Max was much relieved. There was, it is true, a steady stream of visitors, including Reggie Turner (of course) and, to name but a few whose fame survives, A. A. Milne, Sibyl Colefax, Lord Berners, Granville Barker, Ernest Hemingway, Max Eastman, Aldous Huxley, Osbert and Sacheverell Sitwell, Ezra Pound, T. S. Eliot. Max's dear friend from the nineties, Mrs Leverson, also appeared; the Baroness von Hutten came to Rapallo from Portofino, but Florence refused to invite her to the Villino "because she had left her husband and went off with another man who was also married." Gordon Craig and his family lived at a house within sight of the Villino; his son Edward Craig would write that "Ours were no longer a couple of lonely villas on the Riviera. They became more like a couple of well-known cafés on the Paris boulevards where artists and intellectuals dropped in." But visitors were not a distraction or annoyance to Max: aside from a niece of Florence's and Max's sister Dora, the visitors stayed in Rapallo hotels and only called at the Villino. Max by temperament and habit was never bored by leisure or solitude. The busy ant, he once wrote, "sets an example to us all; but not a good one."

In his professional life, although he had pretty much stopped writing, he did some careful "collecting" of himself. He allowed Heinemann to bring out a Collected Edition of 780 sets. "The volumes," Max wrote, "must be as modest in size as they would be in number. They must be in physical proportion to the spirit and ambition of the writer. Also, their aspect must be of a simple-gay kind, as opposed to the ornate-dismal. And though, of course, they would all have to be equal in height, let them at any rate be of all different colours, so that hereafter on shelves every one of them should seem not to have lost utterly its own little soul." The result was a "Harlequin" edition, beautifully bound in ten smart but soft colours. The first seven volumes, 1922, reprinted his seven books; the eighth and ninth volumes, 1924, comprised a selection of his drama criticism (about a third of it), *Around Theatres*; the final and tenth volume, 1928, gathered between hard covers some old material, a few essays, his obituary of Beardsley, an additional parody of Henry James ("The Guerdon"), three fairy tales from the 1890s, and – making their first appearance in print – his play, *A Social Success*, and the satiric fantasy, "The Dreadful Dragon of Hay Hill." This last piece is set in the London of 39,000 BC and demonstrates the quarrelsomeness and discontentedness of the natives and, by implication, the rest of us. The story was inspired by the war and written shortly thereafter; and it is, in my view, among his least successful works. Max called this new book, with his usual scrupulosity about titles, *A Variety of Things*.

By contrast, the 1920s were productive years for Max the caricaturist. He was able to resume drawing and exhibiting his drawings, the public showing of which during wartime would have seemed to him offensive to decency.

It may be good to set down here Max's ideas on the nature of caricature, or at least on the nature of his caricature. His ideas were all in place quite early on, and, like himself, they did not change.

In a 1901 article he described caricature as "the delicious art of exaggerating, without fear or favour, the peculiarities of this or that human body, for the mere sake of exaggeration." But one must always – as if I have not said so often enough already – be alert to Max's irony, and elsewhere he admitted privately that he hoped also to get at the soul of a man, but through the body: "When I draw a man, I am concerned simply and solely with the physical aspect of him. ... [But] I see him in a peculiar way: I see all his salient points exaggerated (points of face, figure, port, gesture and vesture), and all his insignificant points proportionately diminished. ... In the salient points a man's soul does reveal itself, more or less faintly. ... It is ... when (and only when) my own caricatures hit exactly the exteriors of their subjects that they open the interiors, too." (Compare these words with E. H. Gombrich's dictum that the caricaturist "shows how the soul of the man would express itself in his body if only matter were sufficiently pliable to Nature's intentions.")

The true caricaturist, Max insists, portrays these salient points – long noses, puffy hands, the lack of neck – simply as they appear to his distorted gaze; he does not "make conscious aim at exaggeration. He does not say, 'I will go for this "point" or that.' ... He exaggerates instinctively, unconsciously." Max believed that the caricaturist should never draw from the life because he would be "bound by the realities of it" and could not "suborn his pencil to magnify or diminish the proportions." Instead, it is only in recollection of his subject that "the unconscious process of exaggeration begins to work." His manner of operation was to stare at a person for a few moments and draw him later – that evening, or many evenings, or even years later.

Max liked economy of line. His goal was "to have the whole thing as absolutely simple as I can. ... Just boil a man down to the essentials." Again, "In every work of art elimination and simplification are essential. In caricature they are doubly so. For a caricature is a form of wit, and nothing so ruthlessly chokes laughter as the suspicion of labour." As he told Holbrook Jackson, "I like, in visual objects, lightness and severity, blitheness and simplicity. A gloomy complexity is no doubt equally a noble thing to strive for. Morris achieved it in his wall-papers."

Max kept his caricatures small, insisting that caricature could not abide a large surface: "... even as brevity is the soul of wit, so is a small scale not less necessary than an air of spontaneity to the perfect caricature." Big canvases and oil paints, he said, suited only "seriously serious" art. An "average" Max caricature is, by my calculations, about 7 × 12 inches. His tiniest were an inch or two square (on title pages of books). His largest, "The Red Cross Sale at Christie's, April 1918", measures 15 × 30 inches; but as it depicts forty-three individuals, the scale is necessarily small.

Max derided the "foolish convention of a head invariably bigger than its body," which had become for the man in the street practically the definition of caricature, a convention so strong that "it affected even Pellegrini, Daumier, and other masters. ... In a caricature of a tall man the head ought to be not magnified but diminished." On the other hand, some subjects (Swinburne, for one) *had* small bodies, which, along with large heads, constituted "salient points" (see plate 13).

Max summed up his theory:

The perfect caricature (be it of a handsome man or a hideous or an insipid) must be the exaggeration of the whole creature, from top to toe. Whatsoever is salient must be magnified, whatsoever is subordinate must be proportionately diminished. The whole man must be melted down, as in a crucible, and then, as from the solution, be fashioned anew. He must emerge with not one particle of himself lost, yet with not a particle of himself as it was before. ... And he will stand there wholly transformed, the joy of his creator, the joy of those who are privy to the art of caricature.

He would not get much argument on this today, but his conclusion, that the "perfect caricature is in itself a beautiful thing," is another matter. Nor would his explanation have helped:

The beauty of a work of art lies not at all in the artist's vision of his subject, but in his presentment of the vision. If the ladies on the chocolate-boxes were exactly incarnate, their beauty would conquer the world. If Daumier's senators and deputies were exactly incarnate, life would be intolerable. Yet no discreet patron of art collects chocolate-boxes; and that series by Daumier is one of the loveliest and most precious things in the whole world. The most perfect caricature is that which, on a small surface, with the simplest means most accurately exaggerates, to the highest point, the peculiarities of a human being, at his most characteristic moment, in the most beautiful manner.

Beautiful is not a term often used in regard to caricature – certainly not today. Whatever our admiration for the caricatures of, say, Low, Scarfe, Hirschfeld, or Levine, *beautiful* is not a word that leaps to mind with reference to them. But Max's contemporaries, while calling his drawings witty, sharp, cruel, wicked, clever, and murderous, repeatedly described them also as beautiful.

Let's turn briefly to his Leicester Galleries exhibitions. His association with this establishment commenced with a booming one-man show in 1911 ("Max's talent," the *Nation* enthused, "is the finest and most intellectual in English caricature") and another in 1913. After the war, he resumed exhibiting there in May 1921, with even greater monetary success. Max, in London for the opening (nothing else could lure him away from Rapallo), wrote to Florence about this sudden success: "It's odd that I should be such a commercial success in drawing and writing, now, isn't it? I never expected anything of the sort. I just went on doing my best – and not doing *much* of that;

and I think the commercial success is as much due to my leisureliness as to my conscience. I haven't *tired* people." The commercial success (always modest, about £1,400 from the 1921 exhibition) was in part owing to the eminence of "the Browns and Phillipses" of the Leicester Galleries. These galleries were, quite simply, *the* place for artists' exhibitions. They presented the first single exhibitions in England of Cézanne, Renoir, Van Gogh, Pissarro, Matisse, Picasso, Klee, and many others; they also pioneered the practice of loan exhibitions, of French and British artists, including Cézanne, Degas, Gauguin, Van Gogh, Matisse, Picasso, Renoir, Rodin, Rowlandson, Whistler, Burne-Jones, John, Sickert, Steer, Epstein, and others. In September 1921 the Leicester Galleries exhibited Max's Rossetti drawings in a showing of the Pre-Raphaelites; they then gave Max four more individual "triumphs" in the twenties, two in 1923, one in 1925, and another in 1928; they would hold retrospective shows in 1945 and 1952. His connection with the Leicester Galleries led to five books of caricatures, all published by Heinemann: *Fifty Caricatures* (1913), *A Survey* (1921), *Rossetti and His Circle* (1922), *Things Old and New* (1923), and *Observations* (1925).

Amid the rave notices, there were occasional controversies. In the 1921 exhibition Max offended the left-wing press with coarse depictions of the Labour Party. One cartoon, "The Patron," shows a Labour Minister of Education throwing out of his office a poet who had offered to dedicate to him what the Minister calls "your mon-you-mental translation of Pett Rark's sonnits." The *Daily Herald* protested that the only word for the drawing was "vulgar." Max wrote a letter to the editor saying that he had never been called vulgar: "But I must say I feel the epithet inexpressibly refreshing – all the more because it is not undeserved. The drawing in question is distinctly vulgar and so is my inscription on it. Vulgarity has its uses." He had more severe difficulty with the right-wing press, which in 1923 professed shock at his cartoons of Edward VII and one of the future Edward VIII. Otherwise, almost the only complaint concerned Max's draughtsmanship. One reviewer said, "There is, of course, a negligible sense in which he is no draughtsman. He does not, perhaps cannot, and probably does not care to make his figures stand on their feet, or sit in their chairs; yet he is a master of expressive line." Another reviewer put the case thus:

> In terms of aesthetics Mr Beerbohm is not a draftsman at all; he has a delicate sense of color, decorative felicity . . . but he has never learned to draw.

It is only through sheer cleverness that he is able to hold the parts of his figures together, and he invariably comes to grief over the human foot. All his characters descend to shapeless clods. For his own purposes, however, his drawing is consummate, and that is all that can be asked of an artist. He has a genius for likenesses; better than anyone else he understands how to convey the attitudes of his subjects; and his point of view is no less penetrating than original. Add to these humor without venom and refined imagination and you have lifted caricature into the realm of art.

Then, around 1930, quite deliberately and suddenly, he stopped. He feared he was becoming too much a straight portraitist. In 1942, on his seventieth birthday, Max surveyed his career as a caricaturist:

> I can't even guess how I did the earlier [caricatures]. They are so very violent, though I myself was never that. The distortions are so monstrous and so libellous. And yet that was how I *saw* my subjects, not in their presence, but afterwards, in my memory, when I sat down to draw them. And with most of them I was personally acquainted. I marvel that they did not drop my acquaintance. None of them seemed to mind. As time went on, somehow my memory of people's appearance became less tricksy. I began to remember people more or less exactly as they were, and was obliged to put in the exaggerations consciously ... and I have now meekly – but with great regret – laid aside my pencil.

In 1953, at Rapallo, he explained to S. N. Behrman, "Many years ago I found that my caricatures were becoming likenesses. I seemed to have mislaid my gift for dispraise. Pity crept in. So I gave up caricaturing, except privately."

In 1954 Behrman, on his next visit, introduced Edmund Wilson to Max. Wilson, an ardent enthusiast (Max's caricatures, he said, amounted to "a kind of Divine Comedy that he has been working at all his life"), told Behrman afterwards, "He's quite sure of himself. He knows the value of what he has done, both as a writer and as an artist. He doesn't give a damn about having all his caricatures collected and published, as I suggested to him they ought to be. He doesn't even know where many of them are. He knows very well that somebody else will have to worry about all that someday."

CHAPTER TWENTY-FOUR

Representations

How many plates or photographs should adorn a biography? I think it pretty much agreed among book people that shoppers and browsers go first to the plates. And for some readers of biography, the more the better. Still, a biography shouldn't have too many illustrations, certainly not a short one like this, lest it become a pictorial biography. Then, too, one should beware of the temptation to put too much faith in photographs, especially snapshots, as showing us not only what the person *really looked like* but also what he really *was like*. Max Beerbohm was not often photographed. In 1897 he supplied a magazine editor with a pen-and-ink sketch of him by Walter Sickert, explaining, "I never am photographed, else I would have sent you a photograph." But, even if we had many photographs of him, I should not be anxious to include many here. Not only are most inadequate or misleading, but, in Max's case, we possess in his caricatures an abundant source of more expressive representations of him and of his circle. Of course I am including a few photographs in this book, but anyone who understands the art of caricature knows that a good caricature looks more like the man than the man himself does, certainly more so than a photograph or snapshot.

On this last point I draw on the eminent art critic Ernst Gombrich for sanction (as I don't do this sort of thing often, please bear with me). He writes, "All artistic discoveries are discoveries not of likenesses but of equivalencies which enable us to see reality in terms of an image and an image in terms of reality." Accordingly,

What we experience as a good likeness in a caricature, or even in a portrait, is not necessarily a replica of anything seen. If it were, every snapshot would have a greater chance of impressing us as a satisfactory representation of a person we know. In fact only a few snapshots will so satisfy us. We dismiss the majority as odd, uncharacteristic, strange, not because the camera distorts, but because it caught a constellation of features from the melody of expression which, when arrested and frozen, fails to strike us in the same way the sitter does.

Hardly any person alive today has laid eyes on Max or the people he drew, but that is all the more reason to rely not on photographs but on his caricatures. Max himself urged that "The perfect caricature is not a mere snapshot. It is the outcome of study; it is the epitome of its subject's surface, the presentment (once and for all) of his most characteristic pose, gesture, expression." Accordingly, by way of illustrating this history, I have included here a few surface epitomes: of Max himself; and of Turner, Rothenstein, Wilde, Whistler, Swinburne, James, Kipling, King Edward VII, persons important to his private or artistic life; and of course Rossetti, whom Max never saw. Zuleika Dobson and (just barely) Enoch Soames are also represented. Choosing eight pages of typical colour drawings – given the import of watercolour to so many of his caricatures – was not easy. But you will get the idea.

The drawing of Florence reproduced in plate 17 is not a caricature, but a fanciful drawing of her on the terrace at the Villino. Max wrote to Reggie Turner in June 1913, "I have been doing a lot of drawings of Florence, 'from the life'. . . . It is great fun." We know that he did not draw caricatures "from the life" because in doing so he would, as he put it, be bound by the realities of it. And he almost never caricatured women, much less the serious-minded Florence. It is probably fitting that Florence, whom Max so adored, and whom so many others found hard to take, should come down to my readers not in some old unflattering photograph but in this light and whimsical drawing. This was evidently how he saw her in those early years. There may be just a touch of caricature in this multi-image drawing, but for the most part it conformed to Max's straightforward (as opposed to his usual "distorted") gaze. He must have thought the drawing good or he would not have kept it. Looking at this imaginative yet "realistic" depiction of her, one almost wishes he had done more in this line. But no, he stayed within his own artistic limits as he perceived them. This economy, he firmly believed, was a large part of his success as both writer and artist.

Something should be said about the almost over-abundance of self-caricatures. Among the roughly 2,100 caricatures listed in the Hart-Davis *Catalogue* a whopping 97 are self-caricatures – making Max himself his own favourite subject by a good margin. The closest competitors are King

Edward VII and George Bernard Shaw, with 72 and 62 entries respectively. In many of the self-portraits the artist shares the stage with others, forming part of a group portrait, as in "Some Persons of 'the Nineties,' " where he is one of a dozen worthies, including Wilde, Rothenstein, Yeats, Beardsley, Soames, *et al.* (plate 23). Still, the proportion of self-caricatures is surprisingly high. You can't imagine any other caricaturist of note doing that many self-portraits. Max's penchant for drawing himself can be linked, indeed traced, to the kind of writer that he was. Even in his fiction, and certainly in his reviews, he was a personal essayist, and the essayist's aim, as he put it, is to bring himself home to his reader. Virginia Woolf says that Max's writings gave us only himself: he had no message; instead he "so consciously and purely" brought his personality into his writing that it permeated every word he wrote. His triumph, she says, is the triumph of style. Woolf's words apply nicely to Max as caricaturist. His graphic style, though so varied, is intensely personal; it permeates his caricatures of others and *a fortiori* his self-caricatures. From the elfin, childlike figures of the early 1890s (see plate 6) through to his mature years, Max is always round-eyed, heavy-lidded, and dandily dressed. He is ever the impertinent spectator, unshockable, looking as if he could believe anything, no matter how ridiculous, of any man, himself included. For, much as he disapproved of egoistic introspection, he was (as I have insisted all along) genuinely self-aware. In 1905, while writing to his future wife about how at Dieppe he was still playing silly practical jokes and writing letters in disguised hands, he interrupts himself:

> What a lot of writing about myself! But it isn't egoism in the ordinary sense of the word. I am not thinking "I am I" and must be interesting to everyone else. I am something more than I – a detached and puzzled spectator – detached, yet knowing more about myself than about any other subject, and offering myself humbly for the inspection of others. I think there is a difference between this and egoism.

Artists work best with what they know, and he knew himself best. Moreover, if the words may be excused in this context, self-portraiture also fitted in neatly with his belief that in a good caricature the artist mocks what he loves. A decent amount of *amour propre* was something Max did not lack.

The few photographs and self-caricatures reproduced here show something of Max the dandy. Indeed any representation of him stresses his dress. In the caricatures he is almost invariably well turned out, often in evening clothes. Even when depicting himself at his writing table (plate 15), he will concede nothing to informality except the slippers on his feet. He praised the male costume of his time for "its subtlety and sombre restraint, its quiet congruities of black and white and grey," and because it produced "a supreme effect through means least extravagant." And he positively venerated the ubiquitous top hat (as in, for example, plate 6). By 1940 he looked back at it as "a thing of the past; almost a museum piece," although for him it remained "a black but shining old monument." The top hat, Max wrote, "is very sensitive. . . . It alone among hats had a sort of soul. If one treated it well, one wasn't sure that it didn't love one. . . . I feel I may justly claim to have deserved the affection my hats had for me."

Of course Max had plenty to say about dandies, beginning with one of his earliest essays, from which I shall quote only his words on that other great treatise on clothes, Carlyle's *Sartor Resartus.* While Max finds it annoying and pathetic that "anyone who dressed so very badly as did Thomas Carlyle should have tried to construct a philosophy of clothes," he finds in Carlyle some real, though ironic, wisdom on the subject: " 'A dandy . . . is a clothes-wearing man, a man whose trade, office, and existence consists in the wearing of clothes. Every faculty of his soul, spirit, purse, and person is heroically consecrated to this one object, the wearing of clothes wisely and well.' Those are true words. They are, perhaps, the only true words in *Sartor Resartus*." Max was twenty-three when he wrote these words, but he would never for a moment have considered repudiating them.

Today the Museum of London has some of Max's clothes, and the Victoria & Albert Museum has on permanent display a suit and a walking stick that belonged to him.

CHAPTER TWENTY-FIVE

Radio Days

To hear Max's admirers talk on the subject, you would think he was a weekly broadcaster for the BBC. But the fact is that beginning in 1935 and concluding in the year of his death, 1956, he made exactly twelve broadcasts. Occasionally the BBC would re-broadcast one of his talks; and he made two other brief radio appearances, a two-minute reminiscence in 1951 as part of a programme on the music-hall singer Marie Lloyd, and a four-minute memorial talk in 1952 on his friend Desmond MacCarthy. His own proper broadcasts, if you were to average them out, come to about one every two years. Averaging in this way is a bit misleading, for Max gave his broadcasts very irregularly: three in 1935–36, two in 1942; and one in late 1945; then, after he and Florence returned to Italy in 1947, he recorded in Rapallo, and his talks were later broadcast, one each in 1949, 1950, and 1954; two in 1955, and the final one, posthumously, in June 1956. Not exactly a constant presence. As earlier, he wasn't going to "tire" his audience (or himself) by coming before them too often.

But there is no doubt that Max was a hit on the radio. The idea had come from the BBC. A producer there, Moray McLaren, hearing that Max was visiting England, wrote and asked if he would give a talk as part of a series called *Revisited*. Might Max like to revisit London? It's unlikely that any other subject could have lured him to try something so new as broadcasting. He was always eager to talk about the old days. Then too he had never opposed radio in the way he would later oppose television. For all his deprecation of the twentieth century and its gadgets, he liked the BBC – "a wonderful triumph of variety and soundness," he told Reggie; he liked the woman announcer's voice, and those of Chesterton, King George, and Gracie Fields; he was amused at Shaw – quite "capital" at acting but "no good in a 'talk': much too platformy and grimly determined to be a vigorous hefty youth."

Max wrote back saying he was interested, but also rather terrified at the prospect of "radiating" on the subject of London: "I am essentially a private, non-radiant person, by nature and habit. Only a rather heavy bribe would tempt me forth to address *urbem et orbem*. I should want – I was going to say £100; but won't grossly say that: I will delicately say £90. Do you think this outrageous?" The executives at the BBC thought so (other writers in the series were being paid £12) and asked McLaren to make the case to them in writing. He did so. "Max Beerbohm," he argued, "is about the only living writer of English who is universally liked. He is no Shaw or Wells with admirers and enemies; as far as I can see, he only has admirers. For years now he has been read by generations of undergraduates who, when they have long ceased to be undergraduates, have read him again and again and found him as delightful as ever." McLaren prevailed. Max had also made it a condition that the producer, and Florence, first listen to him speaking into a microphone for five minutes to determine that his voice "would not irritate the public and shame the B.B.C." That dry run went off successfully; next he demanded and got seven or eight rehearsals. He was a fussy perfectionist, but he knew what he was doing.*

The first talk, "London Revisited," was aired live on Sunday evening, 29 December 1935, and was a huge success. Siegfried Sassoon – admittedly a fanatical admirer – said, "I felt as if I were listening to the voice of the last 'civilised man' left on earth." Rebecca West – not a fanatical admirer – is quoted as later having said the *very* same thing, and having added, "Max's broadcasts justify the entire invention of broadcasting." Next, the following April, Max spoke on "Speed" and in July on "A Small Boy Seeing Giants" (the politicians famous in his boyhood).

Max would not give another radio talk until half a dozen years later. In autumn 1938, anticipating the advent of war, he and Florence again returned to England, living briefly in Bayswater and then, from 1939 to 1944, in Surrey as guests of Sydney and Violet Schiff, at Abinger Manor Cottage. In many people's minds Max's broadcasts have come to be associated with the war, in spite of his having given only two during those years. But even before these 1942 wartime talks, if David Cecil is correct, Max's broadcasts had inaugurated "a new chapter in the history of his art." They certainly changed

---

*In 1954, Douglas Cleverdon, recording Max's talk on Henry James for later broadcast, moved the operation to a hotel room in Rapallo because of the noise from the road outside Max's house. During the recording session, Cleverdon and his assistants had "to crowd into the bathroom" because Max insisted on being alone with the microphone. He worked at the five-minute talk for two hours.

the size of his audience: he estimated (only partly in jest) his readers to number 1,500 in Britain and 1,000 in America. After the first three broadcasts, he was, Cecil says "a national figure." During the previous quarter of a century, he had been viewed, quite rightly, as a figure not just from the past but of the past. Now he was present, and on the great popular medium: "His voice and manner were a living reality in every house in England that contained a wireless set." Max's other biographer, Samuel Behrman, was if anything more enthusiastic still, saying that it was odd that Max, "one of the least popular writers in the world should have become, next to Winston Churchill, the most popular broadcaster in England during the most critical moment of its history. ... he had millions of listeners." The part about Churchill might be deemed an exaggeration. "Maximilians" are enthusiasts – they don't seem to be able to help themselves – and Behrman was no exception. Moreover, Max did have millions of listeners, notably for the two talks in 1942, one on "Music Halls of My Youth" and the other on "Advertisements." The BBC had an enormous audience, especially during the war. What else was there?

In his radio talks Max announced himself as "an interesting link with the past" – this was always his hook into his material. He had lived in London when it was a congeries of towns and villages; he knew the world before the speeding automobile; as a boy he had seen Lord Randolph Churchill (Winston's father) and Joseph Chamberlain and Lord Rosebery going into 10 Downing Street; he could tell about hearing – he would even sing a few bars – old music-hall performers like Albert Chevalier, the Great MacDermott, Gus Ellen, Harry Freeman, and Dan Leno; he knew inside out the London theatre world of the 1890s and 1900s, including that vanished institution, the actor-manager – Henry Irving, George Alexander, and his own brother; he could tell his audience about eccentrics like George Moore, and the American actor Nat Goodwin who loved to talk theology ("I once read a book called *Paley's Evidences. Paley* was a great Englishman, you ought to be damned proud of him. It's easy enough to be an Atheist, like Ingersoll.... Paley knew what he was talking about. Fine.... Paley convinced me.... I don't say every word of the Bible's true. No, sir. But the Sermon on the Mount – well, it's fine"). And Max would talk about Hall Caine, W. B. Yeats, Henry James, and about an old man, Sylvester Hethway (sometimes Herringham), who remembered Rossetti and his friends.

Max's focus in his broadcasts was broadly speaking the "glittering" Edwardian era, the last ten years of Victoria's reign and the first decade of the twentieth century. These years were alive and fresh to him; they had been his own years as a visible participant on the London scene. Max always considered himself a late-Victorian/Edwardian, and, whether in Rapallo or (during two world wars) in England, he refused to enter the so-called modern era. He did not grow with the times. He never liked the twentieth century. Was this a failing? He himself always believed that staying within his limitations was at the core of his success. After the Edwardian era, a time during which he was near the centre of what was going on in the arts, he stayed put. This evinces a conservative temperament which, overridden for a time during his youth (if he ever had a youth), came eventually to the fore and stayed there. But surely we can't hold this against him. We need conservators, curators of the past. No one could have been better suited to revisit this particular past because in a sense he never left it. For others, the present and the intervening years came along and swept away or at least obscured the past. Shaw, for example, had all these years kept so abreast of the times that he would have had difficulty in achieving the effect Max had. For Max, the past remained present. From the day he left the London scene in 1910 he was for nearly half a century the most eloquent embodiment of and expression of the bygone Edwardian years. And during the last twenty years of his life, these BBC radiocasts provided him with a new and satisfying platform for telling people about that era. For the nostalgic note that pervades them he made no apology. When, immediately after the war, he published the first six talks in a small book – bulked out with a handful of essays and called *Mainly on the Air* – he wrote, "What civilised person in these days (unless he has a passion for such things as science or sociology) isn't nostalgic?"

The persona projected in these broadcasts is naturally quite different from that of the sprightly young writer of the 1890s or even from that of the mature essayist of the next two decades. His age he exaggerated. In 1935 he was sixty-three. Of course by the time of the last broadcasts he was in his eighties. His tone is fatherly, or rather grandfatherly; he champions the good old days. Occasionally he can sound a bit of a crank, an old man lamenting change and new machinery. But even when he is complaining, his mood is soft, modest; and so he gets away with it. The effect on his first listeners was not just pleasant, it was cheerful. Let's listen for Max's radio-talk tone,* in this example from "Advertisements," broadcast on 18 September 1942:

> Ladies and gentlemen, I am afraid my subject is rather an exciting one; and as I don't like excitement I shall try to approach it in a gentle, timid, round-about way. I am all for the quiet life. That is a deplorable confession, I suppose. I remember that many people were irritated and reproachful when, as a youngish man, I wrote in some newspaper, or in some book, that my ideal of happiness was "a four-poster bed in a field of poppies and mandragora." London, when I wrote those words, was not so large a city as it has since become, but it was too large, and too civic, for my taste, and great always was my pleasure in getting away from it, for a while, whenever I could: away from the hustle and jostle that ought to have been so congenial to me.
>
> In 1910, when I was thirty-seven years old, I did altogether get away from it, to a little house on a coast-road on the gulf of Genoa. A very quiet coast road, traversed mostly by rustic carts and horses; a road on which a motor-car created excitement; a road on which little children ran races during a great part of the day.

He recounts how he had come back to England during "what we ingenuously called the Great War." On his subsequent return to Italy he found the coast road "magnificently asphalted" and crowded with motor cars and motorbikes: "the heartiness of their hooting and of their mostly open exhausts was a great improvement on the cries of those little boys and girls who had been wont to run races, and could no longer do so ... I wish, Ladies and Gentlemen, I could cure myself of the habit of speaking ironically. I would so like to express myself in a quite straightforward manner. But perhaps it's as well that I can't; for if I could, my language might be over strong for Sunday evening." And thence on to the noise in London, quieted, tragically, during the present war, and thence to the noise of advertisements, and so on.

---

* Recordings of Max's talks survive, though you must go to some trouble to hear them. The BBC Sound Archive recordings are restricted to internal use; however, you can listen to some of the broadcasts at the National Sound Archive in London ("Music Halls of My Youth," "Nat Goodwin – and Another," "George Moore," and "Hethway Speaking") and at the Library of Congress in Washington, DC ("First Meetings with W. B. Yeats" and "London Revisited"). Max is also to be heard on an old Angel Recording #35206 *Sir Max Beerbohm Reading His Own Works* ("The Crime" and "London Revisited").

The part about his ironic turn of mind is particularly noteworthy. A year earlier Max had actually volunteered to hold forth on "Glimpses of Royalty," telling the BBC, "I have often (in writings as well as in drawings) mocked at [Royalty], as I do at all things of which I am fond. But I don't think any mockery would creep into my broadcast." This drew an apologetic reply from F. W. Ogilvie, Director of the BBC: "Will you think us difficult and stupid people if I say frankly that we should be afraid of misunderstanding on the part of some of our wide audience?" Ogilvie tells Max that the BBC wholly accepts his assurance that there would be no mockery in his talk, but it believes that listeners "tend to read into broadcasts what they expect to find in them." Max wrote back that he fully understood "your feeling that people at large might rather expect me to be ironical about the royal processions and ceremonies I have witnessed – and would construe my respectful and even emotional remarks as bids for unholy merriment." He would leave the royal family alone. After all, two years before this, the King had knighted him.

CHAPTER TWENTY-SIX

Royalty

Some people were of the opinion that Max would have done better had he refused the knighthood King George VI offered him in 1939. And it's true that hearing him constantly referred to as "Sir Max" can grate on one's nerves. But Max himself had no hesitation about accepting the honour. It was not just that his brother, for instance, had been knighted, or Will Rothenstein. The argument from example meant nothing to him. What he liked, I think, was the irony of it. "I shouldn't have liked it when I was younger," he wrote to a friend, "for it would have cramped my style. Now it's all right." Back in the 1890s Max's essays seemed almost obsessed, in an unflattering fashion, with royalty. In "Arise Sir — —!" he writes:

Knighthood is a cheap commodity in these days. It is modern royalty's substitute for largesse, and it is scattered broadcast. . . . [Yet] even now the number of those who are not knighted exceeds the number of those who are. Time, doubtless, will reverse these figures. It is quite possible that, in the next century, forms of application for knighthood will be sent out annually to every householder and be thrown with other circulars into the waste-paper basket. Further still in the future, knighthood may be one of the lighter punishments of the Law. "Forty shillings or a knighthood" sounds quite possible.

But knighthood was a side issue. His real preoccupation was with Edward Albert, "Bertie," Prince of Wales, later King Edward VII. Am I alone in thinking Max rather liked him? Everyone else who has approached the subject thinks he despised Victoria's eldest son, but their opinion fails to take into account Max's sense of fun, his love of irony, his delight in anything touching the ridiculous. I may be wrong. At any rate, the early essay "Diminuendo" (1895) bespeaks his fascination with the "prodigious life" of the Prince of Wales:

What experience has been withheld from His Royal Highness? Was ever so supernal a type, as he, of mere Pleasure? How often he has watched, at

Newmarket, the scud-a-run of quivering homuncules over the vert on horses, or, from some night-boat, the holocaust of great wharves by the side of the Thames; raced through the blue Solent; threaded *les coulisses* [spent a lot of time backstage]! He has danced in every palace of every capital, played in every club. He has hunted elephants through the jungles of India, boar through the forests of Austria, pigs over the plains of Massachusetts. From the Castle of Abergeldie he has led his Princess into the frosty night, Highlanders lighting with torches the path to the deer-larder, where lay the wild things that had fallen to him on the crags. He has marched the Grenadiers to chapel through the white streets of Windsor. He has ridden through Moscow, in strange apparel, to kiss the catafalque of more than one Tzar. For him the Rajahs of India have spoiled their temples, and Blondin has crossed Niagara along the tight-rope, and the Giant Guard done drill beneath the chandeliers of the Neue Schloss. Incline he to scandal, lawyers are proud to whisper their secrets in his ear. Be he gallant, the ladies are at his feet.

The Prince could not be expected to strive after things of the mind: "I do not suppose that, if we were invited to give authenticated instances of intelligence on the part of our royal pets, we could fill half a column of the *Spectator*. In fact, their lives are so full they have no time for thought."

However, it was not Max's writings that made people believe he disliked Edward, but his caricatures. Both as Prince of Wales and as King, Edward was Max's favourite and second most frequent target. But, since Max drew himself even more often, you can't argue hostility from sheer numbers. Was it their content? Were the Edward VII carictures unusually savage? Look at the excruciatingly ugly caricatures of Wilde, who was a friend, or those of Turner and Rothenstein, his best friends. The argument about physical ugliness or ungainliness or big noses* doesn't hold, either. The legends to the King Edward caricatures could be cruel, but so were many others involving friends – Gosse, Moore, Harris, Shaw.

The sexual innuendo or even bluntness of some of the Edward VII caricatures is, I grant you, surprising. The King's insatiable womanizing was an

---

* Max said, apropos of the King, "The noses of fat men do not follow suit with the rest of them as they age. The noses become, if anything, sharper, thinner." In "A Constitutional Monarch" (plate 10) Edward's nose assumes proportions that make it special even among the many "monstrous" variations Max inflicted on the human body.

unavoidable theme for his most attentive caricaturist. A series of eight drawings, exhibited at the Leicester Galleries in 1923, is jokingly titled "Proposed
Illustrations for Sir Sidney Lee's forthcoming Biography." The drawings
show "H.R.H." in each decade of his life, always with a woman in the background; the final drawing depicts Edward in heaven, with halo and harp, the
royal initials having been changed to "A. E." (Angel Edward). The right-wing
press was outraged: "Teutonically brutal," "A scarifying exhibition," "The
end of Max Beerbohm," the work of "a shameless bounder or a stealthy
Bolshevist." Max wrote to the Leicester Galleries saying, "No question of
principle is involved. The question is one of taste merely," and if they as pro-
prietors of the gallery thought it better to remove the offending drawings,
they should feel free to do so. The caricatures, Max said, "were conceived, as
you know, in a spirit of light-hearted fantasy; but if the public is likely to read
any shadow of seriousness into them, and accordingly to regard them as
unkind and even 'disloyal,' I think it would be well to avoid this misunderstanding of my disposition." The Leicester Galleries withdrew the drawings.
Eventually the Royal Family purchased them for Windsor: "The tenants keep
them behind a panel in the drawing room," Max recalled for Samuel
Behrman. "I am told that when they have people they are cozy with, they take
them out from behind the panel and show them." That series is actually
rather tame compared to "Illustrating the force of ancient habit" (plate 11),
a drawing that shows the King visiting a French convent and saying to the
Mother Superior, who has lined up all her young nuns for his inspection,
"Enfin, Madame: faites monter la première à gauche [So, Madame, let me see
the first on the left]."

For Edward's son and successor, George V, Max had, and no argument
about it, genuine affection. Max attended the opening of Parliament in 1914
and wrote to Florence of seeing the procession of the King and Queen:

> And after they had passed I found myself with tears in my eyes and an
> indescribable sadness – sadness for the King – the little King with the great
> diamonded crown that covered his eyebrows, and with the eyes that
> showed so tragically much of effort, of the will to please – the will to
> impress – the will to be all that he isn't and that his Papa *was* (or seems to
> him to have been) – the will to comport himself in the way which his wife
> (a head taller than he) would approve. Oh such a piteous, good, feeble,
> heroic little figure. I shall never forget the sight.

He thought George V a "transcendently decent and loveable King." Still, for private circulation Max wrote a "Ballade Tragique" in which a lady-in-waiting and a lord-in-waiting quarrel to the death over who is duller, the King or the Queen. Rumour had it that this poem was a sore spot with King George and Queen Mary. "Kind friends sent it to them," Max explained.

On the death of George V in January 1936 Max wrote to a friend, "I'm sadly doubtful of the future effects of E. 8. But of course he *may* turn out all right." But of course, as all the world knows, he didn't. Edward had already become involved with Mrs Simpson, and had shown himself dangerously friendly with Nazi Germany (he would remain a Nazi-sympathizer for a time even after World War II began). Max, as early as 1922, had drawn a cartoon that "divined" trouble to come. Called "Long choosing and beginning late [Milton, *Paradise Lost*]," its caption purported to be an extract from *The Times* of 10 November 1972:

An interesting wedding was quietly celebrated yesterday at the Ealing Registry Office, when Mr Edward Windsor was united to Miss Flossie Pearson. The bridegroom, as many of our elder readers will recall, was at one time well-known as the "heir-apparent" of the late "King" George. He has for some years been residing at "Balmoral," 85 Acacia Terrace, Lenin Avenue, Ealing; and his bride is the only daughter of his landlady. Immediately after the ceremony the happy pair travelled to Ramsgate, where the honey-moon will be spent. Interviewed later in the day by a *Times* man, the aged mother-in-law confessed that she had all along been opposed to the match, because of the disparity between the ages of the two parties – the bride being still on the sunny side of forty. "I had always," she said, "hoped that my Flossie was destined to make a brilliant match."

This caricature was one of the items which, after public outcry, was withdrawn from the 1923 Leicester Galleries exhibition.

All this notwithstanding, in what may be called an instance of good sportsmanship on the part of the Crown, Max was knighted, on 14 June 1939. Always the dandy, he took special care with his dress. After the ceremony, he wrote to a friend, "My costume yesterday was quite all right. . . . Indeed, I was (or so I thought, as I looked around me) the best-dressed of the Knights, and quite on a level with the Grooms of the Chamber and other palace officials. I'm not sure that I wasn't as presentable as the King himself – *very* charming though he looked."

CHAPTER TWENTY-SEVEN

Kindred Writer

In 1941 G. M. Trevelyan, historian and Master of Trinity College, Cambridge, got in touch with Max, who for a second time was living out the duration of a world war in England. Trevelyan wanted Max to deliver the Clark Lectures. Max declined. He had thought about it carefully, he told Trevelyan, but had "failed to ferret out one single subject about which I know enough to enable me to say enough, or anything like enough, about it. I have views on a great number of subjects, but no great coordinated *body of views* on any subject. I have been rather a light-weight; and mature years have not remedied this defect." But when the following year Cambridge asked him to present the next Rede Lecture, he accepted. It was only one lecture, and he had a subject close to his heart and one on which he felt he had something to say: Lytton Strachey.

The two men had been friends but not intimates. Then *Eminent Victorians* appeared in 1918, and Max wrote to Strachey thanking him "for the immense pleasure" the book had given him:

> You are finely considerate of your reader and of your art. One can sit comfortably back and just watch you with perfect confidence, knowing that the end of each essay will be as perfect as its outset. . . . Each of your essays is *globular* in effect – no angles, no points out-sticking; a lovely rotund unity, shining and unyielding.

The workmanship of Strachey's sentences, Max continues, is wonderful, pure and "so laboriously filtered," yet "full of animation"; his English is without affectation or eccentricity yet so clearly personal. Then too, there is Strachey's "quite wanton *joy* in the variations of human character" and his gift for dramatic narrative, his "constant power of *visualizing* a scene, great or small, essential or by-the-way – Rome in 1870, or Gordon at Khartoum, or the Archdeacon of Chichester speeding in his phaeton 'between the hedges' at night." What, Max enquires, will Strachey do next? Max himself hopes Strachey will want to say more about Victorian times:

Present times, obviously, don't provide you with good material; and the immediate past – the past one can all but touch – is (to me) so much more enchanting than any other past. And there are so many great and little Victorians whom I positively hear clamouring from beneath their marble slabs that you should write about them – a nobly disinterested wish that does them credit, I think.

Even with Max's correction (Lord Rosebery, not Lord Hartington, had had ambitions to be Prime Minister, win the Derby, and marry a Rothschild), this six-page letter was one to turn the head of any writer, novice or veteran. Strachey was delighted. It is true that back in 1906, recovering from a bout of illness, he had refused Desmond MacCarthy's invitation to meet Max Beerbohm. He didn't want, he said, to be bored. By the next year, he was somewhat changing his tune, telling a friend that Max's Carfax caricatures were "charming ... many of them really beautiful, and some like Blake – all (to my mind) the height of amusement." And in 1917 he was "carried away" by the Grosvenor Gallery exhibition of the Rossetti caricatures: "[Max] has the most remarkable and seductive genius – and I should say about the smallest in the world."

Then in October 1919 Strachey received an inscribed copy of *Seven Men*. He wrote back:

> It would be futile for me to try to say how much I like everything you write. But perhaps what I enjoy and admire most of all are the occasions when you suddenly shoot away from your Classicism into sheer redundant fantasy – the letter to Queen Victoria for instance, or the conversation between the envelopes.* It is these moments, it seems to me, that show that you are – there is only one word for it – inspired. These are heavenly moments, though there are others when the inspiration seems to come from elsewhere. Certainly before you wrote *Savonarola Brown* you must have made it up with the Devil.

---

* In "Enoch Soames," Max, spending that distracted June afternoon in 1897 waiting for Soames to return from the British Museum, fancies himself writing to the Queen, so "full of the garnered wisdom of sixty years of Sovereignty," and asking her advice in a "delicate matter" concerning Enoch Soames, "whose poems you may or may not know ..."; in "A. V. Laider" Max, remarking on his fascination with envelopes returned in the post and pinned to hotel letter-boards, offers an example of the "frequent dialogues" between "the young bright envelopes," still hopeful and eager about being claimed, and "their dusty and sallow seniors," cynical and resigned to never reaching their addressees.

Next, rumour came to Rapallo that Strachey was working on the most
eminent of all Victorians, the Queen herself. Much pleased, Max wrote to tell
Strachey that reading Victoria's letters had made him think about "the extraordinarily congenial problem that Q.V. offers to you in her tough strength
and ability and the delicious *personal* (never *positional*) silliness in which she
abounds" (a shrewd distinction that seems to have informed Strachey's
book). Max also drew a caricature of Strachey in his "royal connexion" – surrounded by images of the Queen, nibbling on his pen "and trying hard to see
her with Lord Melbourne's eyes." Arriving in London in the spring of 1921
to arrange an exhibition, Max asked Strachey to visit him so that he might
"professionally stare at him" to verify the image he had drawn from slight
acquaintance. (Strachey, with his sugar-loaf beard, his immensely long legs,
his long, limp, antennae-like fingers, his body stooping like "a sloppy asparagus," was a fine subject for caricature.) Strachey obligingly called on Max at
his hotel. "I went yesterday," Strachey wrote to his brother, "and found him,
very plump and whitehaired, drawn up to receive me. 'Let us come out on to
the balcony, where we shall have a view of the doomed city.' He begged me
to turn my profile towards him, and for a minute or two made some notes on
the back of an envelope. He was infinitely polite and elaborate, and quite
remote, so far as I could see, from humanity in all its forms. His caricatures
are to be exhibited in three weeks – 'if England still exists.'"

Having returned to Italy, Max wrote to Lytton's mother, saying how
pleased he was to learn that she was not vexed with the caricature of her son:
"One does what one can. I have the dubious blessing of having been born a
caricaturist; and it is always the men whom I respect most that I caricature
with the greatest gusto. This is not a very satisfactory form of homage. But,
such as it is, there it is." Furthermore, he lays claim to "the gift of rapture over
your son's writing" and explains that he rather selfishly and narrowly regrets
the recognition these two books had brought Lytton; Max wants "the base
feeling of feeling 'superior'" in championing him against "the giddy vulgar."
Lady Strachey then answered, calling Max "the greatest living master of
style," and this in turn drew the rejoinder:

Oh, believe me, Lady Strachey, that is not I, that isn't me! – *that* is your
son Lytton. I, at the age of forty-eight, have gradually, after years of
founderings and fumblings, arrived at a way of writing that is rather like
the way *he* arrived at when he made his first step from the starting-point.

But even now I am, and shall always be, a rather tricky writer. Whereas L. has *no* tricks – is a pure classicist who somehow makes the language play tricks *for* him – while *he* maintains a perfect dignity. It must be lovely to be L.

To Reggie, Max writes: "Have you read Lytton Strachey's *Queen Victoria?* That I *am* a Stoic is proved by my having no jealousy of him at all, though his mind and his prose are so like mine and so exactly like what I should have loved mine to be. For sheer divine beauty of prose, and for clairvoyance of mind in dealing with past personages, and for wit, and for much else, nobody comes within a hundred miles of him."

In December 1930 Max worked hard to get Strachey into the Athenaeum Club under Rule II, i.e. by special invitation. His campaign included a resolve, sent in writing to members of the Committee, that unless Strachey was admitted he would resign "as a protest against the doltishness of a Committee that prefers essentially unimportant big-wigs to a man of genuine distinction. ... I should greatly miss the Athenaeum, which I love. But my love for the art of English prose is ever deeper; and I should delight in my self-sacrifice in its cause!" Strachey came in at the top of the poll. This was April 1931. A few days earlier, Strachey had asked Max's permission to dedicate *Portraits in Miniature* to him. "I feel immensely proud," Max wrote back, "that you should wish to dedicate a book to me. Much older though I am than you, my admiration for your prose, since first I knew it, has had the fresh wild hot quality that belongs to a very young man's feeling for the work of a great congenial veteran. I have always felt, and shall always feel, such a duffer and fumbler in comparison with you. But I shall be better able to disguise this feeling when my eyes shall have seen my name in your new book." Max was in fact but eight years older, though with his early success in the nineties he seemed a full generation older. Strachey's book appeared in May, dedicated "To Max Beerbohm with gratitude and admiration." By the following January, Strachey was dead. Max took down the book and wrote in it the famous line from Catullus, "And now Brother for all time, Hail and Farewell."

Did he *mean* all this? this almost cloying regard for Strachey's writing? Did he really rate Strachey's prose above his own? I believe he did. In a letter written in 1927 to Virginia Woolf he had remarked, "I dare say posterity will agree with me that Lytton Strachey's prose is, *on the whole,* the finest English prose that has been written." Max had a way – and it is not a fault found in many artists of satiric bent – of overrating artists and writers whom he admired. His regard for the early novels of Meredith and the early poems of Swinburne seems excessive today. Sometimes, to be sure, posterity corroborates Max's enthusiasms – as for Daumier's caricatures, Maupassant's stories, James's prose. But about Strachey posterity quickly had its doubts. And so Max seized upon the 1943 Rede Lecture to make public and expand upon (and temper somewhat) his private appreciations of Strachey.

He quite expectedly attacked the "vulgar" and "silly" notion that Strachey was a debunker:

> That he was not a hero-worshipper or even a very gallant heroine-worshipper may be readily conceded. ... Assuredly, he was not an artificer and purveyor of plaster saints or angels. He was intensely concerned with the ramifications of human character. He had a very independent mind and was an egoist insofar as he liked finding things out for himself and using his own judgment on what he found. ... He had, like the rest of us, imperfect sympathies.

In *Eminent Victorians* Strachey, while recognizing the greatness of Florence Nightingale, was annoyed at the "necessary grit" in her character; and he clearly favoured Newman over Wiseman: "He was essentially, congenitally, a Newman man. Who among us isn't?"

As for the other allegedly disrespectful book, *Queen Victoria*:

> Aren't there in the Elysian Fields two other worthies who have reason to be grateful to the supposed iconoclast? – Queen Victoria and the Prince Consort? The Prince in his life-time had never been popular; and after Sir Theodore Martin's saccharine biography, he had become a veritable mock. I never heard a kind word for him. The Queen, who in my childhood and youth had not only been revered but worshipped, was, soon after her death, no longer in public favour. Her faults had become known, and her virtues were unheeded. This is not so now; and is not so by reason of Lytton Strachey's fully judicial presentment of her with all the faults over which her virtues so very much preponderated. And it is, by the same token, through him that we know the Prince, not as just dreadfully admirable, but as someone to be loved and to be sorry for.

In places the Rede Lecture is candidly autobiographical:

I can, if you will let me, lay claim to one little modest negative virtue. I have always been free from envy. In the year 1900 I had been considered a rather clever and amusing young man, but I felt no pang whatsoever at finding myself cut out at my own game by a sudden new-comer, named G. K. Chesterton, who was obviously far more amusing than I, and obviously a man of genius into the bargain. In 1918 I was young no longer, and I think I amused people less than I had. I had subsided into sober irony. Well, here was an ironist of an order far superior to mine. And here was a delicately effulgent master, a perfect master, of English prose. And in my joy there lurked no asp of satisfaction that here was not, in my opinion, a man of genius. Very exquisite literary artists seldom are men of genius. Genius tends to be careless of its strength. Genius is, by the nature of it, always in rather a hurry. Genius can't be bothered about perfection. Each of the four essays in *Eminent Victorians* was, as a work of art, perfect.

The preference for talent over genius is quintessentially Maximilian, as is the preference for narrow, more focused, less ambitious artists. For Max, Strachey was not just a kindred writer; he was a later version of himself. When he says that Strachey is the perfect master of English prose, he means of the kind of prose he himself writes. Strachey's work, like Max's, was "escapist." Are we to be angry with Strachey, Max asks, for quite impenitently staying away from any current event?

Even for spirits less fastidious than Strachey's, there is, even at the best of times, a great charm in the past. Time, that sedulous artist, has been at work on it, selecting and rejecting with great tact. The past is a work of art, free from irrelevancies and loose ends. There are, for our vision, comparatively few people in it, and all of them are interesting people. The dullards have all disappeared – all but those whose dullness was so pronounced as to be in itself for us an amusing virtue. And in the past there is so blessedly nothing for us to worry about. Everything is settled. There is nothing to be done about it – nothing but to contemplate it and blandly form theories about this or that aspect of it.

This is no more than we would expect from the creator of *Rossetti and His Circle*, the writer who always looked back to the Edwardian era, the BBC's "curious link with the past." The Strachey/Beerbohm identification extends to Max's words on satire: Strachey is no satirist in the "robust" and

"fundamentally grim" fashion of Juvenal or Swift. Strachey, rather than sati-
rize, mocks, and "Mockery is a light and lambent, rather irresponsible thing.
'*On se moque de ce qu'on aime*' ... Strachey was always ready to mock what
he loved. In mockery there is no malice." These are of course the very words
Max uses elsewhere to explain his own *modus operandi*. And no one ever
thought of calling Max robust or grim, either in his prose or in his caricatures.
Strachey's prose, finally, is "never precious" and, "though classical, is entirely
natural, and rather shy. He makes no attempt to dazzle. He is not even afraid
of clichés. He can be very homely." Words more appropriate to Max's own
late prose would be hard to come by.

Lytton Strachey: The Rede Lecture was published in 1943 as a slight booklet conforming to wartime paper restrictions. It sold, to the surprise of
Cambridge University Press, more than 10,000 copies.

CHAPTER TWENTY-EIGHT

A Chekhovian Story

Lytton Strachey, in his preface to *Eminent Victorians,* writes that the historian of the past "will row out over that great ocean of material, and lower down into it, here and there, a little bucket, which will bring up to the light of day some characteristic specimen." One such bucket-like exploration of the vast Beerbohm archives brings up Camille Honig. In 1944, towards the end of the war, Honig, Polish *émigré* journalist/writer, was giving a talk to British soldiers of a Searchlight Group in the village of Abinger in Surrey. A gunner told him that there lived in the village a gentleman "who used to write in the papers." Some thought him a foreigner – perhaps a Dutchman – he had a funny name though he spoke English "bettern'n some of us." One believed he had been a music-hall star who had lost his voice; indeed this soldier claimed to have heard him attempt to sing on the radio. The name? Sir Max Beerbohm. He was "a proper gentleman" and Lady Beerbohm a "real lady" who "does all sorts of things" for the soldiers. Would Honig like to meet him? The gunner takes Honig round to a cottage, accompanies him to the back door, and with an air of "It ain't my fault," introduces him to Lady Beerbohm and disappears. Lady Beerbohm, all smiles, acts as though she expected the visitor. A novelist, Honig wrote, would have accurately described her as "exquisitely petite and simply charming." (Isn't it nice to hear a good report of her?) Later in the visit she offers him "Polish coffee," coffee with cocoa in it, something he had never heard of and deemed an innocent libel on his people; whereupon she served "delicious" non-cocoa-added coffee.

Honig's account calls to mind Max's visit to Swinburne. Like Max half a century earlier, Honig is nervous about meeting his hero:

I found Sir Max, the greatest living handler of the English language, studying an English dictionary. And, mind you, not, as you might have easily expected, a volume of the Great Oxford Dictionary, or the Shorter Oxford or at least the Concise Oxford ... but one of those cheap, common-or-garden dictionaries, which I, poor perplexed un-Englishman, would have thought utterly degrading to use. Closing the dictionary and waving, so to speak, all conventionalities asides, Sir Max and Lady Beerbohm welcomed me most heartily. They share the art of dispelling the awkward embarrassment and silence that falls after such an introduction ...

Of course Honig, like all Max's visitors over the years, is struck by his appearance:

He looks as elegant and neat as one of his exquisitely turned-out phrases. He wore a well-cut, double-breasted light grey suit, black socks, black shoes well polished, blue striped shirt (I think), a dark tie with an old-world pearl pin it it. His cheeks are fresh and ruddy; his eyes are a childish grey-blue. His moustache, white with yellow tobacco stain, and the white soft trimming around his naked shiny head with the huge bulging forehead which reminds you either of an overdeveloped precocious child or of the popular idea of genius; rather a musical genius than a painter or writer. There is something, in his forehead, of the gentle ironic exaggerations of his own caricatures of the Nineteenth-century Great.

Honig finds Max speaking "as he writes – in the grand manner, and he illustrates his choice sentences with superb gestures and facial expressions, gay eyes, and a voice husky, dramatic and most pleasant." Max, we are told, does not talk, he tells stories (that's precisely what Gide had said of Wilde), and when he tells a story, the listener "has the uncharitable feeling that it has been rehearsed, and one thinks of some grave philosophical comedian talking like Henry James." Lady Beerbohm – as the deferential Honig invariably calls her – intervenes: "We know everything about ourselves – do tell us something about *yourself.*" Honig recounts something of his experiences as a Pole in England, prompting in Max a "Chekhovian story" of a wild Frenchman escaped from France to England and crying "Vive l'Angleterre libre! Vive la liberté!" in a pub where his enthusiasms are greeted with embarrassing silence. Two dart players gaze at him as at a lunatic, two men at the bar order two more pints and continue their talk about dogs, trying their best to ignore the whole incident. You must, Max tells Honig, wonder at us, "coming to this Island with your natural exuberance, and the cold callous attitude of our people to the foreigner must have shocked and exasperated you. We are a queer species, but we don't mean to be like that; it's more, I think, our confounded fear of making an exhibition of ourselves, that we don't show the foreigner a heartier welcome." Honig presses forward to ask Max questions: Why does he not write his memoirs? What is his opinion of present-day writers? What of the future? Why does he not write something, however slight, for today's readers? The answers are as one would expect: Max dislikes memoirs, and writing has always been such terribly hard work for him. As for the present, much less the future, he does not understand it: "Essentially I belong to the Nineteenth Century. My world has died." When the talk drifts to the horrors of Nazism, Max wants to hear something about Poland, but he understands when Honig, "not wanting to grieve him unnecessarily," soon changes the subject. Does Max know the Baltic? Honig knows Memel in Lithuania where Max's ancestors on his father's side had come from. Max shows his visitor pastel portraits of his grandparents, married there in *1785*! His own father, like Max himself, had been the last of many children. Max is pleased with his own proximity to the eighteenth century.

But here is a small shelf of French books, including Proust.

Honig: "How do you get on with Proust?"
Max: "I can't read him – at least not much. He wrote magnificently sometimes, but he was a sick man, he had not the energy to compress, he drowned himself in a sea of literature. I have never been a great reader, but with Proust I could not get along at all. No, these books are not mine, they belong to my friend who has lent me this cottage."

(The friend was Sydney Schiff, a novelist who wrote under the name "Stephen Hudson," and a friend and translator of Proust.) The talk shifts to the Russian writers. Max: "I know, I know that Tolstoy has written the greatest novel. But I get so confused with their names. I never know who is who in a Russian novel." Moreover, he could not comprehend or appreciate "their eternal brooding, their preoccupation with the soul, the Universe, and their self-laceration. And above all their superstition." "Superstition?" Honig asks, lifting his eyebrows. "Yes, all Russians are superstitious, I think."

The goodbyes said, Honig, once outside the house, realizes he has forgotten his cane, re-enters, apologizing, and begins to make for the door a second time. Exclamations of "Oh no!" from Max and his wife. A terrible thought strikes Honig: had he taken the wrong cane? But no, he is motioned to a chair. "Don't you know it is very unlucky to come back after you have said good-bye. You must never do that without sitting down again before you leave!"

Not long thereafter, early on the Sunday morning of 3 August 1944, a German flying bomb hit Abinger church and drove parts of the debris through the cottage. E. M. Forster, who also lived in Abinger, was the first to reach the Beerbohms. He found them shaken but unharmed; they had been sleeping on a mattress under the kitchen table. The cottage was nearly demolished, and neighbours thought it a miracle that Max and Florence survived unhurt. Max wrote to the Schiffs, "Would that the idiotic bomb had continued its idiotic course further than the Church and on yonder to one of the many fields where it could have fallen so harmlessly. But one is thankful that it didn't do more mischief than it did. ... What horrible years of history to have lived through! And yet, for Florence and me, how vast an amount of happiness there was in the dear Cottage!" They stayed with friends in the vicinity for a while, then moved to Flint Cottage, Box Hill, Dorking, Surrey, the house where Meredith had lived so many years and where Max had visited him; and finally to a house lent them by Ellis Roberts near Stroud in Gloucestershire. The deaths of Sydney Schiff in November and Will Rothenstein in February, the two men who had sheltered him during two wars, further saddened Max. The war struggled to its end. He had very little money. Clement Attlee offered him a Civil List pension of £250, but Max with great politeness refused it: he did not deem himself poor enough to deserve charity. Both he and Florence longed for Italy. In the spring of 1947 Florence went to Rapallo to reclaim the Villino and set it in order after the depredations of war. She then came back to England, and together, in September, they returned to Rapallo, this time for good.

CHAPTER TWENTY-NINE

Sacred Cow

To set down all the tributes from artists and (especially) writers that came to Max in the later years of his life would be wearisome. Here are just a few. First, the public kudos: honorary doctorate, the University of Edinburgh, 1930; knighthood, 1939; honorary doctorate, Oxford, 1942; honorary membership ("representing England"), National Institute of Arts and Letters, New York, 1943; honorary fellowship, Merton College, 1945.

For his seventieth birthday, on 24 August 1942, the newly formed Maximilian Society* clubbed together to honour him with a party at the Players Theatre and a cache of seventy bottles of difficult-to-obtain wine (they managed only sixty-three). Alan Dent was the guiding force. Membership was by invitation but otherwise required only "devotion to 'Max' and his works." The seventy-eight members, all distinguished in the arts, included Lord Berners, Cyril Connolly, Desmond MacCarthy, Clive Bell, Augustus John, John Gielgud, Leonard Woolf, Graham Greene.

Nineteen fifty-two, the year Max turned eighty, was marked by a large retrospective exhibition at the Leicester Galleries in May. Critical praise was universal (*The Times* extolled Max's "remarkable triumph in rescuing an essentially popular art and using it to make comments of such extreme sophistication"; the *Observer* said the Edwardian era ought to be called "the Maximilian Period"; the *Spectator* asked, "Was ever a group, a period, a society pickled with such fastidious precision?" *Apollo* labelled Max "an English Institution"). Next came another John Lane combined edition of *Works and More* followed by the Penguin edition of *Zuleika Dobson* (Max detested "cheap" editions and had for years blocked the reissue of the book in

* There is a rumour that a second Maximilian Society has existed in the US since 1985. It is listed among learned societies, but investigation shows that members do little beyond having an occasional dinner and pledging never to pay dues or to do any work on Max – no papers, lectures, articles, etc. Their conviction is that by doing nothing they will do about as much good as do most single-author societies.

an inexpensive format). Throughout August the press used his eightieth birthday as an occasion for pouring out tributes to "The Faultless Max" (as Bertrand Russell's *New York Times* article put it). The *Manchester Guardian* would later ask: "Whose eightieth birthday was ever more publicly celebrated than the Rapallo hermit's?"

In Rapallo, the birthday itself was marked by a very private luncheon given him by a few friends. These included Selwyn and Tania Jepson, who, by assisting in the reprinting of his books and the mounting of the Leicester Galleries exhibition, had put some much-needed money in his pocket, and Sydney Roberts, who in 1941 had committed the folly of publishing a little booklet *Zuleika in Cambridge,* for which may God forgive him – Max did. The celebration took place at Montallegro, at a small country inn up in the mountains above Rapallo where Max occasionally came to escape the summer heat. Here he was presented with a case of wine from the Maximilian Society, congratulatory telegrams from all sorts of people, including Winston Churchill, and, highlight of the occasion, a leather-bound (in red morocco by Zaehnsdorf) volume of handwritten birthday tributes from nearly fifty distinguished friends and admirers. A few reminisced about the old days: Eric Parker, a contemporary at Oxford, recalled walking with Max "through Merton quadrangles and under Merton archways" and playing cards and roulette with him and Reggie Turner; Philip Gosse, son of Edmund Gosse, remembered the very first visit Max made to one of his father's famous Delamere Terrace parties in 1896; Robert Graves told how "The queer young [Charterhouse] masters of Max's schooldays had become queer old masters by mine ... duck-gaited Girdlestone ... and ineffable A. H. Tod who ... used to bawl 'Ye vile fellows! First ye cut ye'r construe and then ye try to fu-u-ule me!'" Of course one expects eightieth birthday tributes to be gushing and extravagant, and they were:

E. C. Bentley said, "... for at least fifty years Max Beerbohm's work has been a necessary part of my mental life."

Christopher Sykes, after comparing Max's prose to Mozart's music, declared, "There is no writer of English in my generation fit to unlatch your shoes."

G. M. Trevelyan said Max was the first of humorous short story tellers and the "*only* drawer of beautiful outline which is also funny."

Harman Grisewood of the BBC called Max the network's "most distinguished contributor."

Kenneth Clark said that Max's *Works* had shown him while still a boy how prose "could have a life of its own: a shape, a texture, a sound, a living voice ... something which gave me then and has given me ever since, the same delightful sensation as music and painting"; and that Max's drawings had been "the first non-realistic works of art I ever enjoyed. ... No one else had been able to wrap the truth in such an exquisite cloak of fantasy."

T. S. Eliot, not venturing on slight acquaintance to address Max directly, wrote in the third person: "He is the defence and illustration of the benefits to a writer of the discipline of the classics; the illustrator, rather than the apologist, of urbanity and the qualities of English prose style now falling into neglect."

John Betjeman, John Masefield, and Walter de la Mare complimented Max in verse. Evelyn Waugh, amid the hyperboles, his own included, offered a homely anecdote. He told how in 1929, as a young man at a dinner party, he had been just barely introduced "to the object of my worship." Then, the following day:

> Fate offered me one of those very few second chances. I found "Max" standing in the hall of my club, waiting for a luncheon guest. Should I accost him? I glanced and sidled and he, generously diagnosing the symptoms, came to greet me. I said, what a pleasant event it had been yesterday. He agreed, and added that he was anxious to see the portrait I was working on; Tonks had spoken highly of it. In that ghastly moment his friend arrived. I slipped away broken. ... I returned hours later to the club and was handed a letter by the porter. It was addressed – could it be? – in the famous script which I had read with a magnifying glass on the reproductions of so many immortal drawings. The Master had observed my discomfort, had identified me from the servants, had made enquiries. He wrote to apologize for his "intolerable offence." He had known my father well, he said. He even pretended to have read something I had written. He hoped to see me again. He was mine sincerely. At that time I lived mostly among people who thought bad manners rather *chic.* They were the hallmark of the '20s. I suddenly heard a voice from a better age and it has rung in my ears ever since.

Carol Reed, one of Herbert's children from his secret second family (and therefore Max's nephew), said, "Although I have long known you through the delight and excitement of your writings and drawings, it was only recently

that I had the great joy of meeting you. ... Much Gratitude for the Great
Pleasure you have so often given me."

I believe the birthday book organizers would surely have asked Virginia
Woolf for some words, had she been still alive. For her public accolades were,
as we have seen, as generous as these 1952 private tributes. She might have
gone back in time, as many of the others were doing, and told of an exchange
of letters in 1927: Max had written to her saying that he considered hers the
best of all modern criticism but found her novels tough going; he apologizes
for holding in his "stodgy" old way that there was only one good method of
narrative – "Homer's, and Thackeray's method, and Tolstoi's and Tom's,
Dick's, Chaucer's, Maupassant's, and Harry's." She replied that his letter had
reached her as she was starting out for the funeral of Thomas Hardy:

> I had a ticket as my father's daughter. When I read your letter, I said to my
> husband, "Now that Mr Beerbohm has praised me I have a right to have a
> seat on my own account." This mood of presumption was struck down
> instantly. I had to go to bed for a week. Or was it the chill and thrill of the
> touch of an immortal hand on my shoulder? Aren't you responsible for my
> week in bed? For you see I look upon you as one, perhaps the only one,
> who is withdrawn far, far above us, in a serene and cloudless air, imperish-
> able, aloof. And then suddenly you let down a ray from your sky and it
> rests – behold! – upon me!

As for her fiction, she tells him she can't help writing the way she does. She
writes her novels, she says, to amuse herself: "I don't defend them; I don't
read them; as for expecting you to read them, the thought makes me shudder.
But I think I could say a word in favour of freaks in general. After all there is
Tristram Shandy, [Peacock's] *Gryll Grange*, *Zuleika Dobson*: all my favourite
works." She closes, "I can't tell, and shan't attempt to tell you, what an exhil-
aration it gives me to think that any word I have written has pleased you."

It is all a bit too much, is it not? As one reviewer of Cecil's biography complained, "in literary and artistic circles, from the start of his career until his
death, [Max] was a sacred cow. Never once, so far as I know, was he attacked
by any critic worth listening to, and this is not a healthy sign." I have been
hunting desperately for this attack and leapt upon these sentences from Vita
Sackville-West's letters: "It always makes me cross when Max is called 'the
Incomparable Max.' He is not incomparable at all, and in fact compares very
poorly with Harold Nicolson, as a stylist, a wit, and an observer of human

nature. He is a shallow, affected, self-conscious fribble – so there." This was in 1957 in a private letter to Harold Nicolson, her husband, who was an outspoken and public enthusiast for Max.

Where are we to find something else negative? I can uncover nothing except an article called "The Child and the Man in Max Beerbohm" by Roger Lewis, published in 1984 in a journal called *English Literature in Transition*. Lewis claims Max advocated "a cult of laziness": "Instead of punctual creation, Beerbohm teased his audience with sporadic manifestations. What his whole attitude evinces, in fact, is a peculiarly late Victorian and Edwardian trait: that of refusing to grow up." He "stayed a child," and, of course, "The guilty secret which Freud in Vienna was discovering was that the child inside us all is not destroyed by age but merely denied." Good to have that explained. But Max, Lewis says, also "inspired boyishness in others"; he was "an indolent [perfectionist] who earned the reputation of being major because he stubbornly remained minor. . . . Beerbohm is a cartoonist and not a fine-artist; he wrote short stories rather than novels; his gift for parody absolved him from having to think up new stories on his own. . . . Beerbohm is a dapper doodler. His attempt at sustained work, *Zuleika Dobson,* quickly founders"; and, what is worse, *Zuleika* has that "tasteless, mass-suicide ending." Talk about leaving a man alone with an irony. Lewis blames Max for "presaging" the actual extermination of a generation of young men in the war that started three years after the novel's publication in 1911; Max's Duke of Dorset "is an intimation of the chivalrous Rupert Brooke who would soon be ordering the bugles to blow out over the rich dead." Jaysus! as James Joyce would have exclaimed, This is better than a play. Lewis goes on to say that we should compare Beerbohm with a character from an Iris Murdoch novel who says, "I am not famous for anything in particular. I am just famous."

I have gone on too long with Roger Lewis, but he is pretty much all I could find. It would have been better had I discovered deflations of Max by, say, Oscar Wilde, Aubrey Beardsley, Henry James, John Galsworthy, Joseph Conrad, Edith Wharton, Arnold Bennett, Graham Greene, E. M. Forster, William Empson, Edmund Wilson, W. H. Auden, James Thurber, Truman Capote, Muriel Spark, Tom Stoppard, John Updike – but alas these are all on the other side. Lewis *contra mundum*. I don't think we can say that here at last is the missing attack by some authority worth listening to. If we are going to have a case against Max, it must come from elsewhere. I'll do my best in the next chapter.

CHAPTER THIRTY

The Case Against

Julian Barnes, in his novel-cum-biography *Flaubert's Parrot* (1984), has a chapter called "The Case Against." It comprises a series of accusations against Gustave Flaubert and his work. Quite uncannily, many of these complaints, as set forth by the book's narrator, Geoffrey Braithwaite, can be alleged against Max Beerbohm. Here are some of them:

That he hated democracy.   Max did not hate what he called the Demos; he just refused to clothe the Demos with divinity; he feared a levelling down; he admitted that in the long run this levelling down was inevitable and right because it brought more happiness to more people. He merely felt sadness. If nearly everyone got into the middle class – a development altogether laudable in regard to the lower classes – what would happen to the aristocrats, such a marvellous source of ridiculousness and fun? You should know too that although he and Florence had day help at the Villino, he was for the abolition of actual servanthood, an "unnatural" and "demoralising state of existence."

That he didn't believe in progress.   If you are serious, you are making yourself an easy mark. It is true that Max was not much of a believer in progress. He hated the kind of progress that tore down lovely old parts of London and put up large, characterless buildings. Max was troubled by speed, especially as seen in the automobile and aeroplane. He came, only in later years, to tolerate the telephone. But he did see real possibilities for the spoken word on radio, and, as we have seen, was himself an infrequent but effective performer in that medium. On the other hand, he would have nothing to do with television. In 1955 the National Broadcasting Company in New York offered Max, who never had much money, $3,000 to do a few television talks. A representative of the company visited him in Rapallo: "You see, Sir Max, it will all be very simple. Our people will come and arrange everything. You will sit, if you like, where you are sitting now. You will simply say, 'My dear friends, I am very happy to be here addressing you.'" Max replied, "Do you wish me to start with a lie?"

That he wasn't interested enough in politics.   My client respectfully pleads guilty. He never voted. He did take a great interest in politicians; he believed that most people, like himself, were fascinated by the "purely personal side of politics": the costermonger says, "Good old Winston!" and the fashionable woman says, "I do think Mr Balfour is *rather* wonderful!" People relish the drama of conflict between interesting individuals, and the House of Commons provided many specimens of these. He went there for entertainment and inspiration, found both, and drew hundreds of caricatures of politicians. Moreover, he became intensely English and patriotic during the two world wars, and during both tried unsuccessfully to volunteer for some kind of war work. Earlier he had felt ashamed of England's involvement in the Boer War (Kipling's kind of war, he said) and did a series of cartoons harshly opposing it. Sounds almost political. In 1954 he signed a petition of the Hydrogen Bomb National Committee calling for an end to the menace of atomic warfare.

That he didn't involve himself in life.   Isn't it all right for someone to be more spectator than player – especially if one is such an amusing spectator? Besides, from about 1894, when he left Oxford, until 1910, he *was* a player. He dined out almost every evening of his life; he ate well, appreciated good food and wine, took his holidays abroad; he was an excellent guest; he talked; he charmed people; he wrote; he drew caricatures; he became famous; for twelve years he produced a weekly play review for the *Saturday*. He didn't fight a duel, attempt suicide, or run off with another man's wife. True, he was slow – having hesitated for about fifteen years – about taking the plunge into matrimony.

That he tried to live in an ivory tower.   Yes, think of Rapallo as an ivory tower if you will. Point conceded. But please to remember that his best work, both as prose writer and as caricaturist, came after his so-called retirement to that lovely place in 1910. And remember all those hundreds of pilgrimages that people made to the tower, over a period of some forty years, and how graciously and helpfully he received these visitors.

That he was a pessimist.   Say rather realist. Max was very fond of men and women, and they of him; his reputation from youth to old age was that of a kind, sympathetic, amiable, generous person. Of course he was a satirist and caricaturist, and for some people this means he was cruel. And he was a reviewer of plays. He did not, it is true, expect too much of human nature, agreeing with Sydney Smith that it was a sorry business at best. Still, Max usually found people amusing, which went for much. He was also very fond of dogs (I don't know if this helps).

That he didn't believe Art had a social purpose.   You've got me there. He didn't.

Enough of charges borrowed from those against Flaubert. Here are complaints more specific to Max himself:

That he never grew up.   Amateur psychologists are forever saying things like this, and they really do not deserve a rejoinder. It is true that Max continued to play practical jokes all his life, that he spent many hours "improving" books – supplying fake dedications, transforming plates and photographs, altering texts, supplying glosses and comments. He assiduously studied Queen Victoria's handwriting so that a copy of *More Leaves from a Journal* might be inscribed from her to "Mr Beerbohm the never-sufficiently-to-be-studied writer, whom Albert looks down on affectionately." Max's library also boasted a copy of *When We Dead Awaken* inscribed "For Max Beerbohm critic of who the writings fills with pleasures me. H. Ibsen." Max's book improvements were not for the public; Florence didn't care for this kind of levity, and the books were seldom shown to anyone. They were for his own enjoyment. Besides, from these pranks there evolved what can be called a genre of his own, namely the illustrated title pages of books, whereon he drew caricatures of the authors, just beneath their names, sometimes incorporating publishers' devices into the caricature. He produced some fifty such, most of them now in the Beerbohm Room at Merton. I once showed an illustrated article on these title pages to the eminent scholar/writer Gordon Ray. He said they did indeed reveal a remarkable art but not one he should like to see widely practised. Of course not. No one else has seriously attempted this particular art. It grew out of Max's flair for the portrait caricature – wherein he was in a class by himself. (So truly in a class by himself that I am reminded of the words of the widowed Nora Joyce, when asked if she remembered other writers, Joyce's contemporaries, such as André Gide. No, she didn't: "Sure, if you've been married to the greatest writer in the world, you don't remember all the little fellows.")

That his caricatures were cruel, that they hurt people.   You have a point. It's probably true that even his friends were more often than not only pretending to be pleased that Max had "got" them. He himself admitted that caricature is of necessity an unpopular art involving "a frank disregard for the feelings of the victim or the remonstrances of his friends." On the other hand, we know Max's defence: that caricature "implies no moral judgement on the subject"; that he had no need to make men whom he reverenced less ridiculous than those he despised; that, moreover, he always mocked what he loved. I have, following Max, insisted all along that his artistic concerns were primarily aesthetic. W. H. Auden thinks they were primarily moral. Perhaps with a nod towards Keats's negative capability – the aptitude for remaining in uncertainties, the contentedness with half-knowledge – we can see validity in both assessments. Auden claimed that when Reggie Turner said there was in Max a streak of "cruelty simple and isolated" he meant that

> an artist whose eye immediately detects moral failings in his subjects and whose hand instinctively reveals them is bound to seem cruel. It was not personal animosity which made the drawings of Oscar Wilde and the Prince of Wales so deadly (Wilde, indeed, was his friend); he simply could not help revealing the moral truth about them – that Wilde was a man "whose soul had swooned in sin and revived vulgar" and that the First Gentleman of Europe was an ineffable bounder. It is this immediate clarity of insight, free from all malice or prejudice, which makes Max superior to most caricaturists, even to Daumier. Even his most devastating portraits never strike one as unjust; one never feels that for personal or ideological reasons he had decided to uglify his victim.

Auden extends this idea to Max's literary judgements: Shaw's "indifference to individual human lives" Max saw as a "moral defect." Conversely, Auden quotes Max on Henry James: "Greater than all my aesthetic delight in the books is my moral regard for the author"; James in his books is a "preacher" of great moral fervour, "one whose outlook on the world seemed to me so fine and touching and inspiring, so full of reverence for noble things and horror of things ignoble." As for cruelty, what if Max did take moral pleasure in attacking men and ideas that he despised, like Kipling and his jingoism? What's wrong with a little antipathy towards pomposity, affectedness, self-absorption, self-importance, vanity, humbug? Ask Thackeray. Ask Daumier.

That he had peculiar tastes in literature.   He didn't care for Hall Caine, Mrs Humphry Ward, or Clement Scott. Nor did he find a great deal to rave about during his twelve years as drama critic of the London stage. Up the ante, you say: how about Shaw? Surely *there*, you protest, there you do find poor judgement. Well, as it happens, posterity is having some second thoughts about Shaw, and for the very reasons Max set forth. It doesn't matter. Max had genuine reservations about Shaw's work, though he was deeply ambivalent. But we've covered this ground. Shakespeare? Wasn't Max of two minds about Shakespeare? No, not really, just about the idolaters and the over-doers. He suggested that the theatre give Shakespeare a rest and declare an outright moratorium for a few years on productions of *Hamlet*. That's not so terrible. The only real shock (no surprise that he liked Thackeray, Trollope, and Boswell) is Jane Austen. Max told an unidentified woman correspondent, who enquired about an obscure reference in *Mansfield Park*, that he had never read the novel and that Jane Austen "has always left me cold – or, rather, hot with shame at not being able to read her." But if you believe everyone's tastes must conform to the consensus on great writers, including Jane Austen, then your thinking about human nature may be as unsound as Shaw's or Plato's.

That his tastes in art of all kinds remained frozen after he moved to Italy. Well, yes, they did. He was thirty-seven. Does everyone have to stay up to date? I once heard Stephen Spender say that most people have only one decade in which they are really at home, in which they know what is good among new developments in various arts. For Spender it was, he said, the 1930s. For Max, it was actually two decades, the 1890s and the first ten years of the twentieth century. He did appreciate Lytton Strachey, but then, Strachey also looked to the past. Max failed to keep up with the acknowledged giants of the first half of the century. The works of D. H. Lawrence, for example, gave him little pleasure. Although willing to admit Lawrence's "unquestionable genius," Max thought his prose "slovenly" and the man himself "afflicted with Messiahdom." When shown a copy of Joyce's *Finnegans Wake* (admittedly an easy target) shortly before being made Sir Max Beerbohm, he leafed through it and remarked, "I don't think he will get a knighthood for that!" When Edward Marsh wrote to ask Max if he would allow the Contemporary Art Society to commission Graham Sutherland to paint his portrait, Max declined, telling Marsh that although he had in his time been "a ruthless monstrifier of men," he was, like the proverbial bully, a coward. Privately, he told Samuel Behrman that in Sutherland's portrait of Somerset Maugham –

which Marsh in his letter had held up as a masterpiece – "Maugham looks as if he had died of torture." (Winston Churchill and his wife, who destroyed Sutherland's portrait of Churchill, evidently felt the same way.) Max admired *The Old Man and the Sea*, the only Hemingway he ever read, saying it was not so much a novel as a poem. He thought, on hearing "Prufrock" read aloud, that he liked T. S. Eliot, but on trying to read more of Eliot's poetry, he found his admiration had been for his friend's reading, not for T.S.E. That Eliot – who had once proposed raising money to buy Max a wireless set – so admired Max is beside the point, I suppose.

That he didn't like classical music, that he preferred the music halls.   I don't see this as a failing. Moreover, he did love Puccini. Please do not say you think Puccini the music-hall equivalent among opera composers. That would be appropriate only if you appreciated the music hall. Max did praise Wagner for creating opera music capable of drowning out the singers and the all-too-talkative audiences in Covent Garden.

That he "was in panic flight through most of his life from two things – his Jewishness and his homosexuality."   Malcolm Muggeridge wrote this in 1965. Muggeridge was a 1930s leftist journalist turned conservative and fanatical Roman Catholic (in later years he would appear on TV saying how he was just longing to die and go to heaven). His words try to make it appear that it was only Max's *denial* that was wrong. But we are on to that game. The suspicion that Max had Jewish origins rests on the following "evidence": the oddness of his name (a corruption of the German?); the fact that his father came from Eastern Europe; that many of his closest friends, including Will Rothenstein and Reggie Turner, were Jewish; and that his wives were Jewish. In 1903, Max himself, asked by Shaw if he had Jewish ancestors, replied:

I am *not* a Jew. My name was originally Beer*boom*. The family can be traced back through the centuries in Holland. Nor is there, so far as one can tell, any Hebraïsm on the distaff-side. Do I *look* like a Jew? (The question is purely rhetorical.) Does my brother Herbert look like a Jew? (Still more rhetorical.) That my talent is rather like Jewish talent I admit readily. And that is the sole reason for this pedantic denial and explanation. If I were a Jew, I should be rather a matter of course. But, being in fact a Gentile, I am, in a small way, rather remarkable, and wish to remain so. Suppose *you* were not an Irishman; and suppose someone, misled by your two chief characteristics – the love of dreaming dreams, and pugnacity – were to accuse you of being an Irishman: wouldn't you be annoyed, and eager to put him right?

Fifty years later, Max wrote to Hesketh Person, who was working on a biography of Herbert:

> I should be delighted to know that we Beerbohms have that very admirable and engaging thing, Jewish blood. But there seems to be no reason for supposing that we have. Our family records go back as far as 1668, and there is nothing in them compatible with Judaism. .... Our great-aunt Mathilde spent some years at the court of the Emperor William I, and married General von Unruh, military governor to the Crown Prince Frederick (who in my childhood, when he came to London, used to send for my father). Another Beerbohm, Anna, married General von Pape, who acted as standard-bearer at the funeral of the Emperor William. As anti-semitism was rife in Germany throughout the nineteenth century, these marriages into military circles would have been quite impossible.

Max's putative Jewishness amounts to a non-question. A valid question, indeed objection, concerns the cruelty of some of his caricatures of Jews, especially the huge noses he gave them. The largest nose – aside from that of King Edward VII – he gave to Reggie Turner, his closest friend. Of course things that were in only slightly bad taste before Hitler now appear immeasurably worse. That Max was perceived as Jewish and that he himself agreed that his talent was Jewish are engaging issues but beyond the focus of this chapter of indictments.

We looked at the homosexual/heterosexual/asexual question in some detail in earlier chapters. To repeat: we simply do not know anything of Max's (physical) sexual life. His psychological life was on the evidence romantically heterosexual. The rest is speculation, informed or otherwise. Confident, unadorned assertions like Muggeridge's are unhelpful. Not that we have any need to know, in any case.

That he lacked ambition.   I let Max, writing in 1940, answer this one: "What about *My Ambitions?* To this sharp enquiry, I can only reply with bowed head, that I never had any. I had merely some modest wishes – to make good use of such little talents as I had, to lead a pleasant life, to do no harm, to pass muster." He produced some fifteen volumes of prose and thousands of caricatures.

You may be accusing me of setting up soft, easily debunked objections and then airily dismissing them. And you are quite right in saying that the case against as given here isn't particularly forceful, try as I have done to make it so. You may also have accused me of unfairness to Roger Lewis, or of breaking a butterfly on a wheel. All right, here at last is a serious, thoughtful reservation. It's all the more worth paying attention to because it comes from one of Max's greatest enthusiasts, W. H. Auden. And, yes, it was Auden, I now confess, who wrote those words quoted in the last chapter about Max being a sacred cow never attacked by anyone worth listening to. I have been saving this aspect of Auden till now. The following lines appear near the end of the lengthy review of Cecil's biography that Auden wrote for the *New Yorker* in 1965:

> Greatly as I admire both the man and his work, I consider Max Beerbohm a dangerous influence.... His attitude both to life and to art, charming enough for him, when taken up by others as a general cultural idea, becomes something deadly, especially for the English, an intelligent but very lazy people, far too easily bored, and persuaded beyond argument that they are the *Herrenvolk*.... "Good sense about trivialities," he once wrote, "is better than nonsense about things that matter." True enough, but how easily this can lead to the conclusion that anyone who attempts to deal with things that matter must be a bore, that rather than run the risk of talking nonsense one should play it safe and stick to charming trifles.

Auden next quotes another familiar passage from Max: "How many charming talents have been spoiled by the instilled desire to do 'important' work! Some people are born to lift heavy weights. Some are born to juggle golden balls." Here, Auden says, Max "slyly suggests that minor artists may look down their noses at major ones and that 'important' work may be left to persons of an inferior kennel, like the Russians, the Germans, the Americans, who, poor dears, know no better. The great cultural danger for the English is, to my mind, their tendency to judge the arts by the values appropriate to the conduct of family life." Auden sees English people's talent for charming, entertaining domesticity as a "threat to their artistic and intellectual life." The focus has moved from Max's practice to English mores generally. Then Auden draws back, saying that Max's kind of charm, which would be deadly and suffocating in nine out of ten artists, was not so for Max. Moreover, and finally, we are told – something of a leap – that it was really not Max's fault that he was knighted and buried in St Paul's Cathedral: "His charm was, and still is, irresistible, and, which is unlike many charmers, there was nothing phony about him, because, as Chesterton perceived, he did not 'indulge in the base idolatry of believing in himself.'" The argument is a bit disjointed, but Auden's reservations are valid enough, once he retracts them. Surely no one is proposing that people should set up as imitators of Max's life or art. That's partly what we mean by inimitable.

Enough.

CHAPTER THIRTY-ONE

Necrology

When you live to be very old, you find your friends have died. Asked in 1953 if he knew a certain artist, Max replied, "No, he was after my time. The fact is, that almost everybody today is after my time." To have lived into one's eighties in Max's time was to have lived very long indeed. His contemporaries were most of them dead, and the elder contemporaries of his youth long dead. Most of the friends of even his middle age were dead. From his formidably long roster of friends I catalogue here only some of the better known, together with a few of his characterizations of those who have received scant or no mention in these pages, in the interest of enlivening the list. These names and dates serve to complement Max's assertion that he was a curious link with the past and help to position him among his many notable friends and acquaintances. It's nice to recall that all of them can be seen in Max's caricatures – lest we should forget what they really looked like.

Naturally, the few survivors Max knew from Rossetti's circle died early on:

James A. M. Whistler, prickly genius, in many ways a model for Max, died in 1903. See Chapter 7.

Algernon Swinburne, for Max the divine singer, died in 1909. See Chapter 21.

George Meredith, whose early novels Max once loved extravagantly, also died in 1909. Max had contrived a number of visits to his aged, deaf, and partly paralysed hero. He found him "florid and splendid like his books." They talked of laughter, and Meredith said Max "had it." Shortly before the old man's death, Max visited once more: "Meredith was charming again. He seemed a little older than last year, but was just as full of talk and laughter. He seemed to have felt the death of Swinburne deeply. . . . He said he himself would soon be 'under the grass with the Prussians walking over him.' Also, that three years of Prussianizing would do England a lot of good. He also had a scheme for a raid on France, to capture five hundred or so of French women, to brighten the breed of the future."

Theodore Watts-Dunton, Swinburne's rescuer from drink and poetry, died in 1914.

Edmund Gosse, who as a young man had known Swinburne and Rossetti, who had become a kind of social patron of Max among the literary set, died in 1928. In 1925 Max dedicated a collection of caricatures, *Observations*, to Gosse. Max's second largest, and second most crowded caricature (twenty-eight identifiable people), "The Birthday Surprise," commemorates a bust of Gosse presented to him on his seventieth birthday. The drawing rests on the ridiculous assumption that Gosse, who had sat for the sculptor for nearly a year, started back in shocked surprise when presented with the finished product. The caricature hangs in the Savile Club where Max and Gosse were prominent members.

Hall Caine, the youngest and, for Max, the least admirable member of Rossetti's circle, lived on, in spite of Max's persecutions, until 1931.

From the days of Max's mildly unconventional youth, his Oxford and *Yellow Book* days, he was to outlive everyone:

Aubrey Beardsley died in 1898, aged 25. In an obituary Max wrote of how Beardsley's *Yellow Book* drawings first excited the wrath of reviewers and the public, how he had been urged to study two bogus drawings that he himself had inserted in the magazine under fictitious names, and how, next, a "plague" of imitators in England and America attempted in vain to ape Beardsley. His fantastic art was unique, inimitable. In his brief, tragic life, Beardsley embraced, Max said, "a larger measure of sweet and bitter experience than is given to most men who die in their old age." Yet Beardsley – and here Max's words seem self-referential – had remained always

> rather remote, rather detached from ordinary conditions, a kind of independent spectator. He enjoyed life, but he was never wholly of it. This kind of aloofness has been noted in all great artists. Their power isolates them. It is because they stand at a little distance that they can see so much. No man ever *saw* more than Beardsley. He was infinitely sensitive to the aspect of all things around him. And that, I think, was the basis of his genius. All the greatest fantastic art postulates the power to see things, unerringly, as they are.

Oscar Wilde died in 1900. See Chapter 4.

Henry Harland, editor of the *Yellow Book*, who overcame his scruples about publishing an undergraduate and brought out Max's first truly public work, the *succès de scandale* on cosmetics, died in 1905.

Leonard Smithers, first publisher of Max's caricatures in book form, died in 1907.

Charles Conder and John Davidson, two close friends from Max's early years on the London scene, died in 1909 (both are caricatured in "Some Persons of 'the Nineties,'" plate 23). Conder, a painter of dreamy "romantic elegance," had been one of the "august elders" – he was four years older than Max – to whom Rothenstein introduced Max in 1893. Fifteen years later Max was telling Florence, "I am going to the Conders again tonight. Theirs is one of the few houses that I really like going to." The morbid Scottish poet John Davidson was an equally dear friend. "I never can read his writing – his violent buffeting of clouds may be very fine, but means nothing to me," Max wrote to Florence. "But for himself I have great affection. He is, in his way, authentically a man of genius; and has all the sweetness of his tribe." His death by suicide prompted Max to tell her, "It is a tragic end to a tragic life. I wish I could banish it from my mind."

Robert Ross, Wilde's faithful disciple and the gallery owner to give Max his first one-man exhibition in 1901, and three more between then and 1908, died in 1918.

John Lane, Max's first publisher, lived until 1925. Max wrote to his widow: "I shall always remember with gratitude his very many acts of kindness to me – including his kindness in, as it were, 'discovering' me when I was an undergraduate at Oxford. It was he (and, a little later, Aubrey Beardsley) who first urged me to become a writer."

Walter Sickert, painter and great friend, a fellow admirer of the London music halls in the 1890s, died in 1942.

Lord Alfred "Bosie" Douglas lived until 1945. After Wilde's death in 1900, Douglas converted to heterosexuality and married Olive Custance, a wealthy unconventional woman with lesbian tendencies. He also converted to Roman Catholicism, in which faith he remained ardent the rest of his life. He was a frightful snob, a vicious anti-Semite, and, like his father, an incurable litigant. At the 1918 libel trial of Noel Pemberton Billing, Douglas, inveighing against "perversion," testified that he thought Wilde "had a diabolical influence on everyone he met. I think he is the greatest force of evil that has appeared in Europe during the last 350 years." Douglas named Ross and Turner as principal members of the evil "cult" of Oscar Wilde. Many people believe Douglas hounded Ross into his grave. In 1923 Douglas served several months in prison for criminal libel: he had written that Winston Churchill, while First Lord of the Admiralty in 1916, had, in conspiracy with wealthy Jews, blown up a British ship and falsely blamed a German torpedo; this he had done to kill Lord Kitchener who was on route to Russia where he would have "nipped in the bud" the revolution by replacing "Bolshevik Jews" with loyal Britons. Douglas continued always to regard himself as a sonneteer of Shakespearian brilliance.* In his old age, out of religious motives, Douglas "forgave" Oscar his sins, especially as Oscar had (although unconscious) been received into the Catholic Church on his deathbed. Douglas was probably, as Max had said in 1893, at least partly mad. Max kept his distance but had no unkind words for the man who had occasioned Wilde's downfall.

Moving forward to some of Max's friends from the years of his great popularity on the London scene, 1896 to 1910, we find some remembered and indeed some illustrious names:

Henry James died in 1916. He has been frequently mentioned in these pages. Max counted himself a loyal Jacobite; from James he got "the finest of all literary joy."

William Heinemann died in 1920. He and his successors became Max's primary publishers, both of his caricatures, beginning with *The Poets' Corner* in 1904, and of his prose, beginning with *Zuleika Dobson* in 1911. Max found him "a charming person to deal with" – as well he should have, given the fanatical control Heinemann allowed Max over the smallest details of his books, not just the commas and dashes in the text, but everything in regard to type, margins, paper, bindings, labels, and jackets.

Lord Northcliffe (Alfred Harmsworth), the great newspaper czar, who had given Max a column in the *Daily Mail* and later sent him to write on Italy, died in 1922. Harmsworth had also admired Max's caricatures but hesitated to publish them in *Vanity Fair* because he thought them libellous; he wanted, as Max said, caricatures that pleased their subjects, omelettes with no eggs broken. Into old age Max loved to repeat a story about Lady Northcliffe's portrait: "There stood the Academician trembling before Lord Northcliffe.

---

* A recent biography by an Oxford undergraduate, Douglas Murray, attempts to show Douglas as "in many ways [a] lovable figure"; it also argues for the excellence of Douglas's sonnets, but makes the tactical error of printing several of them.

'Do you approve, m'Lord, of her Ladyship's pose?' Lord Northcliffe, scarcely glancing at his wife ... in a demolishing voice, 'I don't care a damn, my good man, as long as you use the most expensive paints.'"

Joseph Conrad died in 1924. On Conrad's death, Max wrote to his widow describing her husband as "a man of great genius whom the world had for many years neglected, whom the world (in its stupid but decent way) had at last made much of, and who (fundamentally sad though I suppose him to have been, like most men of genius) was pleased a little – ironically pleased, but genuinely pleased – by the humdrum worldly success that had overtaken him." Conrad himself credited Max's parody in *A Christmas Garland* as having signalled his arrival as a writer.

John Singer Sargent, the hugely successful portrait painter, "the Van Dyck of our times," died in 1925. Max often met Sargent, along with Henry James, at society functions, where the two were permanent ornaments. They had in common, Max said, a hesitant manner of talking: "They seemed to chop the sentences out of themselves, with great preliminary spouting, as of whales." Max recalled Sargent being asked at a dinner party about portrait painting: "He began to heave and pant, but he did get out an amusing definition: 'A portrait is a painting where there is always something not quite right about the mouth.'"

Thomas Hardy died in 1928. Max knew and admired Hardy and his work. Of a stage adaptation of *Tess of the d'Urbervilles* in 1900, Max wrote of how dismaying it was to see a book one loved debased:

> "Tess," more than most books, should have been saved from the stage. Some novels, as being merely melodramatic, deserve no better fate than being foisted upon the stage. Others, as containing no melodrama at all, and being, therefore, unlikely to attract the public, are allowed to rest within their covers; but, if they were dramatised, at any rate they would not be degraded so unspeakably as is "Tess." For "Tess," as a book, is full of melodrama. The melodrama in it is made beautiful by the charm of Mr Hardy's temperament. One sees it softened and ennobled through a haze of poetry.

I doubt a better explanation exists for the pleasure that painful novel gives to most people. Upon Hardy's death, Max wrote to his widow, telling her of his own memories of her husband from the Savile Club and Gosse's house, memories of his "youthfulness and peculiar modesty and unlikeness to anybody but himself – memories of his very beautiful manners, manners that one admired all the more because something in his eyes betrayed that his thoughts were perhaps a-roving to other and higher matters of his own"; Max told her too of his even more treasured later memories: "It was wonderful to see, in [Hardy's] old age, youthfulness merely sublimified, and his idiosyncrasies undimmed and more lovable than ever."

Bohun Lynch, the first to write a book about Max, also died in 1928.

Frank Harris, a marvellous editor, a rascal but a lovable one, who told the truth only when his invention flagged, died in 1931.

Arnold Bennett also died in 1931. Max judged – and he is not alone in this – Bennett's *The Old Wives' Tale* one of the great novels of his time. Henry James disagreed and asked Max " 'What's it all about?' ... Why, I told him, it's about the passing of time, about the stealthy merging of youth into age, the invisibility of the traps in our own characters into which we walk, unwary, unknowing." Max's reading of this book had occasioned his getting to know Bennett; he wrote to the author telling him that on finishing *The Old Wives' Tale* he had "felt a real void" in his life and invited Bennett to lunch: "I know I should like you, in my humble way; and you'd probably like me – *c'est mon métier* to be liked by the gifted: I somehow understand them."

George Moore died in 1933. Max, for all the fun he had with this "true eccentric," declared that a man like Moore "must be judged by what is fine in him, not by what is trivial." Moore's fine qualities, Max wrote, included his honesty of mind, his modesty about his own work, his freedom from jealousy, his "loving reverence of all that in all arts was nobly done." But above all Max prized

> that inexhaustible patience of his, and courage, whereby he made the very most of the gifts he had, and earned for himself a gift which Nature had not bestowed on him: the specific gift of *writing*. No young man ... ever wrote worse than young Moore wrote. It must have seemed to every one that here was a writer who, however interesting he in himself might be, never would learn to express himself tolerably. ... Some of the good writers have begun with a scant gift for writing. But which of them with no gift at all? Moore is the only instance I ever heard of. Somehow, in the course of long years, he learned to express himself beautifully. I call that great.

John Galsworthy also died in 1933. He and Max, friends but not intimates, valued each other's work. Max once described Galsworthy as a "dry man but sympathetic [who] looks very like his manner of writing," a provocative notion, especially from a caricaturist.

T. E. Lawrence died in 1935. Max did not know him, but said of Lawrence's translation of the *Odyssey*, "I would rather not have been that translator than have driven the Turks out of Arabia."

G. K. Chesterton died in 1936. He is frequently linked with his friend Hilaire Belloc, who lived until 1953. The ambitious religious and social views of Chesterton or Belloc held little attraction for Max. Of Chesterton's *What's Wrong with the World?* (1910), he said, "very cheap and *sloppy*, though with gleams – gleams of gas-lamps in Fleet Street mud and slush." In Belloc's writings he found "splendid things abounding" in the midst of "a lot of absolute chaotic rot."

William Butler Yeats died in 1939. Max first met Yeats at a dinner given by Leonard Smithers to mark the publisher's launch of the *Savoy*, where Yeats annoyed Max by ignoring Smithers's unsophisticated wife and talking errant nonsense about diabolism. In a 1954 broadcast, Max said:

> My wretchedly frequent failure to find definite meanings in the faint and lovely things of Yeats – my perception of nothing but some sort of mood enclosed in a vacuum far away – has always worried me very much. . . . I often had the pleasure of meeting Yeats, and I liked him. But merely to like so remarkable, so mystic and intense a creature – to be not utterly under his spell whenever one was in his presence – seemed to argue a lack in oneself and to imply an insult to that presence. . . . I always felt rather uncomfortable, as though I had submitted myself to a mesmerist who somehow didn't mesmerize me.

Privately he was less repentant, writing to Florence: "Me [Yeats] drives to excesses of grossest philistinism, sympathetic though I generally am to men of genius. A genius he is of course; and geniuses are generally asinine: but his particular asinineness bores me and antagonizes me."

H. G. Wells died in 1946. Max knew and liked Wells, but had no sympathy with his faith in science or his social idealism and utopianism. Samuel Behrman wrote of Max that he "shied away from lunacy not only in its violent forms but also in its milder forms, one of these being utopianism. . . . He had a horror of utopians, a suspicion of 'big' ideas." Wells's prose troubled him as well. Writing to Shaw in 1903, Max asked, "Have you ever seen a cold rice-pudding spilt on the pavement of Gower Street? I never have. But it occurs to me as a perfect simile for Wells's writing." In 1921, when Reggie Turner sent Max a copy of Wells's *Outline of History*, he replied, "You *couldn't* have given me a present that I should have hated more."

Holbrook Jackson died in 1948. His book *The Eighteen Nineties* (1913), whatever its shortcomings, such as not mentioning Enoch Soames, had been dedicated to Max and had helped inspire Max's aforementioned caricature "Some Persons of 'the Nineties.'"

To push on to the Bloomsbury circle, whose members, although close to him in age, represented the next generation. Three were important to him:

Lytton Strachey, the twentieth-century writer with whom Max felt the closest kinship, died in 1932. See Chapter 27.

Virginia Woolf died in 1941. No one ever ranked Max's writing higher. He admitted his difficulty (being himself old-fashioned) in appreciating her fiction, but considered her criticism the best of modern times.

Desmond MacCarthy died in 1952. He was Max's closest friend among the Bloomsbury coterie. Max recorded for the BBC a brief memorial piece on his old friend: MacCarthy was not only one of the finest of talkers, he "was an equally keen listener, a great educer of talk from other people. He would lean forward, a picture of receptivity, very often murmuring pensively 'I see – I see.' He was also a great user of that attractive, that beguiling phrase 'And tell me.'"

Then, in a category by himself, George Bernard Shaw. See Chapter 9. He died in 1950. The "most salient" man of letters of Max's time, born in 1856, he had seemed to live on for ever. Asked in old age whether he missed any of his contemporaries, Shaw replied, " No. I miss only the man I was," drawing from Max the comment, "When I think of the gay and delightful people he knew ..." Max thought it particularly silly that Shaw had ordered his ashes to be strewn in the garden of his country house at Ayot St Lawrence, among the roses. "Imagine! Among the *roses!*"

Two special cases dating back to Max's undergraduate days I have saved for last.

Reggie Turner died in Florence on 7 December 1938. Max wrote to Sydney Schiff:

I had known him so long; he was the earliest of my great friends, and remained always the greatest – and will remain so. ... I think his life had been on the whole a happy one, full of interest and fun. Of course he had been too sensitive an observer and feeler of things to be genuinely and uninterruptedly happy in such a world as this. But he had had a good share of happiness. And now he is beyond the reach of the other thing, and is at peace, dear fellow.

Will Rothenstein died on 14 February 1945; Max wrote to his widow:

Our dear Will, it is grievously sad that he is gone, that we shall never again see him and hear him. He was the oldest of my friends. He was, absent or present, a part of me. There was no man whose mind and heart impressed me so much as his. I learned so much from him when I was quite young, and I have gone on learning from him ever since. He was always extraordinarily kind to me – and indeed to how many other people! ... Death is a horrible thing. I hate to think that Will's great heart and brain ... are at work no longer, well though they have earned their rest. His life was a surpassingly full one.

Max won't descend into sentimentality; and never, on the occasion of the death of friend or relative, does he give the slightest hint of even a hope for an afterlife.

Rudyard Kipling died on 18 January 1936, and George V died two days later. "I am told," Max wrote to a friend, "that Mrs Kipling (née Balestier) very much resents the death of the King at so solemn a moment."

CHAPTER THIRTY-TWO

Ministering Angel

In 1927 Will Rothenstein, who in the 1890s had done so much for Max, did something, all unknowing, that would again eventually have a profound and beneficent effect on Max's life. Will introduced him to Elisabeth Jungmann. Born in 1894 at Oppeln, Upper Silesia, the daughter of a prominent German-Jewish lawyer, she spent much of her life helping famous men manage their lives. Tall, striking, intelligent, she served from 1922 to 1933 as personal secretary and assistant to the writer Gerhardt Hauptmann, who wintered in Rapallo. In 1933 Elisabeth was to fall in love with and attach herself to the ageing German poet and man of letters Rudolf Binding. He died (one account says "in her arms") in August 1938. A year later she fled to England, where Will Rothenstein provided her with a place to stay at Far Oakridge. She worked for the Jewish Central Information Office in London; she next became research assistant for the Political Intelligence Department, an arm of the British Foreign Office. After the war she worked at the Control Commission for Germany and Austria, where she laboured for "the cultural revival of Germany."

Max took warmly to her from their very first meeting, in Rapallo, when she translated for him and Hauptmann, Max knowing no German and Hauptmann no English. She was young and vivacious. She managed to be on good terms with Florence, who seems not to have minded Max's "delicately flirtatious" attentions to her. Elisabeth visited the Beerbohms frequently at the Villino and, later, regularly at Abinger during the war. Max wrote a letter of testimony to the Aliens Tribunal urging her qualifications for British citizenship; he wrote her a warm letter of condolence when in 1942 her mother died while being transported to Auschwitz. After the Beerbohms returned to Italy in 1947 she was one of the few cherished visitors from their old days and practically the only guest who slept at the Villino rather than in a Rapallo hotel. On one of those visits, in the summer of 1948, Max asked for her address and phone number and pencilled them onto the flyleaf of a volume of Siegfried Sassoon's poems. "We won't tell Florence about this," he said.

On subsequent visits he asked Elisabeth if the phone number would still find her. They had tacitly agreed, in view of Florence's failing health from heart trouble, that should anything happen to Florence, Elisabeth would come to him. Florence, to her credit, seems to have endorsed the "secret" arrangement. In January 1951, Max telephoned Elisabeth. She left her job, came by the first train, arrived two hours after Florence died on 13 January, and stayed permanently.

She took immediate charge. Alone, she accompanied Florence's body to Genoa for cremation. When the urn disturbed the Italian servant, she had a gardener row Max and herself out on to the Gulf of Tigullio to scatter the ashes. She organized the household, which she found in an "antediluvian state." The Villino had a new, healthy, hardworking mistress. Max still would never have to make a cup of tea for himself. More crucially, her presence revived him. He was seventy-eight and physically fragile when there entered his life this devoted, self-sacrificing woman who seemed to manage, exactly to his liking, everything from meals and medicines to correspondence and visitors. Most importantly, they enjoyed each other's company and conversation; he came to love her; she almost literally adored him.

Elisabeth was doubtless a more pleasant and a more social being than Florence. She had a sense of humour; she admired every aspect of his work, right down to the "improving" of books by altering texts and forging inscriptions. To tear up one of his scrawled caricatures as "disrespectful" would have been to Elisabeth a sacrilege. As far as Max's friends were concerned, Florence was not a hard act to follow. The testimony of one guest, Kenneth Rose, in contrasting the two women as hostesses, was typical: "Elisabeth Jungmann . . . gazed contentedly but silently on her Max, only occasionally leading him from one dazzling anecdote to another. (How different, I fear, from Florence, who had an equally inspired gift for interrupting him over some triviality at the very climax of a story.)" We, like Max's friends, tend to be rather hard on Florence. But this would have angered him. If he seems to have taken her death rather in his stride, it is because he was not given to pining. Of course he was saddened by it. "I wish she could have lived as long as I," Max wrote to an old friend. "But I am grateful for the forty years of happiness that she gave me." It was not as if he forgot Florence or disregarded her wishes. Elisabeth tells how later on Max, rummaging through old letters, found one from her and burned it: "She wrote nice letters. But she thought she didn't quite express herself clearly enough. I had to promise her that I would destroy her letters . . ." Again,

Elisabeth came upon a photograph of Florence taken in 1950 and told Max she thought it good: "I don't find it good," he said. "One cannot laugh or smile like that, eternally." An hour later he looked at the photograph again, tore it up and burned it. In August 1954 his old flame Constance Collier, as full of energy as ever, arrived at the Villino unfatigued after having driven nine hours from Venice. She told Max he looked as young as ever, rather overwhelmed him with her gusto, announced the terrace "divine," stayed an hour and a half, returned to her hotel, and the next day motored back to Venice. Before leaving she took Elisabeth aside and told her she liked her but had not liked Florence: "She never let him talk. She was frightfully ambitious. . . . [Max] is the only man I loved & love . . ." A few days later Constance wrote Elisabeth an "affectionate & sweet" letter, adding that Florence had taken Max away from all his friends. Elisabeth told this to Max. "What impudence!" he said. "Of course, I wanted to be far away – that's why I went to Italy."

There is no denying that Elisabeth Jungmann gave him a new lease on life. No less an authority than Max's personal physician said that "only after Florence's death when [Elisabeth] began looking after him, did he come to life again in a much more serene unworried sounder way"; Elisabeth became "more than a wife to him, much more." Rupert Hart-Davis says that no one ever loved Max as did Elisabeth Jungmann. I was inclined to think this an exaggeration. Surely Max's mother and sisters, not to mention Florence, had loved him. But on reading Elisabeth's diary for the years from 1951 to 1956, I almost think no one ever loved anyone so much as she loved Max. During the five years she served as chatelaine of the Villino Chiaro, her one obsessive care was Max's well-being. To her he was as a piece of "precious porcelain." If she did not go as far as her opposite number at I Tatti, Nicky Mariano, who is said to have warmed Bernard Berenson's wristwatch each morning, it was only because Max did not wear a wristwatch. We catch the flavour of Elisabeth's devotion in letters she wrote to him in 1952 when she travelled briefly to London to see Max's exhibition and visit her doctor. To her "Dearest Sweet Angel" she relates how the London reviews of the exhibition are "expressing their beholders' enchantments, their bewitchedness, their wonder at an incredibly rare, heavenly, amusing, lovable angel's genius. . . . Sweet angel, do give me a line how the irritation in and & around the g..... behaves? how the dear beloved eye is? And what book have you taken up to read? ... Darling angel, it *will* be too heavenly to be back with you soon! Meanwhile be blessed, be loved! Your devoted Elisabeth."

From her diaries we know, daily, the state of the weather and of Max's health: "– a new little injury on right hand! Opening the shutter he hit himself"; a "slight cough"; a "touch of the flu"; eye cataracts. "A slight itch on the back made him move his hand in that direction. The braces cause two big bruises!" Elisabeth, who had served as a nurse in the First World War, would have thought any medical attention on earth insufficient for her charge. She frequently summons Dr Giuseppe Bacigalupo, who had succeeded his own mother as Max's Rapallo physician. Dr Bacigalupo dutifully attends his patient, brings specialists, consultants. Elisabeth is mildly impatient with Bacigalupo's verdict of "quite the same"; she finds it hard to accept that age is wearing Max down and that nothing can be done to slow the process. He so relies on her that she forgoes even short trips into town ("I'd much rather stay here, with the angel, & not cause him that little anxiety"). His physical sensitivity increased: "I think he was born," Elisabeth explained later, "with several skins less than other people." He was distressed by a harsh voice or a door slammed (though he managed always to tolerate the continuous din of "infernal" traffic outside the Villino). A point of her special concern is the nights – each is assessed: horrible, bad, fair, better, good, etc. We know his nightmares, to which he was especially prone in these years: he dreams that he has to walk, like a kitten, on the ledge of his terrace; that he is "walking on the edge of a precipice, being attacked by everybody"; that he finds himself in a tunnel and suddenly hears a train coming; that a boy is constantly hitting him over the head with a folded journal; that he has "to show some drawings to King Edward & there were so many, they went on rushing past his eyes even after he'd woken up"; that he is lost, unable to find his way in a huge hotel; that he has to argue with many eminent men, among them Gilbert Murray, but has "no brain to argue with"; that he has to get to a play but cannot find a cab. Frequently he dreams of not having money, for bills, for taxis, even for the underground.

The diaries touch also on less troubling matters. Sometimes Max supplies glimpses of the past: the occasion, for example, on which he smoked his first cigarette, at a dinner party given by Herbert in Manchester immediately after taking his entrance exams for Oxford in 1890: "I sat next to Hare, the famous comedian, and during the evening smoked 5 or 6 cigarettes. . . . I must, also, have drunk too much champagne, for – although I enjoyed the party throughout – I was violently sick all during the night." (Max continued to

smoke Italian cigarettes and drink wine at lunch and dinner until the very
end.) We learn that Henry Irving's private secretary, Q. F. Austin, was
"among the first to encourage me. He praised my earliest things very much."
Max tells Elisabeth that his friend Granville Barker was called to America to
advise on "the millionaires' theatre":

> One of the millionaires: "Which is the greatest of all theatres in Europe?"
> Gr Barker: "I think the Scala in Milan is said to be the greatest ..."
> The American: "*We shall double that*," with quiet confidence, putting his
> hand down on the table, somehow confirmingly.

Max recounts how in 1907 he went three times to a fortune teller: "The
woman read me my future from my hands, said to me that my fame would
remain with me throughout my life, without diminishment. She also said
that ... I would either make a long journey or stay abroad."

Again, "M. tells me of a music hall entertainment at the Empire, Leicester
Square, to which he & Florence were taken by William Nicholson because
Max was parodied there. He found it wildly amusing, but Florence was angry
& horrified."

But more often the diary is concerned with small daily happenings, or near
happenings: Max completes an entire *Times* crossword puzzle, "a difficult
one"; he sings music-hall songs, including "If I were the only boy in the world
& you were the only girl"; he has "great pleasure" in permitting the Randolph
Hotel to be decorated with murals of *Zuleika Dobson* (by Osbert Lancaster);
he enjoys a laugh when he learns that certain learned people have been search-
ing among the writings of Abraham Lincoln and among the classic Greek
writers for the line he had himself invented, in Greek and in English, "For
people who like that kind of thing, that is the kind of thing they like." He
often read "a whole book" in one day. He relishes E. F. Benson's *As We Were*
and a biography of Henry Irving; he pronounces Françoise Sagan's *Bonjour
Tristesse* "a bad & vulgar book, badly translated. It shows the decline, the
decadence in France." He turns down an offer from the *Sunday Times* for an
article on a "decisive happening in life which became a turning point": "I
wouldn't know about what to write. Perhaps my meeting with Florence. It
did alter my life completely. But this is too private. Perhaps my being,
through the William Nicholsons, introduced to the Baroness von Hutten:
they brought me here to this coast. Otherwise I may never have come to live
here on this gulf." He draws a caricature of Henry James for Elisabeth, "&

afterwards gave it a light blue wash. But he sighed and complained about his eyesight 'My drawing days are over' etc & apparently the eyes did trouble him a lot & vision wasn't cleared. Poor Angel." He composes limericks on "The Illustrious Inebriates" including J. S. Mill and Disraeli. He reads a radio broadcast by Bertrand Russell on "The Road to Happiness": "Russell is a bore; but he is a bright bore, which is the worst of bores." In February 1955 he is "rather upset at receiving a letter from the Times Literary Supplement saying that the Maximilian Society had renewed [his] subscription 'with love & homage' for one year, until 11 Jan. 1956. 'To receive this kind of charity jars! I don't like it!' etc. At my firm protest & disagreement: 'I'll try to dismiss it from my mind.'"

The biggest event of these years was the already alluded to eightieth birthday party (24 August 1952) up on Montallegro, where he is showered with "masses" of telegrams and flowers and presents: "Main gift the beautiful red-saffian [Morocco leather]-bound book of tributes to Max. [Tania Jepson] hands it to him in the little room where we are to have our party, he is quite overcome. Furthermore, he receives a lovely cigarette box of wood, 2 bottles of French champagne. . . . a delightful party apart from the slow service." The menu had included ravioli, chicken with mushroom and potatoes, birthday cake and fruit. "S.C. [Roberts] made a charming little speech & M. thanked. . . . M. so happy. Guests went down at 4 (after snapshots). We gathered together at 7 for supper, Tania and M. and I. M. in bed. We waited the 9:55 broadcast 'The Seventh Man', tributes by Frank Swinnerton, Michael Sadleir, Compton Mackenzie, Robert Graves, Gordon Craig, Osbert Lancaster. . . . The great day was beautiful."

The diaries also mention guests from these years – the Thornton Wilders, Oliver Brown of the Leicester Galleries, Alan Dent, president of the old Maximilian Society, the adoring Dutch academic J.G. Riewald, Montgomery Hyde, M.P. Sometimes Elisabeth records her own impressions: Edmund Wilson "astounds" her with his "startling knowledge of Beerbohmiana"; Lilli Palmer brings her guests, Laurence Olivier and Vivien Leigh: "they were all very charming indeed. L.O. looks extraordinarily young, whereas V.L. has already too many little lines under the eyes."

One great service Elisabeth did not just for Max but for his later admirers was to facilitate (though she could never have done so had Max not wished it) the visits of S. N. Behrman. Behrman, playwright, biographer, and *New Yorker* writer, was to serve, briefly, in the last four years of Max's life, as a kind of Boswell to Max. The two men became good friends, quite at variance with the received notion that a person in his eighties can't form a new and deep friendship. Max genuinely liked Behrman, and Behrman worshipped Max. Behrman knew his visits resembled Max's to that other survivor from the past, Swinburne. Here was Max, friend of Oscar Wilde and Henry James and George Bernard Shaw; Max, who had known Whistler and Meredith, here he was on the terrace at Rapallo, pleased, even eager to talk about his memories, and in so doing, telling Behrman and us much about that past and about himself. Behrman's five visits formed the basis of a seven-part Profile he would publish, after Max's death, in the *New Yorker*. It was the longest piece ever published in that magazine, and came out in book form as *Portrait of Max*, in 1960. This book is a solid part of the record, and anyone writing on Max is indebted to S. N. Behrman; he or she is also indebted to Elisabeth Jungmann, for she orchestrated the visits, made them pleasant for Max and delightful for Behrman. She fetches books, she suggests openings, she draws Max out, she subtly steers the conversation; she makes possible these interviews – which is what they are – in spite of the fact that Max never gave interviews. He seems even to have consented to Behrman writing up his visits for the *New Yorker*.

Samuel Behrman, with help from Elisabeth, persuaded Max to write out an anecdote he had been fond of repeating about Henry James. Max, after first protesting that he was "beyond composition," put down on paper what came to be a five-minute contribution to a BBC programme of recollections of Henry James. Entitled "An Incident," it told how in the spring of 1906 (1909 actually) Max took part with Henry James in a little episode that itself seemed strangely Jamesian: Max was walking along Piccadilly towards his club, the Savile, intent on reading "The Velvet Glove," a new story by Henry James that had just appeared in a new monthly review. Half-way to his destination Max is accosted by James himself, who had been slowly making his way from the other direction. James announces himself just come up to London from Rye and asks Max if there is any new exhibition of pictures he should see. Max recommends the Grafton galleries, and James asks if Max would like to act as his guide:

> I felt much honoured – and yet, to my great surprise I heard myself saying instantly "Well, I'm afraid I can't. I have to be in Kensington at half-past three."

"What," Max asks, "had prompted me to tell that fib? ... It was mainly my aforesaid impatience to be reading 'The Velvet Glove' ":

> And here I was now in the Savile, reading it. It was, of course, a very good story, and yet, from time to time, I found my mind wandering away from it. It was not so characteristic, not so intensely Jamesian a story as James would have founded on the theme of what had just been happening between us – the theme of a disciple loyally – or unloyally? – preferring the Master's work to the Master.

This little tale, written and recorded in 1954, was, fittingly enough for someone who so revered the Master, the last thing Max wrote for publication. It was broadcast posthumously in June 1956.

CHAPTER THIRTY-THREE

An Ending

Elisabeth Jungmann's diary for 1956 makes sad reading. Max's health declined steadily. He suffered increasingly, his physician said, from a gouty form of rheumatism, cardio-circulatory troubles, anaemia, and a nervous hypersensitivity that made him jump up at unexpected sounds. Nonetheless, on 10 March Elisabeth made a brief overnight trip to Milan – she was gone fewer than eighteen hours – to see a ballet based on Max's *The Happy Hypocrite* (*L'ipocrita felice*, libretto by Franco Antonicelli, music by Giorgio Federico Ghedini). Dr Bacigalupo had urged her to go. She arrived at La Scala just as the ballet began and thought the performance "very sophisticated & charming" but the music "not over impressive." Next morning she took an early train back to Genoa, then another to Rapallo, and, as there was no taxi available, "ran home in 27 minutes." Angela, the cook, awaited her, pale and worried: Max was not "bene." Dr Bacigalupo had come and administered injections, one for his heart, one to calm him. Elisabeth found Max awake, but breathing heavily, with a death-like rattle in the throat ("röchelnd"), his face "pale almost to whiteness, but oh, holding my hand & asking questions & listening to my account (which I tried to give in a way as harmless & cheerful as possible) & then telling me of a Marionette theatre he had seen in Venice, the grace, the beauty, & fun of it, & recovered more & more! Angela said: 'Gli ha dato la vita!' "

He rallied somewhat and a few days later even managed to smoke half a cigarette. But on 26 March he took a bad turn: "... at 5 a.m. gasping for breath, oppressed, in great misery.... Took him in my arms, a cushion propped up between my chest & his back, & tried to calm him. 'I can't go on like that – I can't ... what am I to do?' I soothed him & caressed him, gently, tender. 'I love you – I love you' he said repeatedly." At noon Dr Bacigalupo and his mother came and suggested Max be moved to the Villa Chiara, their private hospital a mile away. Elisabeth recorded:

The transport was a great torture to the darling, in all its awful phases. ... he felt wretched, was violently sick. The "bed" moved up & down & we were thrown right & left in the many curves although the driver didn't drive too fast. I held Max in my arms most of the time to ward off the worst of the bangs & shakes. At the Villa Chiara it was found that the trag-bahre [litter] was too long for the lift. My heart sank still more. To be shifted again would be unbearable for the darling. Then the thing was put in diagonally – & at last he was in his comfortable bed.

He knew he was dying. He knew that although he had been lucky all his life, his luck had run out. He had told Florence, in 1905, that he could stand life only when it was made pleasant for him, which it usually was; he had been, he admitted then, "pampered rather than otherwise" with the result that he did not like life unless it offered him "something nice every day." And such had been pretty much the case for the next fifty years, until now. His end would not be quick or painless.

His English physician, Dr Leo Rau, wanted him to come to a London hospital, but Max refused to return to London an invalid; he also refused to be transferred to Rome, where better medical facilities were available. At the Villa Chiara he was carefully watched over. Previous biographers have implied that Max suffered from deficient medical care. The evidence does not bear them out. Bacigalupo, an able and astute physician, assisted occasionally by his mother (who had earlier been Max's doctor), by specialists he called in, and by Dr Rau, did all that could be done. Max was beyond hope of recovery. The truth was that no medical care could have satisfied Elisabeth, who took a room adjacent to his and practically never left his side.

Max was not a good patient. "I have no capacity for bravery," he told Elisabeth, ". . . the nurses will soon lose patience with me." When on 11 April a severe attack of cardiac asthma left him much weaker, he said, "I've seen my mother suffering, & my sister Agnes suffering – Herbert had a wonderfully easy death (he was peeling a peach & ate it & all of a sudden he was dead) –, & Constance, after she'd had a serious operation . . . but nothing was like my own suffering this morning, nothing." He could not bear for Elisabeth to be away for a moment. He feared she might have gone out to dine with the visiting Dr Rau: "How *could* I ever have thought of going out in the evening on such a day, or ever! But he *will* have the blackest conception of every thing, poor angel." Elisabeth was under enormous stress: "I get so worn out by his great disastrous pessimism. I don't want ever to show him how it gets me down."

In the midst of all the pain, they get married. Secret plans had been afoot for some months: under Italian law Elisabeth as a widow would much more easily inherit all of Max's possessions and copyrights (he had made a will entirely in her favour in 1951). But more than this, he wants to be married to her; he knows she desires it, and his only fear is that he will be too weak to sign. Their close friend Tania Jepson arrives for "the great day," a bright and sunny 20 April:

> After endless writing, done in the lounge by a worthy secretary, in huge books – Libri di matrimonio – at 4.31 the Sindaco with another nice Würdenträger [dignitary] came into M's room, with it. 4 witnesses: Dr B, his mother, his wife, & Tania. He put on a feierlich sciarpa [ceremonial scarf], green – white – red, with embroidery, & put several questions first to M. then to me (name of father, mother, etc), then read a statement about the marriage, then asked the great question which M. answered with a lovely smile & a "Si"; so did I; everybody signed. M was supported by Dr B. – & the ceremony was over ... the relief!!!

Max tells her he thinks the names Elisabeth and Beerbohm go together nicely.

Occasionally he can take his mind off his bodily collapse. He worries that a friend of Behrman's for whom he had "improved" some printed pages of *The Happy Hypocrite* might not have realized that the additions were meant to be funny. He admires a "beautiful lavender shadow" cast on the wall by a sunset and recalls that Gordon Craig had taught him the beauty of shadows. He remarks that the green labels on the hospital glassware are "an ugly green." His mind wanders; drowsily he repeats lines from Virgil and from his beloved Swinburne.

But for the most part he is overwhelmed with ailments: fever, swellings, ear infections, eye trouble, bedsores; at times he "shrieks wildly! It cut right into one's heart." Nightmares and "oppressiveness" haunt his nights and nearly break Elisabeth. She writes, "He suffers agonies. He suffers intensely from even what would appear to be slight discomforts. He is just unable to bear them, to adjust himself, quite unable. He is not in control of his mind."

By 5 May, the strain is showing on Elisabeth: "I was at the end of my tether. ... It was terribly difficult today. I didn't know what to say to those endless complaints, fears, discomforts. A nervous breakdown, I felt, was certain to come." On 11 May, "The house echoes with his screams. I fled, but they followed me ... enormous. Talked afterwards angrily & splendidly about the 'senseless torture' to Dr B. ... But the despair, the pessimism, the gloom!" By 12 May Max is saying, "There is not one part of my body that hasn't betrayed me."

14th May: "... a rather big swelling, glandular, shows. Dr B is alarmed. Face ashen, general state wretched. 'The tips of my fingers feel numb. ... My arm trembles. ... You could not wish me to live on like this. You cannot blame me if I long to die ... I would have loved to live with you serenely as before – but I cannot continue like this ...' Light vomiting. Swelling hurts. Pulse very poor."

15th: "Povera Elisabetta," he keeps repeating. "I am desperate, hopeless ... I dread the night. ... How can I possibly survive the night?"

16th: When Dr Bacigalupo asks him how the swelling is today, he appears not to understand and instead quotes Swinburne, "Even the weariest river / winds somewhere safe to sea."

17th: If Elisabeth tries to leave his room even momentarily, "his eyes follow me anxiously & he'll stop me in the door with his 'Dear Elisabeth!' or 'Don't leave me!' Only when he is asleep do I dare to slip out of the room."

18th: He tells Dr Bacigalupo *Grazie per tutto* (the only Italian words his doctor ever heard him utter).

19th–20th: The doctors think he will not regain consciousness; but he does, briefly:

> "Did you sleep well?" I asked. "No" he said very clearly. Held my hand firmly in his. 7 pm. Another injection ... which calmed him. He grasped my hand firmly & held it, & so I sat with him, for hours.

He slips into unconsciousness. I am tempted to think that, *just possibly*, his mind drifted back, as Lytton Strachey has Queen Victoria's do in her last moments, back through numerous decades, lighting upon sunny views from his terrace over the Mediterranean; upon the peaceful churchyard at Abinger; upon his dazzling dress on being knighted or his first appearance before a microphone; perhaps King Edward appeared, or his mother and Reggie witnessing his marriage, or a breathless Henry James hesitating along Piccadilly; or a young Bernard Shaw with his bicycle, or Oscar Wilde before the fall, fat, purple-faced and idolized; or quiet Mob Quad of Merton College, or himself a small boy outside Number 10 Downing Street; or his big carrot-topped brother taking him to lunch. But these are merely biographer's fancies. He just wanted it over. *Cedo junioribus*, he had written at twenty-three, sixty years previous, I give way to younger men: "I belong to the Beardsley period. Younger men, with months of activity before them, with fresher schemes and notions, with new enthusiasm, have pressed forward since them. *Cedo junioribus*. Indeed, I stand aside with no regret. For to be outmoded is to be a classic, if one has written well. I have acceded to the hierarchy of good scribes and rather like my niche." Of course he was not thinking these words, either. Elisabeth, exhausted, took a few hours' sleep, during which time Max died, shortly after 2 a.m.

The final irony would be the burial of his cremated ashes in St Paul's Cathedral. Elisabeth had superintended the dressing of the body in Max's dark blue "utility suit," and arranged for a short service at the Anglican chapel of San Giorgio in Rapallo. She accompanied the body to Genoa for crema-tion. On 31 May she arrived, with the ashes, at Dover and British Customs: "Had to go, with my casket, to a special office &, altho officials were polite & nice, lost too much time to catch 'Golden Arrow.'" After a late arrival at Victoria Station she went directly to Hampstead Parish Church, planning to have Max's ashes buried next to Herbert's. But the great world intervened. Elisabeth was summoned to meet with the Dean of St Paul's; and the funeral ceremony took place in the Cathedral on 29 June (very ill-attended, accord-ing to Evelyn Waugh – though it is gratifying to find that Vyvyan Holland, Oscar Wilde's son, was in the congregation). I can't find that Max ever men-tions St Paul's in his writings. But the idea of being buried among the famous would have appealed to his sense of fun – as had his knighthood. There he would be, comic writer and caricaturist, in the crypt with Nelson and Wellington and Alexander Fleming, the discoverer of penicillin. The one association that comes naturally to mind in connection with Max and St Paul's Cathedral is Sydney Smith. Smith, Dean of St Paul's more than a century earlier, had been known in his day as "the wittiest man in England." Perhaps for that very reason, he was never memorialized in St Paul's. But he was one of Max's heroes, a man who could amuse and laugh at people yet somehow usually not offend them.

CHAPTER THIRTY-FOUR

Today

In July of the year 2000 I went to inspect the chief places of Max's career, from birthplace to burial place. It's hard to explain exactly why, but these kinds of visit are a necessity for the biographer. Why are not words and pictures enough? To this I can say only that they are not enough. Even when the visit to the actual places in no way changes what one has written or even will write about them, the biographer must see them for himself. I had been many times to London and many times to Oxford, indeed had worked in the Beerbohm Room at Merton College on three or four occasions. But never had I come as Max's biographer. For me, this time, these places became places of pilgrimage – embarrassing, laughable as it may seem. The writer of another's life is in some ways a crazed, obsessed person.* Who else would stand in the street taking pictures of obscure and undistinguished-looking houses? Who else would be so moved by very ordinary, everyday places like Orme Square?

I started at the wrong end, as it were, that is, with St Paul's, Christopher Wren's great cathedral. Here at least it is all right to stand in awe – at one of the world's largest and most impressive churches. It seems odd that Max's ashes should be buried in such a place. For his ashes are actually here. (Most of the memorials are simply that, memorials and not grave markers; since 1936 burials in public buildings have been prohibited "except under special circumstances," which circumstances evidently obtained in Max's case in June 1956; or, it may be, cremated ashes are accepted.) Admission to the crypt costs £5. A guide, a woman from Italy, directed me towards the front right, where, she said, I could easily locate the plaque. And sure enough, there it was, a simple, severe, black stone bearing the legend:

---

*The obsessed enthusiast can, by visiting the Harry Ransom Humanities Research Center at Austin, Texas, view some amateur film footage that Alfred Knopf (Max's American publisher) took of his authors. Max appears for about two minutes, coming into and out of Knopf's London office in Bedford Square and walking along the pavement. He wears a bowler hat and carries a walking stick. He looks stylish and sprightly. The year is 1928.

MAX BEERBOHM
Caricaturist and Writer
1872 – 1956

The ashes are buried under a stone (marked M.B.) directly beneath the plaque. His memorial shares a wall with five others – four sculptors and architect Edwin Landseer Lutyens. The opposite wall is entirely occupied by one large memorial to Max's friend and frequent target, John Singer Sargent. It's a considerable honour to be commemorated in St Paul's. About 300 heroes of the nation and of the arts are memorialized or buried here, beginning with Wren himself, and including, most spectacularly, Nelson and Wellington; but also Florence Nightingale, William Blake, Joshua Reynolds, Frederick Leighton, John Everett Millais (the connection with the Royal Academy of Arts seems strong). The crypt is the biggest anywhere and today also houses a restaurant called the Refectory, and the Crypt Café which, the visitor information leaflet claims, serves as "the perfect place to enjoy a snack or light lunch in a comfortable atmosphere or simply to relax and watch the world go by." The official guide booklet, a large, colourful glossy affair, makes much of Max's presence.

On the following day I took a taxi around to Max's four London residences, all fairly close to one another. Fifty-seven Palace Gardens Terrace in Kensington looks the grandest today, situated just above and "terracing" the park and swank embassy row, and not far from Kensington Palace itself. It has a blue plaque, and even though there are some 500 such plaques in London, this kind of official recognition is not to be sniffed at. To qualify, the person must be regarded "as eminent in his sphere by a majority of the person's own profession or calling." No problem there. That his name should be known to "the well-informed passer-by" is a bit trickier. At any rate, Max's plaque was erected in 1969 – more quickly than most people so commemorated. Among Max's friends and admirers, Aubrey Beardsley got his fifty years after his death, Oscar Wilde fifty-four years after his death; Lytton Strachey, who died in 1932, got his plaque in 1972, Virginia Woolf, who died in 1941, in 1974.

Clanricarde Gardens, the little cul-de-sac where Max grew up, is not far from Palace Gardens Terrace, but just across the line in Bayswater. Today it appears rather down-at-heel and is given over to cheap bed-and-breakfast-style hotels. It is but a five-minute walk to Orme Square, where Max attended school. Mr Wilkinson's school occupied two houses, one of which was destroyed by bombs in the Second World War. I learned this from the present occupier of the remaining house, Diana Peyton. She was gardening in the square and kindly invited me in to see her house. It has no single large room, and she wonders how it could have been a school, but then it was a very small school. By coincidence, Diana Peyton is distantly related to Herbert Beerbohm Tree.

Half a mile east of Orme Square is Hyde Park Place, where the Beerbohms moved in 1892, a thriving street in spite of the heavy traffic on the Bayswater Road, which comes between it and the Park. Nearby, 48 Upper Berkeley Street, at which address the Beerbohms lived after 1897, is located in what appears to be a moderately thriving though unprepossessing neighbourhood, in the heart of what is today called, or so my taxi driver informed me, "Little Beirut."

In Regent Street, just off Piccadilly Circus, the Café Royal, Max's favourite haunt, has become a listed interior. It survives exactly as he described it – an extravaganza of gilding, crimson velvet, opposing mirrors and "upholding caryatids" rising to the "painted and pagan ceiling."

Godalming, a prosperous village in Surrey, home of Charterhouse, is a forty-minute train ride out of London, the train ride that Max disconsolately took exactly fifteen times (three terms per annum for five years), except that Max's train left from Victoria. Mr Brian Souter, the Art Director, gave me a tour of the school. As one would expect, it is somewhat the same, somewhat changed, from what it was in Max's day. Girdlestoneites or Duckites is still there, though enlarged and made more commodious; the boys no longer sleep in one large dormitory but have reasonably pleasant, individual little rooms. Charterhouse Great Hall is still in use, and the boys still answer *adsum* to roll call. There are serious additions: the Ben Travers Theatre, the Ralph Vaughan Williams Music Centre, the John Derry Technology Centre; an astounding athletic facility called the Queen's Sports Centre. And, most marvellous addition of all, girls. The Upper School has about a hundred female students (of 350), who live, as it happens, under Brian Souter's care in their own commodious, newly built house. Souter also took me to the art storage room where a few dozen Max caricatures are kept, and to the headmaster's office, where an additional three or four caricatures adorn the walls. The headmaster, John Witheridge, who may have seen me as a brief but welcome distraction from his task of interviewing parents of prospective students, graciously showed me the drawings. Of these, the most prized is a self-portrait (bearing the legend "They call me the inimitable ..."), a study for the finished drawing which is in the Mark Samuels Lasner Collection (plate 15). Perhaps the headmaster knew the Charterhouse caricature was a preliminary version, perhaps he did not; I said nothing on this. Next, at the library, Archivist Shirley Corke got out records, class lists, photographs, and copies of the *Greyfriar* which first published Max's drawings; also a large cache of his caricatures done at Charterhouse, those that convinced me that Max's style and finesse developed very early indeed. Nicely, Shirley Corke, in the company of her parents (her father, Sir Edward Bridges, was Secretary to the Cabinet during the Second World War), met Max around 1945 at the Burford Bridge Hotel, in Surrey, not far from Meredith's old house at Box Hill where Max was staying. She says that Max "talked in paragraphs" while everyone listened attentively. He seemed, she recalls, to be able to think a long way ahead while speaking; perhaps, like all great talkers, he tended to repeat stories he had already delivered elsewhere. She remembers his courtesy, his gentle manners, how "unalarming" he seemed to a young girl. For myself, talking to someone who actually met Max Beerbohm is a little like touching the hand that touched Jesus.

At Oxford, in the Library of Merton's Mob Quad, the huge Beerbohm archive awaited me: thousands of letters, numerous manuscripts, memorabilia of all kinds – baptismal certificate, passports, visitors' books from the Villino, countless press clippings, reviews, obituaries. The latest addition is Max's 1892 undergraduate notebook, containing a dozen essays to be read to his tutor and enhanced with caricatures on facing pages. The notebook cost £20,000. Upstairs, abutting the "earliest and most perfect example in England of a mediæval library," is the Beerbohm Room, temporarily closed for renovations but shown to me by Assistant Librarian Fiona Wilkes. It's a lovely room, the walls crowded with Max's caricatures. The windows are carefully shaded with curtains that protect the watercolours from sunlight. On an earlier visit there in 1994 I asked a former librarian about some mysterious markings in the margin of one of the caricatures, whereupon he – also baffled – said, "Well, we must consult the original." Max would have been amused to learn that some of the framed caricatures so carefully guarded from the light are exact-size photographic reproductions; the originals are kept in museum-style drawers. Among the artefacts in the room is Max's small card-table-like working desk at which he wrote and drew for half a century. (See plate 15.) Max's actual room in 1890 – and Randolph Churchill's earlier – was located on the ground floor which today houses the (relatively) new study area of the Library.

Number 19 Merton Street, the tiny house where Max had a tiny room, is today replaced by an ugly, utilitarian late twentieth-century building, looking very much out of place at the head of the narrow, last remaining cobblestoned street in Oxford. It turns out to be the Warden's Residence. Mrs Batch's house, on the Broad, where the Duke of Dorset had rooms, is also gone, subsumed by the New Bodleian. But for the most part, Oxford or certainly the college buildings themselves remain what they were in Max's time, or, for that matter, a good deal before Max's time. The little city of laughter and learning that inspired *Zuleika Dobson* is still there. The emperors are still there, though "they are by American tourists frequently mistaken for the Twelve Apostles." The Mitre Hotel still functions, though come down in the world from what it was in Max's or Zuleika's time. And of course there are women everywhere. Women students, women dons; the Warden of Merton is a woman. Up until a few years ago (say, twenty or thirty) it used to be said that every young woman who attended Oxford (Zuleika of course did not "attend" but only visited for a few fatal days) thought of herself, quietly, as a sort of Zuleika, though this was doubtless a slander on the sex. I don't know how many of today's students, male or female, are familiar with the novel, or what they would make of it. If they wish to read it, *Zuleika Dobson* (like *Seven Men*) is almost always in print.*

I flew to Genoa, thinking how much more time-consuming and yet more relaxing must have been the train journeys that Max took back and forth. I splurged and took a taxi the fifteen miles to Rapallo. Rapallo did not disappoint; it remains, as Max said those many years ago, "this beautiful place." There are a handful of English residents, but most of the visitors and second-home people are Italians, many of them elderly, who come for the temperate climate, the relatively warm winters, the relatively cool summers. Rapallo is today a town of 30,000, three or four times what it was when Max moved

---

* A good audio tape of the novel would be desirable, and nearly came to pass. In 1987 Decca had John Gielgud record the novel, but when the tapes were sent to Rupert Hart-Davis, who for years acted as literary adviser to the Beerbohm estate (in those days Mrs Eva Reichmann, sister of Elisabeth Jungmann), he refused to license the recording because Gielgud had throughout spoken Zuleika as "Zul*i*ka." Max, who once settled the pronunciation by sending a telegram, ZULEIKA SPEAKER NOT HIKER, would have wholeheartedly endorsed the prohibition.

there in 1910. Although the lace-makers that once thrived there are all but gone, the town has a life of its own and is far less dependent on casual tourism than its smaller and in some ways smarter neighbours, Santa Margarita and the overwhelmingly touristy Portofino, a few miles out on the promontory. You can take a breathtaking car ride up to Montallegro where Max sometimes stayed at a hospice run by nuns and where his eightieth birthday was celebrated. The funicular to Montallegro still operates, though on the day I visited it was not, as the Italians say, "functioning."

Not surprisingly, few inhabitants of Rapallo know anything of Max Beerbohm. Max's memory seems to rest chiefly with the Bacigalupo family, and especially with Massimo Bacigalupo, son of Max's physician during his later years at Rapallo. Massimo teaches American literature at the University of Genoa and could tell me just where Hemingway once met Max at the Riviera Hotel (where by coincidence I myself was staying); he reminded me that Hemingway has a character in a short story say "Marsala is what Max Beerbohm drinks." He showed me where Max's neighbour Ezra Pound lived, and he had me shown round the Villa Chiara, located in the hills between Rapallo and Max's house, the private hospital founded by his father, the place where Max died. (It is now a nursing home; the old people can sit in its garden of wisteria vines and, perhaps, enjoy the view of the Gulf.) Massimo comes of a truly cosmopolitan family: his mother was an American, and his grandmother a German-born physician, whose practice extended to many Rapallo expatriates; some of her clientele, including Max, passed to her son, who tended him during the post-Second World War years until his death. It's easy to understand how Dr Bacigalupo and his mother were unhappy about the implications, by both Cecil and Behrman, that Max suffered at the end of his life from inadequate medical attention, an impression given them by Elisabeth Jungmann who, as I have indicated, would have considered any medical attention given Max inadequate. Massimo remembers her well; he recalls her playing St Nicholas for him and his brother. She was a great friend of his grandmother: both women were strong, tall, bony, intelligent, German and – odd thing to say of one's grandmother – "rather sexless."

Aside from the town itself and the mountainous Montallegro, the big attraction for me was naturally Max's house, the Villino Chiaro, calling port of so many hundreds of visitors during Max's long years there spanning five decades. I found myself ridiculously envying them – this long train of visitors, and especially envying Samuel Behrman, who felt very much as Max had when he himself visited the aged and reclusive Swinburne. Behrman has written of the thrill he had on entering that house. His account cannot come up to "No. 2. The Pines," but then, how could it? When I made my way to the house, Max had been dead for nearly half a century. And not only this incontrovertible and obvious reality of the lateness, so to say, of my visit preyed on my mind, but I was prepared on another account to be disappointed: in a tiny, privately printed booklet called *In Search of Max Beerbohm*, Wallace and Corry Nethery had written in 1984 that the house was utterly changed, that a third storey had been added and that the terrace, with its view of the Gulf of Tigullio and the peninsula towards Portofino, this one saving and glorious feature of the Villino Chiaro, had been removed. The Netherys even supply a photograph. Of course I wanted to see the place nevertheless. Massimo had arranged that my visit be made with his niece, daughter of yet another Bacigalupo physician, his younger brother Andrea. This niece, Martina, a twenty-year-old university student, and, like all her family, fluent in English, was the ideal guide and introducer. For the current occupier of the house (really houses, for the adjacent "Casetta" is joined by a stairway to the Villino itself) is Gabriella de Fraia, a fencing instructor, and Martina had been her star pupil, once ranked ninth in the world in the junior category. This itself made for a nice congruity, or incongruity – a fencing instructor mistress of the Villino Chiaro. The person who had previously owned the place, having acquired it around 1960 after Elisabeth Jungmann's death, was one Hagop Dirane Topalian, an Armenian who served as a mysterious agent of King Farouk!

But back to the house itself. All my misgivings had been for no reason. The Villino is exactly as one expected from the descriptions and the old photographs. The terrace still gloriously fronts the Mediterranean, the little garden still flourishes at the back, and the square cubicle in the centre of the terrace, Max's study, with its french doors giving a view of the sea, is precisely intact. The ground floor remains a garage, though, unlike in Max's time, cars are now kept there. How could the Netherys have got it so wrong? Well, there remains the double iron gate that is the entrance to Max's house, the opening in the stone wall that fronts all the properties on the inland or easterly side of the coast road (the traffic is still frightening, but it is much less than it would have been had not the Autostrada taken most of the trucks away). But this gate leads to a passage that moves left before coming to the Villino

Chiaro. Next to the gate is a plaque, saying in English and Italian that Max Beerbohm, writer and caricaturist, lived here (the English predictably enhanced by the inevitable and somewhat wearying formulation "The Incomparable Max"). But the plaque is actually under a neighbouring house. His worshippers make pilgrimages to Rapallo, risk their necks getting out of their cars, and then take pictures of the wrong house.

Two more items:

Martina Bacigalupo sleeps in Max's bed. It came to her via her grandfather and her uncle Massimo. Though a four-poster, it is not a large bed, it is not what the Italians call a "due piazze." Nor is it quite so small as a narrow single bed – "una piazza"; rather it is a "piazza a mezza."

A mile from the house, on the busy road into Rapallo, the little bar/tobacco of which Max wrote so movingly in "The Golden Drugget" is still there. But today so many houses line this road that during the night a string of lights reaches from Rapallo well past the Villino Chiaro, and the light from this establishment is not at all singular or special, as it was in 1910. And even back then, it probably was not really an inn, just a bar, a tavern. Still, how nice that a bar remains there till this day. It was, admittedly, slightly disconcerting to find the place called Flanagan's Pub and advertising "Live Music" and "Karaoke." Like Max, I did not go in. The beliefs that one most cherishes one is least willing to test.

NOTES

SHORT TITLES AND ABBREVIATIONS

Max Beerbohm's Writings

And Even Now   *And Even Now*. London: Heinemann, 1920
Around Theatres   *Around Theatres*. New York: Simon and Schuster, 1954
Garland   *A Christmas Garland: Woven by Max Beerbohm*. London: Heinemann, 1912
Last Theatres   *Last Theatres: 1904–1910*. Intro. Rupert Hart-Davis. London: Hart-Davis, 1970
Letters   *Letters of Max Beerbohm: 1892–1956*. Ed. Rupert Hart-Davis. London: John Murray, 1988
LRT   *Max Beerbohm's Letters to Reggie Turner*. Ed. Rupert Hart-Davis. Philadelphia and New York: J. B. Lippincott, 1965
M&W   *Max and Will: Max Beerbohm and William Rothenstein: Their Friendship and Letters*. Ed. Mary M. Lago and Karl Beckson. Cambridge, Mass.: Harvard University Press, 1975
Mainly   *Mainly on the Air*. Enlarged edn London: Heinemann, 1957
More   *More*. London and New York: John Lane, The Bodley Head, 1899
More Theatres   *More Theatres: 1898–1903*. Intro. Rupert Hart-Davis. London: Hart-Davis, 1969
Peep   *A Peep into the Past and Other Prose Pieces by Max Beerbohm*. Intro. Rupert Hart-Davis. London: William Heinemann, and Brattleboro, Vermont: Stephen Greene, 1972
Rossetti   *Rossetti and His Circle*. New enlarged edn Intro. N. John Hall. New Haven and London: Yale University Press, 1987
Seven Men   *Seven Men*. London: Heinemann, 1919
Strachey   *Lytton Strachey: The Rede Lecture*. Cambridge: Cambridge University Press, 1943
Variety   *A Variety of Things*. New York: Knopf, 1928
Works   *The Works of Max Beerbohm*. Bibliography by John Lane. London: John Lane, The Bodley Head, 1896
Yet Again   *Yet Again*. London: Chapman and Hall, 1909
Zuleika   *Zuleika Dobson*. London: Heinemann, 1911

Biography, Criticism, Manuscript Depositories

Auden   W. H. Auden. "One of the Family" in *The Surprise of Excellence*, ed. J. G. Riewald. Hamden, Conn.: Archon Books, 1974, 159–74 (from the *New Yorker*, 23 Oct. 1965, 227–44)

Behrman   S. N. Behrman. *Portrait of Max: An Intimate Memoir of Sir Max Beerbohm*. New York: Random House, 1960
Cecil   David Cecil. *Max: A Biography*. London: Constable, 1964
Charterhouse   Charterhouse Archives, The Library, Charterhouse, Godalming
Danson   Lawrence Danson. *Max Beerbohm and the Act of Writing*. Oxford: Clarendon Press, 1989
Ellmann   Richard Ellmann. *Oscar Wilde*. New York: Knopf, 1988
Merton   Merton College Library, Oxford
Mix   Katherine Lyon Mix. *Max and the Americans*. Brattleboro, Vermont: Stephen Greene, 1974
Princeton   Robert H. Taylor Collection, Department of Rare Books, Princeton University Library
Samuels Lasner Private Collection of Mark Samuels Lasner
Texas   Harry Ransom Research Center, University of Texas at Austin

* * *

Page

xi "gifts are small": *Letters* 127–9
    triumph of style": *The Common Reader* 1st series (New York: Harcourt Brace, 1925) 222

xiii that of tragedy": *The Symposium*, Jowett trans.
    in the other": Richard Ellmann, *James Joyce* rev. edn (New York: Oxford University Press, 1983) 120
    way than comedy": "Hannah Arendt: From an Interview," *New York Review of Books* 25 (26 Oct 1978) 18
    inevitable dominance": Robert M. Polhemus, *Comic Faith* (Chicago: University of Chicago Press, 1982) 22
    to become solitary": *How to Read and Why* (New York: Scribners, 2000) 23–5

xiv thing they like): *Zuleika* 180
    with these ironists: *Peep* 86

1   Oedipuses, weren't they?": Giuseppe Bacigalupo, *Ieri a Rapallo* (Udine: Campanotto, 1992) 29
    very lovable character": Ms. letter, Samuels Lasner
    excepted, absent-minded: Hesketh Pearson, *Beerbohm Tree* (London: Methuen, 1956) 8

2   was sound asleep": Jungmann, Ms. diary, Merton

gamin [street arab]" ... and high-spirited": Constance Collier, *Harlequinade* (London: John Lane, 1929) 137–8
    my clever children": Cecil 23
    Strange, isn't it?": *LRT* 51
    and more adventurous": *LRT* 293

3   have tempted him": Auden 162

3–4 at that time ... accordingly, was I": *Mainly* 25–6

4   and the rest": *More* 17
    a "coloured lady": Cecil 7

5   right and proper": "From a Brother's Standpoint" (1920) rpt *The Incomparable Max*, ed. S. C. Roberts (London: Heinemann, 1962) 293
    right about *Trilby*": Behrman 61
    success of his life": *Bernard Shaw: Collected Letters 1911– 1925*, ed. Dan H. Lawrence (New York: Viking, 1985) 22

7–8 jealously hoarded ... should not hesitate: "From a Brother's Standpoint," 297–8, 301, 308, 298–9

8   fortune he squandered: Madeleine Bingham, *The Great Lover: The Life and Art of Herbert Beerbohm Tree* (New York: Atheneum, 1979) 6
    Heine's into English: Collier 138

9   face to the wall: Cecil 254

odd, distinguished creature": Ms.
letter, Texas
miserable old age: *Mainly* 38, 46

10 to write English *well*" ... like a
nonagenarian": William Rothenstein,
*Men and Memories: Recollections of
William Rothenstein 1900–1922*
(New York: Coward-McCann, 1932)
370–71; cf. *M&W* 112
cruel and detestable: Pearson 7

12 could be proud: Auden 166
mixed notes are mixéd' ": Charterhouse;
see also George Engle, *Charterhouse
CA News* 22 (June 2000) 5; cf.
"A.L.I.," "A Charterhouse Eccentric,"
undated article, Merton

13 an awful place?": *LRT* 25–6

13–14 goes Max Beerbohm!' " ... that is
all": *More* 153–6

14–15 in being there" ... be grown up!":
Mainly 150–4

15 their personal appearance": Ms. letter,
Charterhouse

16 to further outrages: Ms. letter,
Charterhouse
W. Haig Brown": Ms. letter, Merton

17 made me insufferable" ... of having
left school: *More* 155, 156
Punch and Judy show": William
Rothenstein, *Men and Memories:
Recollections of William Rothenstein
1872–1900* (New York: Coward-
McCann, 1931) 144

18–19 his book, its sepulchre ... hurt nor
fettered: *Works* 149–50, 152, 153–4,
156–7

19 most actual magic": *Zuleika* 191
too much side": Cecil 58–9

20 to dramatize himself" ... the outer
world": Cecil 60–1
Herbert is dead": Bingham 236.
Surprisingly, the words are Robert
Ross's in a letter to Ada Leverson.

20–1 cultivated a mask" ... reveal his
mask?": Auden 160–1

21 happy I suppose: *LRT* 49

22 Lionel Lawson ... Miss L. Henrie:
LRT 8–11

all my friends": *LRT* 184

23 traveling incognito": Stanley
Weintraub, *Reggie: A Portrait of
Reginald Turner* (New York: Braziller,
1965) 184
youthful extravagances": *LRT* 16

24 grown ever warmer: *Seven Men* 4–5
in one of his years ... beautifully
written": Rothenstein, *Men and
Memories ... 1872–1900* 144,
144–5, 152, 146

25 offense in it" ... 'than angry' ":
Behrman 237, 82

26 reverence" for Oscar Wilde: *LRT* 35

27 astonished, charmed": *Oscar Wilde*,
trans. Bernard Frechtman (New York
Philosophical Library, 1949) 1
is quite useless: *Dorian Gray* (London:
Penguin, 1985) 3–4
without being good": *Max in Verse*, ed.
J. G. Riewald (Brattleboro, Vermont:
Stephen Greene, 1963) 8
I should love": *LRT* 57
and ideal treatment" ... Art imitates
Life: *The Artist as Critic: Critical
Writings of Oscar Wilde*, ed. Richard
Ellmann (New York: Random
House, 1968) 301, 304, 319–20

28 tricks they admire": "Waugh's Comic
Waste Land," *New York Review of
Books*, 15 July 1999, 30
and seldom sober": *LRT* 90
fiercely vindictive": Ellmann 324

29 would kill himself": H. Montgomery
Hyde, *Oscar Wilde* (New York:
Farrar, Straus, 1975) 120–1
be no sceptics: *LRT* 32

29–30 rests my foot" ... vainer than
ever": *LRT* 33, 34, 291, 34, 36, 37

30 gates of Beauty: *LRT* 289–90

31 less arduous calling: *Works* 4–5
the neighbourhood" ... upon the
sofa": *Peep* 4, 6–7

32 pen than mine": *Works* 55
cowards of us all": *Works* 63
themselves, so to speak' ": *Works* 107
fat to a fault" ... sensitive, I wonder?":
LRT 35, 53, 73–4

33 find himself infamous": Ts. Merton
ordinary human courtesies": Behrman
85
say in its favour": *LRT* 37
princes understand poets": Ellmann 382
34–9 for Dorian Gray]" ... that is all":
LRT 26, 28, 33, 39, 39–40
35 Will, very shocked?": *M&W* 24
not tell its name": *Letters* 7
equivalent for my love": *LRT* 131
old O.W.'s memory": *Letters* 118
35–6 this time [1894]" ... noticeable
contribution": Ellmann 423, 424, 425
36 was less nimble" ... in female dress":
LRT 97
to the disciple": Ellmann 423–4
37 MAN YOU ARE": Ellmann 417–18
Lewis as his counsel: *LRT* 100
as it is perfect. ...": Ellmann 463
ponce and Somdomite": see Ellmann
438. But even Ellmann has "To"
rather than the incontrovertible
"For"; see reproduction of the actual
card in Sally Brown, *Oscar Wilde
1854–1900* (Catalogue to the British
Library and Morgan Library
exhibitions of 2000 and 2001) 34.
38 great a triumph ... lost his nerve":
LRT 102–4
dossier against Oscar": Behrman 85–6
BBC radio adaptation: *Letters* 198
it is parodying: cf. Danson 79–80.
Danson's book is by far the best
critical work on Max.
from circulation temporarily": *LRT*
141
39 blinds drawn down": Ts., Merton
catch his eye": *LRT* 117–18
of style or incident": *The Complete
Letters of Oscar Wilde*, ed. Merlin
Holland and Rupert Hart-Davis
(New York: Henry Holt, 2000) 855
art in others: *Letters of Oscar Wilde* 856
himself to spit": Ellmann 577
40 might have died: *LRT* 135–8
he had suffered: *Peep* 39–40
42 of the globe" ... to my modesty":
"When I was Nineteen," *Strand*

Magazine, Oct 1946, 51–5
43 "a little risqué": qtd Karl Beckson,
London in the 1890s (New York:
Norton, 1992) 243
Beardsley, by name": *Seven Men* 5
prostitutes and confidence men": Cecil
93
44 myself, "is life!": *Seven Men* 4–6
amber of modernity": *LRT* 63
mention Art again": *M&W* 4; *LRT*
69–70
over the edges!": *M&W* 17
roguishly winking": *LRT* 92
memory of love-making: Beckson 67,
242–4
45 praised "Stella Maris": *The Times,* 20
April 1894, 3
of thing illegal": *Westminster Gazette,*
18 April 1894, 3
"the little busy bore": *Punch,* 5 May
1894, 212
to "pure nonsense": *World,* 25 April
94, qtd. *LRT* 94n
in all literature": *Yellow Book* 2 (July
1894) 281; rpt *Letters* 2–4
a cowardly decadent": *Letters* 2
45–7 in the rouge-pot? ... her a
welcome!: *Works* 99–100, 102,
103–4, 123–4
47 delicate bit of satire" *Yellow Book* 2
(July 1894) 282 ; also *Letters* 2–3
47–8 success of astonishment ... meant for
portraits": *Sketch* 2 (Jan. 1895) 439
48 has been away!": Ellmann 527
for the happier past": *Works* 167
49 paper-bound French novel: Julie
Speedie, *Wonderful Sphinx: The
Biography of Ada Leverson* (London:
Virago, 1993) 80
"turned grey overnight": qtd Sally
Brown, Curator, Oscar Wilde
Exhibition, British Library and
Morgan Library, 2000, 2001; cf.
E. F. Benson, *As We Were* (London:
Hogarth Press, 1985) 316
50 definite – personality' ": *Seven Men* 22
made my entry": *Peep* 68
in the *Daily Mail*": *Seven Men* 22

51 something new and strange": Richard
Davenport-Hines, review of J. Lee
Thompson, *Northcliffe, TLS,* 2 June
2000, 36
a great University": *Peep* 23
who makes himself ridiculous": *Daily
Mail,* 11 Aug. 1897, 4
and a gentleman: *LRT* 119–21
preferring the good": Michael
Holroyd, *Bernard Shaw Vol. I:
1856–1898* (New York: Random
House, 1988) 406

52 lack confidence" . . . invention
flagged": Behrman 123–4
have had to submit!": Cecil 164

53 beyond their reach . . . irresistible *élan:
More* 105–6, 107–8
an artistic touch": *Critic* (NY), Aug.
1899, 752
the gifted author": *Dial* (Chicago), 16
June 1899, 402
very Thackerayan": *Academy,* 13 May
1899, 528

54 to deal with": Ts., Merton
will be grateful": *Athenaeum,* 28 May
1904, 695
envied by the young": *M&W* 163

55 anything at all: *Works* 60–1

56 proprietor who reared it: *Vanity Fair*
Ch. 51
English could be written" . . . of well-
bred writing": Cyril Ray, "News
about Max," *Sunday Times,* 4 Oct.
1855, 8; Gordon N. Ray, *Thackeray:
The Age of Wisdom* (New York:
McGraw-Hill, 1958) 425

57 an educated mind": *New Statesman
and Nation,* 22 March 1941, 302
"unpretentious ease": Gordon N. Ray,
Thackeray: The Uses of Adversity
(New York: McGraw-Hill, 1955)
401, 402
the earth as food and wine": Ray,
Wisdom 429

58 presence of The Master: *The Newcomes*
Ch. 80
no tears are: *Letters* 201

60 is right, always": Ts., Merton

61 squabbles to immortality . . . his
caressing sense of beauty": *Yet Again*
107, 108–9, 109–10, 110–11,
113–14

61–2 in all times" . . . is full of thought:
The Gentle Art of Making Enemies
(London: Heinemann, 1994) 136,
137–8

62 fairyland is before us" . . . his painted
'nocturnes' ": *Yet Again* 116–17

62–3 needs die a poet . . . I suppose, your
own: *Gentle Art* 26–7, 163, 164,
165

63 laud the amber: *Yet Again* 118–19

64 of the Seaside . . . out his genius": *Peep*
9, 14
YOUR HOLE, RAT!" . . . upon a mare's
nest": *LRT* 112–13

65 in his own sphere: *Saturday Review,* 20
Nov. 1897, 540–1
him translate it": *Saturday Review,* 27
Nov. 1897, 592
near his skin: *Saturday Review,* 4 Dec.
1897; cf. *LRT* 125

66 on the business": *Bernard Shaw:
Collected Letters 1898–1910,* ed. Dan
H. Laurence (New York: Dodd
Mead, 1972) 28
so many, so many! . . . deep
footprints": *Letters* 13

67 an important event": *Bernard Shaw:
Collected Letters 1898–1910,* ed. Dan
H. Lawrence (New York: Viking,
1985) 28; cf. Cecil 163
"fervidly" at G.B.S. himself: *More
Theatres* 11
north light of the studio: *Bernard
Shaw . . . Letters 1898–1910* 43

67–8 so great a play" . . . Paddy *malgré
lui*": *More Theatres* 22, 24, 25, 26

68 stage-managed the whole thing: cf.
Danson 86
the incomparable Max": Bernard
Shaw, *Our Theatres in the Nineties,*
Complete Works (London:
Constable, 1930) XXV, 407. Danson
(p. 86) points out that Shaw
borrowed the line about the younger

generation knocking at the door from Ibsen's *The Master Builder*. One wonders how many of Shaw's readers caught the allusion.

68–9 journalist in London ... the Underground Railway' ": *Around Theatres* 1, 2, 3, 3–4

69 less irrelevant subject": *LRT* 300
intellectual prostitute": *M&W* 39
work more difficult": Cecil 166
cabs, the occasional telegram: Rothenstein, *Men and Memories ... 1872–1900* 284

70 the year 1901": *Around Theatres* ix
half so strong: *Around Theatres* 578–9
$5,000 dollars a word: Ms. letter, Beinecke Library, Yale

71 Bliss! Rapture!: *More Theatres* 12–13
habitual criminals of art": *The Artist as Critic*, ed. Ellmann, 358
digression as possible: *LRT* 300

72 aware, he didn't" ... worth writing about": *Letters* 205
processes were vague" ... length becomes amusing": *Last Theatres* 92, 93–4
form of journalese": *Around Theatres* 289
passable English": *Last Theatres* 94

73 Forward! On!": *More Theatres* 444
cheap and nasty": David Cecil, "The Man Who Never Stopped Playing", *Horizon* 3 (May 1961) 38

73–4 standpoint is feminine ... bilious little thing' ": *Around Theatres* 245, 246, 247, 248

74 against '*perfide Albion*' ": *Around Theatres* 30
grown-up persons: *Last Theatres* 66–7
been over-rated" ... of Mr Kipling's work": *More Theatres* 215, 219

74–5 good in the world" ... Kipling is unfit": *Last Theatres* 276, 306, 307

75 misused his genius": Behrman 70–1
of "Samson Agonistes": *Around Theatres* 527

75–6 knowing than I am ... rolled into one": *Around Theatres* 4–5, 6, 7

76 really appreciate him:" *Around Theatres* 75
the British stage": *Around Theatres* 231
making it unique: *Around Theatres* 357

77 keep his temper: *More Theatres* 174–5
does not pander: *Around Theatres* 433–4
sense of mystery": *More Theatres* 38, 39
a higher wisdom ... go on with": *Last Theatres* 512, 512–13

78–9 Dan Leno's genius! ... out to Dan Leno: *Around Theatres* 349, 350

79–80 and killed him...
Curtain falls [on Act III]: *Seven Men* 182–3, 189, 207

80 herein aimed at": Ms. letter, Samuels Lasner

81 tyrannous preoccupation" ... or seen enacted": *Around Theatres* 269, 268
whole thing is wrong": *Bernard Shaw ... Letters 1898–1910* 372
must guard jealously": *Letters* 39–41

82 at his Best" ... the last line": *Around Theatres* 353, 354, 355
it was perfect" ... being ridiculous?": *Around Theatres* 413, 414
Shaw has done": *Last Theatres* 296, 297

82–3 actual world ... like 'Misalliance' ": *Around Theatres* 561–2, 563–4, 564–5

83 temperament again: *Around Theatres* ix
send him my love: Ms. letter, Merton

84 never harmed him"): *Letters* 208n
stage directions": Behrman 24
presentment at all: Behrman 24
or doing nothing": Ms. notebook, Berg Collection, New York Public Library

84–5 serve you right" ... presence of mind": *Letters* 73, 120

85 kind of malice" ... account of him": *Letters* 160, 184
is a REFORMER: *LRT* 231
the drawing in two: Katherine Lyon Mix, "Max on Shaw," *Shaw Review* 6 (Sept. 1963) 100

86 afraid of me: *LRT* 230
body of his fear": *Bernard Shaw ...*

Letters 1898–1910 249
a coarse man: Behrman 23
their own kind": *More* 42–4

87   panache by G.B.S.?: Behrman 43
temperance beverage face": Ts., Merton
down the ages": *Letters* 50
and a pig? . . . with their personalities:
Danson 102, 104, 104–5
in current literature" . . . he is
immortal": *Around Theatres* 272, 175
English gentleman: Danson 104–5

89   and stronger: *More Theatres* 12
I think so: Ts., Merton

90–1 us who hasn't! . . . and fourth items:
Yet Again 247–8, 258–9

91   to the farce: *Yet Again* 19–20

92   quite seriously: Cecil 62

94   grist to Max's mill: Cecil 205–7
modelled on Yeats: Cecil 341
"instructed" his solicitor: *LRT* 173

95   Such was Hans: qtd *LRT* 173–4; cf.
Weintraub 133–4

96–7 are one of them . . . false relation:
And Even Now 128–9, 138–41

97   Georgian atmosphere": Collier 136

98   knew them *all*": Behrman 179

99   of popular singers: *M&W* 2
under the sun-bonnet": *Works* 116

100   my seeing her . . . vitality for that":
LRT 45, 47, 48, 49

101   good and changed: *M&W* 18
Cissie Loftus now" . . . the past
already": *LRT* 72, 95
of her period" . . . in the world":
Speedie 45, 36
to be a mulierast": Ts., Merton

102   on any body": Ms. letter, Samuels
Lasner

102–3 sick of seeing me" . . . female
society: Ms. letters, Texas

103   tried to seduce him: Speedie 40–1

103–4 "brilliant and delightful" . . .
carefully and well": Ms. letters, Texas

104   be sympathetic: *LRT* 101

104–5 "extremely bad taste" . . .
friendship with you": Tss., Merton

105   point of honour: cf. Cecil 129

dangerous friends". . . to marry her":
Ts., Merton
spoke at all . . . all the arrangements":
Cecil 219–20
deeply for her": *M&W* 11

106   unkind about him": Ts., Merton
flamboyant temperament": Cecil
221

107   walking stick": Behrman 295
with Constance Collier": Ts., Merton
the information: *LRT* 154–5
they felt, "refinement": Ts., Merton
to be blamed": Ts., Merton

108   ties of love . . . enough to me": *LRT*
158–9, 161
is on tour": Behrman 229

109   history of art" . . . "the English Goya":
Behrman 262, 198

111   imagined Jenny Mere": Cecil 231
Florence was all brains": Mix 67
foolish and bleated": *New York Times*,
29 March 1906, 6

112   "Barkley" he warned her: Ts., Merton
rest of humanity" . . . *I* met *you* : Ms.
letters, Princeton
hard you tried": Ts., Merton

113   better than anyone: Ms. letter,
Princeton
acknowledge the size". . . other such
subject"): Tss., Merton
so much better: Ms. letter, Princeton
detect the impropriety" . . . gadding
about in London": Tss., Merton

114   Max aetat: 32" . . . approval into
words": Ms. letters, Princeton
it *is* good" . . . lonely without you":
Tss., Merton

115   don't deserve, Constance: *LRT* 158–9
length, I am afraid: *Letters* 44–5

116   those beastly feathers" . . . the vein left
me": Tss., Merton
in decent society!" . . . "The darling
wept": Cecil 282, 285

117–19 and inhuman Hedda" . . .
temporary egoism!": Ms. letters,
Princeton

119   Do go and see . . .": *Letters*, 60
never met you": Ts., Merton

tortures of the soul": *Around Theatres*
500–1
120 to express myself: *Letters* 62
rid of it by venting it!": Ms. letter,
Princeton
as "crude chaff": *M&W* 58–61
121 about Max's heart: *Letters* xi–xii
122 always will be" . . . in hand with you":
Tss., Merton
122–3   all the time . . . wherever we are:
Ms. letters, Princeton
123 been spent that way: Ts., Merton
you very much . . . be so happy: Ms.
letters, Princeton
123–4   behind – will there? . . . perhaps he
isn't!: Tss., Merton
124 is beyond me . . . all about *you*: Ms.
letters, Princeton
124–5   good and all . . . for my
happiness": *LRT* 183–4
125 "downright tiresome": Cecil 299
seem hardly valid": *LRT* 184
126 'It's hardly decent!": Frank Harris,
Contemporary Portraits (New York:
Brentano's, 1923) 131–2
"palpably false": *TLS* 28 Feb. 1924,
128
alone with Florence": Behrman 179
127 gesticulation and 'patter'" . . . being
with her: *LRT* 185–6
he married her!": Ts., Merton
128 plaster hardly dry): *LRT* 189–90
"commodious" rooms: Ms. letter,
Samuels Lasner
dining-out in London": Cecil Sprigge,
"The Last Years in Surrey and in
Italy," *Manchester Guardian,* 24 May
1956, 14
129 place, quite alone: *M&W* 62, 63
and happiness: *LRT* 191
your own, Max . . . Your own Max:
Tss., Merton
130 please come back": Cecil 378
onto the stage: Mary Lago, Ts., "Mrs
Max," 14–15, Merton
lovely and perfect": Ms. letter, Samuels
Lasner
from the 1890s: Cecil 424

link with the past": *Mainly* 34
131 difficult to know": Mix 165–6
Max's clever friends . . . been happy
with him": Cecil 376–7, 453–4, 377
132 own loving Max": Ts., Merton
133 sober and ample": *M&W* 87
134 "infinitesimal defects" . . . ever and
ever": Ms. letters, Princeton; rpt
Lawrence Danson, "Max and Mr
McCall," *Princeton University Library
Chronicle* 47 (Winter 1986), 175–84.
McCall suggested that both sides of
the correspondence be printed as a
private pamphlet, but Heinemann
vetoed the idea. See R. H. McCall
and Lawrence Danson, "Max and Mr
McCall Revisited," *Princeton
University Library Chronicle* 49
(Autumn 1987) 78–86.
135 and ambitious work: cf. Cecil 310f
. . . becomes monotonous": *Bookman,*
June 1912, 425–8. See also J. G.
Riewald, *Sir Max Beerbohm: Man
and Writer* (The Hague: Nijhoff,
1953) 125.
rival your collection": Ms. letter,
Samuels Lasner
136 basis in reality": *Zuleika Dobson*
(London: Heinemann, 1947) "Note"
tragedy too poignant" . . . fantastical-
humourous, reality": *LRT* 208, 209
Gershwin, and Audrey Hepburn:
Behrman 205–6
137 waist to speak of: *Zuleika* 9–10
among the poets": *Seven Types of
Ambiguity* (London: Chatto &
Windus, 1949 [1930]) 176–7
to the author": *Around Theatres* 65
the author's permission' ": Ts., Merton
139 fantasy in our time": *Aspects of the
Novel* (London: Edward Arnold,
1927) 154
is to English poetry: see, for example,
Harold Nicolson: "In no similar
work . . . (with the possible exception
of *The Rape of the Lock*) is there so
dexterous an alternation of the
element of expectation with the

element of surprise," *The Surprise of Excellence*, ed J. G. Riewald (Hamden, Conn.: Archon Books, 1974) 31 (reprinting article from *The Listener*, 25 Sept. 1947). See also F. W. Dupee and David Cecil, *Surprise* 189, 236.

140 mannerisms of them all: *Saturday Review*, 9 Nov. 1912, 579

141 God's point of view": Cecil 406
Ugly, and the False": *Around Theatres* 26

142–3 and the Flemish" ... new artistic dawn: *Garland* 179, 182, 182–3, 184, 185

143 of his bed ...: *Garland* 3–4

144 from the shell!' ": *The Lies of Art: Max Beerbohm's Parody and Caricature* (New York: Knopf, 1972) 143
ineffectively imitating" Max: *Letters* 87
"parodying himself": Leon Edel, *Henry James: The Master, 1901–1916* (Philadelphia: Lippincott, 1972) 387
the unmonocled eye!": *Letters* 86
approach to the Yogi": H. V. Marrot, *The Life and Letters of John Galsworthy* (New York: Scribners, 1936) 353

145 from the Portuguese' ": *Garland* 142
Ibsen and Browning!' ": *Letters* 87
my public existence": *Tales of Unrest* (Garden City, NY, 1923), Author's Note, viii
in *A Christmas Garland*: *Spectator*, 21 Dec. 1912, 1068
right at elections": Ann Thwaite, *Edmund Gosse* (London: Secker & Warburg, 1984) 342

146 frog's-march him!": *Garland* 19
"their brains and hearts": Raymond Mortimer, *Sunday Times*, 26 Feb. 1950, 3
their very minds": *Athenaeum*, 16 Nov. 1912, 590
the perfect jest": *TLS* 7 Nov. 1912, 492

148 anything to touch her": *LRT* 234–6
idea is inconceivable" ... and feelings

expressed": Tss., Merton; cf. Cecil 336, 337

149 an elegant walking cane: Rothenstein, *Men and Memories ... 1900–1922* 212
as the 'sixties": *Letters* 93
in a dense fog": *Rossetti* 48
of 16 Cheyne Walk": Ts., Merton

150 and spiritual composition": Rothenstein, *Men and Memories ... 1900–1922* 314

151 words "Hall Caine": cf. also *Mainly* 76
looking at myself": Henry Treffry Dunn, *Recollections of Dante Gabriel Rossetti* (London: Elkin Mathews, 1904), 17–18
convex round-shaped mirrors": *Some Reminiscences of William Michael Rossetti* (London: Brown, Langham, 1906) 267
called *The Mirror of the Past*": Behrman 41

152 would care to hear": *Rossetti* 49

153 of the Prince Consort: *Mainly* 128–9, 127

154 in art and life": *The Times*, 3 Oct. 1922, 12d
the Pre-Raphaelite Brotherhood": *New York Times*, 5 Nov. 1922, III 7a
as one item": Rupert Hart-Davis, *Hugh Walpole* (London: Macmillan, 1952) 391

156–7 be left alone" ... nothing whatsoever": *Seven Men* 144, 144–5, 148

157–9 on his decade ... I did exist!": *Seven Men* 3, 6, 10–11, 11, 12, 16, 26–7, 37, 43

159 keep his appointment: *The Times*, 20 March 1997, 21 (letter from R. F. Coales)

160 never heard of Lacan: private communication

161 pass into oblivion: *And Even Now* 303–4

163 unexpectedly industrious journalist": Rupert Hart-Davis, *Peep* vii

165 *books* at all": *Letters* 95

168–70 never will not be ... darkness and

Davis (London: Faber and Faber, 1986) 26

invention of broadcasting": Behrman 265

crowd into the bathroom": J. G. Riewald, *Remembering Max Beerbohm* (Assen: Van Gorcum, 1991) 61

196 a wireless set": Cecil 430, 434

196 millions of listeners": Behrman 265
well, it's fine": *Mainly* 71

197 isn't nostalgic?": Ms., Samuels Lasner

198 great part of the day ... for Sunday evening" *Mainly* 47–8

199 into my broadcast" ... unholy merriment": Carman 79, 79–80, 80

200 it's all right": Ts., Merton
sounds quite possible: *More* 137–8

201 are at his feet ... no time for thought": *Works* 154–5, 156
anything, sharper, thinner": Behrman 98

202 a stealthy Bolshevist" ... of my disposition": Tss., Merton; cf. Cecil 398–9
panel and show them": Behrman 90
forget the sight: Ts., Merton

203 and loveable King": Ts., Merton
sent it to them": Behrman 102
turn out all right": Ts., Merton
though he looked": Ts., Merton

204 remedied this defect": *Letters* 204

204–5 shining and unyielding ... them credit, I think: *Letters* 107, 108

205 height of amusement": Michael Holroyd, *Lytton Strachey* (New York: Holt Rinehart, 1968) I, 289, 315
smallest in the world": Holroyd, II, 244–5
with the Devil: Ms. letter, Samuels Lasner
or may not know" ... and sallow seniors": *Seven Men* 31–2, 140–2

206 in which she abounds": *Letters* 117
"a sloppy asparagus": Cecil Beaton, *The Wandering Years* (London: Weidenfeld and Nicolson, 1961) 26
England still exists'": Holroyd, II, 393

206–7 there it is" ... lovely to be L: *Letters* 126–7, 129

207 hundred miles of him": *LRT* 259
in its cause!" ... in your new book": *Letters* 179, 180
time, Hail and Farewell": Cecil 350

208 has been written": *Letters* 166

208–10 imperfect sympathies" ... can be very homely": *Strachey* 10–11, 11, 19–20, 6–7, 12–13, 12, 24

211 some characteristic specimen": (Harmondsworth: Penguin, 1986) 9

211–14 and simply charming" ... before you leave!": *New Statesman and Nation,* 2 June 1945, 551–2

214 the kitchen table: Mix 161
in the dear Cottage!": *M&W* 173–4
to deserve charity: Cecil 461

215 and his works": Ts., Merton
such extreme sophistication": *The Times,* 5 May 1952, 9
"the Maximilian Period": *Sunday Observer,* 11 May 1952, 6
such fastidious precision?": *Spectator,* 9 May 1952, 612
"an English Institution": *Apollo,* June 1952, 159

216 "The Faultless Max": Bertrand Russell, *New York Times Magazine,* 24 Aug. 1952, 18
than the Rapallo hermit's?": *Manchester Guardian,* 20 Oct. 53, 4

216–18 under Merton archways" ... so often given me": Ms. Birthday tribute album, Merton. Waugh published an expanded version of his remarks called "Max Beerbohm: A Lesson in Manners," *Atlantic Monthly* 198 (Sept. 1956), rpt *Surprise of Excellence,* 92–5.

218 Chaucer's, Maupassant's, and Harry's": *Letters* 165
rests – behold! – upon me! ... has pleased you": *Letters* 166–7
not a healthy sign": *The Surprise of Excellence* 173

219 fribble – so there": *Harold Nicolson: The Later Years,* ed. Nigel Nicolson (New York: Atheneum, 1968) III, 373
refusing to grow up" ... I am just

famous": *English Literature in Transition* 27, no. 4 (1984) 297–9. The character is Mischa Fox in Murdoch's *The Flight from the Enchanter*; Fox was based on Elias Canetti, Bulgarian-born German writer, winner of the Nobel Prize for Literature in 1981.

220 called "The Case Against": *Flaubert's Parrot* (New York: McGraw-Hill, 1985) 138–51

state of existence": *And Even Now* 183

start with a lie?": Cecil 491

221 is *rather* wonderful!": *Yet Again* 151

of atomic warfare: Riewald, *Remembering* 61

222 down on affectionately" ... pleasures me H. Ibsen": "The Man Who Never Stopped Playing," 36–7

all the little fellows": Richard Ellmann, *James Joyce* rev. edn (Oxford: Oxford University Press, 1982) 743

223 of his friends": *LRT* 301

uglify his victim ... horror of things ignoble": Auden 170, 171

224 able to read her": *Letters* 97–8

"afflicted with Messiahdom" ... knighthood for that!": Cecil 483, 443

monstrifier of men": *Letters* 219

225 had died of torture": Behrman 148–9

and his homosexuality": "A Survivor," *New York Review of Books,* 25 Nov. 1975, 33

226 to put him right?: *Letters* 37–8

been quite impossible: Ts., Merton

to pass muster": *Peep* 89

227–8 to charming trifles ... believing in himself'": Auden 172, 172–3, 173, 174

229 after my time": Jack House, "Sir Max is still the Incomparable," *Evening News* (Glasgow) *Saturday Supplement,* 26 Sept. 1953, 1

Max "had it": Ms. notebook, Berg Collection, New York Public Library

breed of the future": Ts., Merton

230 with the finished product: cf. Thwaite 494–5

unerringly, as they are: *Variety* 165

231 dreamy "romantic elegance": Cecil 133

like going to" ... from my mind": Ms. letters, Princeton

to become a writer": *Letters* 153

231–2 the last 350 years" ... "Bolshevik Jews": Douglas Murray, *Bosie: A Biography of Lord Alfred Douglas* (New York: Hyperion, 2000) 221, 234

232 of all literary joy": *Letters* 94

person to deal with": *LRT* 204

[a] lovable figure": Murray 4

233 most expensive paints'": Jenny Nicholson "Grazie per Tutto", *Spectator,* 1 June 1956, 755

had overtaken him": *Letters* 151

as of whales" ... about the mouth'": Behrman 231, 232

haze of poetry: *Around Theatres* 68

234 lovable than ever": *Letters* 168

walk, unwary, unknowing": Behrman 248

somehow understand them": *Letters* 65

call that great: *Mainly* 97–8

235 manner of writing": Cecil 262

out of Arabia": *M&W* 149

mud and slush" ... absolute chaotic rot": *LRT* 193, 194

didn't mesmerize me: *Mainly* 105–6

antagonizes me": Ts., Merton of 'big' ideas": Behrman 283

236 simile for Wells's writing": *Letters* 38

have hated more": *LRT* 257

phrase 'And tell me'": *Mainly* 101

people he knew" ... Among the *roses*!": Behrman 194, 24

237 at peace, dear fellow: *LRT* 283

surpassingly full one: *M&W* 174

so solemn a moment": Ts., Merton

238 says "in her arms" ... cultural revival of Germany": Corry Nethery, *The Second Lady Beerbohm* (Los Angeles: Dawson's Book Shop, 1987) 50, 70

"delicately flirtatious": Cecil 417

transported to Auschwitz: Nethery 64

Florence about this": Cecil 477

239 "antediluvian state": Nethery 82
climax of a story)": Nethery 102–3
that she gave me": Ts., Merton

239–40 destroy her letters" . . . much
more": Elisabeth Jungmann, Ms.
diaries 1951–6, Merton

240 of "precious porcelain": Bacigalupo,
Ieri a Rapallo 29
wear a wristwatch: Behrman 195–6
lovable angel's genius . . . Your devoted
Elisabeth": Ms. letters, Merton

241 he hit himself!" . . . that little anxiety":
Jungmann, Ms. diaries, Merton
than other people" . . . "infernal"
traffic: Nicholson 754

241–2 by everybody" . . . the only girl":
Jungmann Ms. diaries, Merton

242 thing they like": *Zuleika* 180. Cf.
Behrman 185–6
"a whole book": Nicholson 755

242–3 decadence in France" . . . under the
eyes": Jungmann, Ms. diaries, Merton

245 to the Master: *Mainly* 132–3

246 at unexpected sounds: Bacigalupo 29

246–7 "not over impressive" . . . his

comfortable bed: Jungmann, Ms.
diaries, Merton

247 nice every day": *Letters* 44–5

247–8 patience with me" . . . the relief!!!:
Jungmann, Ms. diaries, Merton

248 "an ugly green": Behrman 302

248–9 into one's heart" . . . out of the
room": Jungmann, Ms. diaries,
Merton

249 *Grazie per tutto*: Bacigalupo, 32
him, for hours: Jungmann, Ms. diaries,
Merton

250 like my niche": *Works* 160

252 "the well-informed passer-by":
Caroline Dakers, *The Blue Plaque
Guide to London* (London:
Macmillan, 1981) iii

254 a mediaeval library": H. W. Garrod,
qtd. Alan Bott, *Merton College*
(Oxford: Merton College, 1993) 20

255 mistaken for the Twelve Apostles":
Zuleika 5
SPEAKER NOT HIKER: *Letters* 213

257 had been removed (Los Angeles:
Dawson's Book Shop, 1984) 30

ACKNOWLEDGEMENTS

I am grateful to Mark Berlin of London Management for permission to quote Beerbohm texts and to reproduce the caricatures.

My chief debt is to the collector and scholar Mark Samuels Lasner. His collection of Beerbohm manuscripts, letters, books, and caricatures is, if I may be allowed the word in this context, incomparable. He has given me access to these materials, patiently answered all my queries, and shared with me his enormous knowledge of Max.

The manuscript at various states was read, greatly to my benefit, by David Gordon, Neil Grill, Gerhard Joseph, and, as always, by my wife, Marianne. Julia Miele Rodas ably supplied library research and meticulous proof reading. Other help has been given me by Massimo Bacigalupo, Martina Bacigalupo, R. S. Call, Gabriella de Fraia, Mortimer Frank, Stephen Gill, Victoria Glendinning, S. M. Grover, Daniel Lowenthal, Sara Lussier, Bernard Mandelbaum, Diana Peyton, and Colby Willis.

I wish also to thank officers of various institutions: Fiona Wilkes, Julia Walworth, and Michael Stansfield of Merton College Library; Richard Oram and John Kirkpatrick of the Harry Ransom Humanities Research Center, University of Texas at Austin; Mark Farrell of the Robert H. Taylor Collection, Princeton University; Brian Souter and Shirley Corke of Charterhouse; John Nicoll, Candida Brazil, Kevin Brown, and Elizabeth Smith of Yale University Press, London; Dean John Moses of St Paul's Cathedral; and Isaac Gewirtz of the Berg Collection, New York Public Library.

At Bronx Community College I have had the continued support of English department chairs Bernard Witlieb and Frederick De Naples and from President Carolyn Williams, and, at the Graduate Center, from Executive Officer Joan Richardson. I acknowledge generous aid from the PSC/CUNY Research Award Program.

NJH
New York City
Great Barrington, Mass.

Index